MARES!
(Ya Gotta LOVE 'em)
Fifty Stories to Aid and Inspire Mare Owners

Compiled by Betsy Kelleher

Mares! (Ya Gotta Love 'em)
Fifty Stories to Aid and Inspire Mare Owners
by Betsy Kelleher

Printed in the United States of America

ISBN 978-1-60477-547-1

Unless otherwise indicated, Bible quotations are taken from the Holy Bible, New International Version. Copyright © 1973, 1978, 1984 by International Bible Society. Used by permission of International Bible Society. "NIV" and "New International Version" are trademarks registered in the United States Patent and Trademark office by International Bible Society.

www.xulonpress.com

for Cherie –

Thank You –
    for being a part
    of this book project!

    Betsy Kelleker
    2-08

Within each mare –
is the heart of a "woman."

PHOTO CREDITS

Cover photos, front and back, by Linda Snyder of Picture Perfect Photography, Bunker Hill, Illinois. Linda also took the photo of Betsy and Lady, shown with the first story.

Cover photo subject is Jordan Dowdy at 10 years old (taken in 2007), with KT Passionate Kiss (Kissie), a 15-year-old mare. Jordan is the daughter of Ken and Tammy Dowdy of Arlington Stables, Granite City, Illinois. She rides several mares owned by the family and has shown in local horse shows.

> Photo of Kandy ("More Than Blue Ribbons") and Debbie Antognoli by Robb Hess.
> Photo of Katy ("Precious Katy") and Crystal Doll by Jim Wright.
> Photo of Brandy and Doreen Davis ("She Wasn't Very Fancy") by Tammy Meidinger.
> Photo of Lilly ("A Complete Miracle") and Lisa Waltrip by Rosemary Lahmann

In Memory
Of
Paula (Pam) Fortado
Gibson Tockstein

11-18-1946 to 11-15-2007

Acknowledgements

This book would not exist without 37 horse owners who contributed stories besides my own. **_Thank You_** to each one of you for all the time and effort spent in the preparation of each story, plus your patience and cooperation in dealing with editing and other parts of the process! I also appreciate the tears that have been shed in the course of drawing out memories so precious and painful, to be shared with our readers. A special thank you to Mary Wynn Craig, who not only contributed two stories but also helped me edit several others and eased my stressful overload! You are so appreciated! Thanks to Betsy McGee Rice for her copy suggestions and to Erin Landers, who happened to post on a website the very words I had planned to use in my title! A special thank you to both Dianne Doll and Denise Pederson, who have been promoters and encouragers for several years! I have enjoyed getting acquainted with many writers on a more personal basis. This whole experience has been encouraging and heart-warming (we aren't going to mention the frustrations). Again, my heartfelt thanks to each and every writer! I also give thanks to the Lord who has helped me through this project. I hadn't planned to make this a spiritual book, but many writers have done so on their own! God has brought these stories together and I have watched it happen. So I give thanks for His help and I pray each reader may feel His influence along the way.

TABLE OF CONTENTS

Introduction

By Betsy Kelleher

Mares aren't for everyone. Some can be moody, stubborn, cranky, fussy, flighty, nervous, demanding, mean and even dangerous. Others are loving, loyal, protective, committed, tremendously strong and reliable. Mares often require special handling before their best side is evident. If you don't have patience and understanding, and if you don't honestly love their unique personalities, you probably shouldn't own a mare. Even though some horse owners would never own a mare while others prefer them, how you feel about your horse is more important than its gender. Women usually get along better with mares, especially women who accept their own feminine natures. Men who don't understand or respect women will probably have trouble understanding the feminine issues in mares as well. Yes, ladies, our mares are much like us!

This book is about mares, but it's about women, too. It's about the essence of being female and the special qualities of the female gender. It's about a strong need for connection, love and acceptance. And it's about a built-in destiny that can't always be explained. It is the nature of mares to nurture and protect and care for their own. They are the mothers and the babysitters...but they also are the leaders and providers. God gave mares the same loving, affectionate nature that He gave women...and the same inner strength and fortitude. An alpha mare presents additional challenges for human companions, just because her genes tell her she must be the leader of the herd. In a herd of horses, the pecking order determines the leader, and someone's got to do it! In a herd of two, involving horse and human, it's still the same.

Horse trainers tell us to train mares just like geldings or stallions...and to train gaited horses just like non-gaited horses. Basic training for any horse involves a good foundation of common building blocks laid step by step, gaining respect and trust, and developing obedient responses to specific cues. A good trainer considers physical, mental and emotional aspects of working with a horse. A wise trainer understands a mare's moods and needs as well, but that doesn't mean he will allow her to give in to them while he is working toward her training goals. His compassionate handling, however, can be a major influence on her acceptance of the training and her ultimate attitude toward being ridden. A trainer who recognizes and appreciates a human female's unique qualities will be more qualified to work effectively with a mare (in my opinion). I wouldn't want my mare to be trained or cared for by someone who doesn't like mares!

Geldings are often the preferred gender because of their relatively steady, consistent nature. But geldings can be stubborn and mean and spooky, just as much as mares. Beware of viewing "mares" as a collective evil! Each individual horse has a temperament and personality all its own, sometimes influenced by past human mistakes! We can't choose a gelding or a mare or a horse of a certain breed or discipline without also looking at the specific personality and temperament of that specific horse.

Mares usually have more variety in their natures. One day, this mare is a loving, sweet, intelligent creature, nuzzling your cheek and quietly obeying your requests. The next day, this same mare might change into an unknown beast, kicking and squealing and totally out of control! Fortunately, I've never owned that mare but I've heard about her!

Quite often a horse chooses you, sometimes without your knowing, and you must adapt to whatever that horse brings to the relationship. You learn to cope with the problems you encounter and perhaps even grow from the experience. Do you suppose it is possible that God sometimes helps the horse make the choice? Perhaps God gives us the horse we need to help us through our individual journey at a certain time. In that sense, each one is a gift from Him.

Those who prefer mares probably enjoy the special relationship that mares usually desire. You

can ride a gelding, then put him away and go home…
but a mare wants more. She wants your care, your
attention and your love, and then she will give you
her all in return. Doesn't that sound…like a woman?
A mare must respect you before she will cooperate
fully and willingly, and she wants to be treated with
respect herself! She can't be pushed around and still
be happy the next day. If you take your frustration
out on a mare, you will have to make it right before
the working relationship can go on. She will insist
on it, especially if she is the alpha type. Our relationships with our mares are extremely important. Inner
strength often comes from good relationships.

I had a special female friend for almost 30 years.
We connected on emotional, intellectual, spiritual and
mental levels. We talked about horses and life and
everything else and I appreciated her great insight.
She could put my feelings into words before I often
realized exactly what my feelings were. Though she
was several years younger than I was, I found myself
often seeking her advice and reassurance. I have dedicated this book in memory of that friend. Pam was
a "head mare" in every sense of the definition. She
was a caretaker, always in charge to make sure things
were done right and people she knew were properly
cared for. No one I've ever met felt the responsibility
she did toward all of God's living creatures.

When I read Jeremiah 31:3 one morning, I knew
instantly how much I needed to hear it: "I have loved
you with an everlasting love; I have drawn you with
loving-kindness." When we become really aware
and convinced of the reality of God's love for us, it

changes our world. We become like a new creature, changed on the inside. We are freed from guilt and fear and empowered to BE and to DO. We find new direction and new energy. We find joy and peace. I saw that change in my Lady, as she grew to understand that she was secure in my ownership. When she felt my "love," she was able to give herself to me in a way that has humbled me and melted my heart. She has become to me like a friend or a sister or mother, like a **person**. She has taught me about love and kindness.

After my husband bought Lady and discovered her very alpha nature, I tried to "fix" it so he could ride her. I searched for helpful information and found nothing but books on breeding. Four years later, Lady is my mare now and the inspiration for this book. It is fitting that "Walker's Velvet Queen" be the first story.

I wanted a book to help mare owners deal with mare issues and appreciate their mares with a new perspective. This project has taken on a life of its own, however, not exactly what I imagined in the beginning. This is a collection of stories by 38 different mare owners, including myself. There are a few articles in this book by experienced trainers, but many of the stories are from the hearts of men and women paying tribute to a special creature that entered their lives. Some stories are about mares who have crossed that rainbow bridge and they are sad, but only because of a special relationship that once brought so much joy. Many of these stories contain nuggets of wisdom on how to deal with mares and their moods.

I see two threads of something else interwoven and moving within this book. First, the affectionate fellowship of female spirits, both horse and human, as they learn together, work together and celebrate their own female natures. And second, I see within these stories again and again the theme of God's redeeming love…not only for the mares that people have helped, but also for the people themselves.

As you enjoy these stories about mares who have deeply touched lives and hearts, I hope you find helpful advice to apply to your own situation and discover new ways to succeed with your mare. And perhaps you will also find that God's amazing, redeeming love is at work all around us.

At the age of five, Betsy rode her first horse…an uncle's pony (a mare!). Growing up on an Iowa farm, she rode one of her grandfather's work team (a mare!). At age 39, she finally owned her first horse, one that had been her oldest son's 4-H project (a mare!). Now, her greatest challenge is a mare her husband purchased for himself before realizing her true Alpha nature. "Walker's Velvet Queen" aka Lady has provided Betsy's first experience riding a gaited horse. For awhile, Betsy got excited about showing because Lady has such a smooth gait. But the greatest joy is the special loving relationship that has developed between Betsy and Lady.

Lady Is A Teacher

By Betsy Kelleher

My husband was looking for a good trail horse. I had spent weeks searching the internet, calling owners, asking questions, carefully eliminating possibilities one by one to find the perfect horse to meet his needs. In a sale barn, a black Tennessee Walker mare reached out to him with her friendly nose and snuggled her head on his arm and Russ bought her on the spot. Dumbfounded and perturbed, I knew my poor husband had no idea what he was getting!

He had been riding a gorgeous black Tennessee Walker gelding that was very willing but head shy and nervous. He was so frustrated by a lack of bonding with the gelding, I guess it was natural that he would connect with an affectionate mare!

"Walker's Velvet Queen" is registered with excellent bloodlines. She was Iowa born in September (just like me!). She is short and stout, 14.1 (at withers) or 14.3 (at rump), and when we bought her she was six and a half years old. She is now ten. She has a nice head and she's just the right size to mount easily if the saddle is tight enough on her round back. Her white blaze has a cute fuzzy edge and her back ankles show some white with little black patches.

Our first day started on an encouraging note. She did not spook at a yellow plastic bag tied to a long stick, and as I walked her around the indoor arena, she stopped when I stopped and backed when I touched her shoulder with my elbow. She seemed very responsive and I was impressed! Russ couldn't wait to ride her. As she stood by the gate in the indoor arena, he brushed her, I picked out her feet and we saddled her. His saddle didn't fit, so we got my saddle that was built wider over the withers, and we had to adjust the cinch and the stirrups — all while she stood perfectly still, untied, the whole time. He tried to mount and the saddle slipped. We put it back on and tightened it and Russ got up with a chair. She stood quietly for it all without moving an inch.

Then I watched as my dear husband rode her around the arena a few times, and I wondered why she was going so fast. I wasn't used to her speedy little fox-trot gait! She seemed very smooth, but she would rush to the gate, and my husband did not have much control. Thinking I could do better, I got on her. But instead of circling the arena on the rail as I asked, she quickly headed for the gate and I too had very little control. We had forgotten a curb strap!

I later decided that Lady had probably never been in an indoor arena before, and she didn't trust the clicking noise (electric fencer) over the door opposite the gate. I also discovered that she wasn't comfortable with four wheelers, big trucks and tractors. In addition, a truck drove in as we rode (it was late afternoon) and I later learned that Lady's feeding time was whenever her owner came home. I'm sure part of her attitude involved not wanting to miss supper. She is one eager eater!

That one ride on Lady (plus watching me ride her) convinced my husband she wasn't what he wanted. Russ is not a take-charge rider, and Lady is definitely a take-charge alpha mare. I worked with her, trying to "fix" things so he could ride her. I should have known — you can fix Alpha. Lady is a little powerhouse with a strong attitude and a quick mind, but she can also be very sweet and obedient. I learned by experience, however, that if she spooks, I had to be ready! She thinks fast, moves fast, and spins even faster! My first ride down the road by our barn taught me that, when a big dumpster truck passed us. Even though I was able to stay in the saddle when she spun, it took me two years to get over the fear of riding her down that road again!

Lady seemed very nervous at first, and it took her awhile to settle down in her new surroundings. I tried to think of ways to reassure her by touch and voice. I blew in her nose and she gently blew back. Then I decided to not worry about it and just be there with her and focus on quiet thoughts. I couldn't change her alpha mare personality, but I could learn to stay calm (hopefully) and work toward a more confident control. Being "boss mare" has great responsibility;

perhaps she would relax if I convinced her I could handle that position!

I rode her in the indoor area (with a curb strap) until the clicking electric fencer over the door was no longer an issue. After each ride, I led her out to the truck to unsaddle her. We went out and came back to her stall through an entrance much like a hallway, with a cement floor, a solid wood wall on one side and a stall on the other with wire mesh above wood. One day, I had an idea. Knowing she wasn't the best at trailer loading, I decided to work with her in this entrance. I walked her halfway through, stopped her, and asked her to back up. She did what I asked. Then, I asked her to go through again, ahead of me, as I would ask when loading into a trailer.

Even though Lady had willingly walked through that doorway several times before, this time she refused and tried to pull me back to her stall. Since she had told me no, it was my duty now to tell her she couldn't make that decision. I was holding the reins to her bridle, so I merely tightened my hold, putting mild pressure on her to walk forward. She pulled back. I held the pressure until she stretched her neck to relieve it. I released the pressure for a moment, and she stepped back. That was to be expected. I pulled again on the reins, just enough for the pressure to be uncomfortable. She pulled back and I stood there, holding the reins steady and tight, waiting. She finally took a step forward, and I let the reins go slack immediately. She again stepped back. My husband got a chair and sat down at a safe distance to watch. He expressed the opinion that I wouldn't get her through the doorway, and I think he also said something about watching two boss mares butting heads.

Well, of course I had to finish what I'd started! For about fifteen minutes, I did the same thing, holding the reins tight, pulling just enough to make it uncomfortable until she took a step forward, then releasing the pressure. If she stepped back, I would pull again immediately. If she stepped forward and did not step back when I released the pressure, I let her stand a few minutes and praised her. A half hour later, she had come several steps into the passageway and decided she might as well go all the way. It was a moment of the most delicious victory! It was also an important step in our relationship.

A few months later, however, my husband still wanted a different horse, and we traded her off for a quiet little gelding. He rode the gelding before buying and I rode Lady that day. We had such a grand ride through the woods that I actually cried when we left without Lady. Two weeks later, we decided we didn't like the gelding's attitude and we drove all the way back to Kentucky and traded him back for Lady — for me.

I found that Lady was a pretty nice trail horse. I have always enjoyed a horse that is eager to go and Lady is like that. She moves briskly along in her smooth fox-trot-like gait, and she is fun to ride. Now and then, she stops when she doesn't want to go where she's pointed. If we met a person walking on the trail, she would just stop until my husband went on ahead of us, then she would follow closely.

Lady has never threatened to kick another horse on the trail except once during one of our first trail rides. My husband and I had stopped to let our horses eat grass for a few minutes. His horse's tail hit her in the face at one point, and I felt her tense up. I watched the situation, waiting to see what would happen next. As Sammy's long black tail hit her in the face for the second time, I clearly felt her intentions. She whirled quickly, ready to strike. I kicked her hard and yelled "no!" My husband's horse moved out of the way and Lady went back to eating grass.

At first, Lady didn't like being turned out alone, so I put her out with my older gelding, Traveller. She kicked at him. He seemed to like her in spite of her attitude and they apparently worked it out. She was ok with Sammy on the trails, so we tried putting them together in the pasture. For awhile, we put her with one gelding or the other and she would squeal when she first went out, seemingly asserting herself as the "boss lady." Both geldings seemed to understand and they kept their distance. Once she was getting along with either gelding, we tried to put all three together. The two geldings who had been best buddies for years started acting like squabbling, jealous suitors. Lady actually ran across the length of the paddock at one point to come between them! We came close to not keeping Lady because of the situation. The two geldings weren't getting along any more, and none of them came when called! Lady showed a definite preference for Sammy, leaving poor Traveller alone, so we finally put just Lady and Sammy together. They immediately connected. Actually, she connected with him first — hoof to side – before they connected as close companions. Lady obviously favored Sammy, who was also black. They were in the same pasture together for months, and they were in love! We couldn't work with one alone without both of them calling out and fussing. One day, we watched as Sammy lay down to roll and Lady ran across the paddock toward him, whirled and kicked him in the chest several times as he got up. That was the beginning of Lady's solitary confinement. We chose to not take a chance on one of them getting a broken leg. I had lost my first mare that way.

I find that Lady is an excellent teacher. For example, she has taught me the need for more patience. With my old gelding, I open the trailer door and say, "get in there." Lady usually needs a little coaxing and a little waiting, and a very strong hold on the rope! But I have found that quiet patience works best and the job gets a little easier each time. I am also learning to be more flexible. If I turn Lady out and she wants back in, I may put her back in her stall or take her out for a bite of grass or work with her in the arena. I don't tie her unless I am going to be close by, or she will paw a deep hole in the ground!

I am learning to accept things as they are. That means I can ignore Lady's pawing at the gate without throwing things at her. I must clean her stall quickly, however, because she may soon want back in, even though she obviously wanted out the minute she saw me in the barn. If I put her out in the small pasture alone, she will keep coming to the door and looking in to see where I am. She loves attention! No, she demands attention! And she loves her stall because she knows it has a snack in the feed pan and a flake of hay waiting.

Because of Lady, I am learning a new attitude toward working with horses. Maybe I've been with calm, easy Traveller so long that I was getting complacent and careless. I am learning greater awareness, especially when looking for things that might bother a mare's sensitive emotional personality! She will ignore a yellow plastic flag waved all around her, but she will jump sideways entering the arena if someone has left the white plastic chair inside. But then she will go right over to it and smell of it, unafraid.

Russ is learning, too. When I first put Lady out in the little pasture, she wouldn't come in and I had to go get her. One day Russ stood at the gate holding a piece of carrot where Lady could see it. She walked around, eating a bite of grass here and a bite there, getting closer and closer, finally coming to him. Without realizing it, he became the leader that she chose to follow, even though she took her time. The day I first put her out in the big pasture, I let her eat a bite of grain out of a pail before letting her go. When I called her in, holding the pail where she could see it, she came running!

Because of Lady, I am working to control my emotions. My gelding didn't seem to care if I was nervous or in a bad mood. He was always calm and steady and I could relax when riding him. With Lady, my emotions have a definite effect on her actions! I need to be calm and confident because she is very responsive to my moods and dependent on my leadership. I can't have a calm authority over her without controlling myself first.

Lady is most definitely an "alpha" mare and unpredictable at times, but she has the most loving personality. I want to "fix" her headstrong spooky nature around noisy big things coming toward her, but I can't make her not be an alpha mare. I need to learn to be calm myself, to be a confident, quiet and gentle master she can depend on.

I want to be a teacher and caretaker more than a forceful master. I've found from experience that a horse's problem will not go away if I never work with it. Allowing a horse to remain fearful is dangerous. But if I can work with Lady to increase her confidence in me, we form a stronger connection – a loving bond. She knows I love her, and it does affect her behavior.

My husband now says, "I'm glad we got her back. I think you need each other." I am very glad to have her back, too. Even as I continue to work on her "issues," however, I have the feeling that she is still the "boss lady!"

Lady has such a nice gait, I decided to show her. That idea actually grew from all the arena riding I have done (because I was too scared to ride her out on the road!). She had done pretty well in a couple of shows two years ago, and I decided to try again this last summer. First show of the season, and I was excited! I planned for plenty of time to load Lady into the trailer, and I walked her one step at a time toward the trailer ramp, telling her all the while how much I wanted to show others how wonderful she was. She shocked me by eagerly walking right into the trailer, first try! She did quite well for me that day, although we didn't get any blue ribbons.

Next show date, I was a bit worried about the forecast of possible rain. I tried to do everything as I had done before, walking Lady slowly toward the trailer, talking about going to the show. As we got to the ramp, Lady took one sidelong look at me and started backing away. From there on, it just got worse. I finally lost my patience and used the end of the lead rope on her rump. That didn't help. My husband got into the trailer and tried to pull her in. She backed away even more. It started to rain. The ramp got slippery and my husband fell. That did it. I put Lady back into her stall, with another slap on the rump and no hay snack. As it turned out, the show was cancelled because of heavy rain. If Lady had loaded, we would have had to come back in a downpour.

I tried to "make up" with Lady afterward, but I soon realized something was wrong. She acted mad, pouty, hurt and aloof for almost two weeks! Even though I talked to her (yes, I apologized!) and rubbed on her favorite spots, she refused to respond in her usual affectionate way. I was beginning to worry. Other people who knew her also noticed. So I slipped some extra chamomile tea into a couple feedings, and we finally had a breakthrough.

I knew from experience that Lady best responds to patience and persistence and force just gets her too excited. But her refusal to load was inappropriate, and saving me a trip in the rain was no excuse. I felt guilty that I had taken out my frustration on Lady, and I knew I should have stayed calmly focused instead.

I was surprised that Lady had loaded so quickly for the first show. I had been excited that day, but my inner feelings were positive and focused and I was patient and calm as I led her to the trailer. I had added some flower essence to her water and a little extra chamomile tea in her feed, as well as the Moody Mare supplement. I still think it all helped!

For the next show, I was so focused on loading my mare that I didn't think about her feelings. Was there something in ME that caused her resistance? Or was it because I hadn't given her all the calming stuff? I really needed to "listen" to my mare a little more instead of trying to force her.

At one point I sensed a change in this mare, and I know the day it happened. A massage therapist was working on Lady and I was telling the story about trading her off and getting her back, and all the while Lady was nudging me with her nose, and watching me intently, and nudging again. I guess I was pretty much ignoring her. Suddenly, she gave a fast nip at my shoulder! Startled, I was glad for a heavily padded jacket. The therapist, also very surprised, said, "I think she is trying to get your attention!"

Lady definitely had my attention at that point. I scolded her soundly, but thought carefully about the situation. We had been talking about the possibility of selling one of our horses. I think horses understand more than we realize. I started talking to Lady like I would a person, and I explained to her that I did not intend to sell her, in spite of any talk. She was my horse, and I was her owner, and that was it. I may have made that decision at the very moment I told her, and I can't rule out the possibility that her actions had some influence on me! But having said it, I intended to keep my word. Even to a horse.

That afternoon, after the massage, I rode her in the outdoor arena and out into the big empty pasture. We had a grand ride, much like the ride in the Kentucky woods the day we first traded her off. She was calm and obedient, and she gave me a smooth consistent gait. I'm sure a relaxing massage helped. But since then, every ride has been a joy. She is more responsive to lighter cues, without over-responding as much as before. Perhaps Lady has just taught me to give consistent, specific cues, with a gentle touch. Anything else doesn't get the response I am after! She consistently seems more relaxed and more focused. I am enjoying her more and becoming more adventurous in our training goals.

At first, I wondered if this change in Lady might be the result of a certain supplement containing copper. Someone told me that mares need copper, and since I was giving her a hoof supplement, I changed to one that contained copper. But then I checked my records and found she had been on this supplement long before the massage. No, the change in Lady started right after the massage.

I have decided that Lady's new serenity comes from feeling she truly belongs to me — a feeling of being loved, if you will. Perhaps she was uncertain about her own security. She knows about auctions, about horse sales, and about being traded off. I've ridden her for almost four years, and we have had several "discussions" regarding which of us is in charge. I don't allow her to push me around and I try to be more alpha to earn her respect. I know that discipline is part of loving.

Lady is definitely my horse, a loving girl who nuzzles me and gives me kisses, but she is not exclusive. Lots of fellow boarders love on her and she loves back. Her black head is always over her stall door, ready for visitors. She is very demanding, however, and anyone who has the nerve to walk by her stall without giving her proper attention will probably be startled by a squeal and a loud bang as she kicks the wall!

One day I had witnesses! I entered the barn, going first to my Traveller with a hunk of carrot. Lady's head was over her adjoining stall door, expecting a carrot of her own. She got it, and I moved back to check Traveller's water.

A loud bang and a high pitched squeal told me that Lady was disappointed! Immediately, I jumped into her stall, scolding her loudly. She cowered in the back of her stall, looking for a place to escape from my apparent high level of anger. My husband stood nearby, chuckling at Lady's antics. Another woman who loves Lady and probably gives her as much attention as I do, was also right there watching.

Debbie at first couldn't believe our sweet Lady would act that way. But she saw it for what it was worth — a simple demand for attention from a headstrong female!

I really wasn't as mad as I tried to sound, and after I came back out of the stall, I stood there by the door, talking to Debbie and my husband for a few minutes. Lady slowly came from the back of her stall to stand by the door, and then reached her head over the door toward me.

"Look at that," one of them said. "She's trying to make up with you."

Lady was reaching out her nose to me, her big beautiful eyes intently looking at me with her usual depth and personality. I moved a bit closer to her, and for a couple of minutes, we blew in each other's noses. I really do love this mare. I tried to scare her into not kicking her stall and a few minutes later, she was reaching out to me, as if to say, "But we're still friends, right? You aren't really mad at me, are you?"

And I blew back in her nose, to tell her, "Of course we're still friends. You're my Lady."

Connie Owens came out of the womb loving horses and wanting to learn everything she could about them. Her father took her to a riding stable when she was ten. She spent summers there helping care for the horses and leading riders on the "hour ride." There she met people who wanted her to show their horses, which she did for 15 years. She met her husband Mel and "learned she had a lot to learn." They started a Hunter/Jumper stable, taught many riders and trained many horses, some of which went on to perform with the Olympic Pentathlon Team. They found the 80 stall boarding stable they owned didn't allow time to form relationships with the animals with which they loved to work, so they decided to train race horses. They were successful trainers for 14 years. There have since been some off and on years of race training, hunter training, judging, and giving lessons, and Mel is still sharing his knowledge and experience through lessons and clinics. The formation and publishing of the Illinois Horse Network, an all-breed monthly newspaper that informs the Illinois public of state and national news, keeps a now "old woman" busy.

One Big Mare!

By Connie Owens

The riding stable where I worked as a kid had no mares in the rental string, but there were privately owned mares in the main barn. Somehow a couple of them got close enough for one to slice through the other's hide, a gash about a foot and a half long, along the muscle crease from the point of the rump toward the gaskin. That was the first lesson I learned about mares. They kick.

When I was a little older, I rode, trained and showed a pair of geldings, a Walking Horse and an American Saddlebred. We also had a Palomino mare that I rode Western. She was always a problem because she was, by necessity, turned out with the boys. Gelded or not, boys will sometimes be boys. It's never a good idea to turn mares and geldings out together.

After I met and married my husband Mel, we started our own stable and handled many mares. We bought and sold horses of all types. Mel had a way with mares and they always seemed to like him. He was never demanding, but gave them assignments that they could accomplish and they always worked hard for him.

One time we bought a really cute strawberry roan from an old horse dealer. She must have been part draft. She was a little over pony size and pretty hefty, but she had a beautiful head. When we were looking her over she was a little light behind and the dealer attributed it to her shock when he gave her a shot in the rump. We took her home and worked on her for weeks. I was showing Mel how much she had relaxed to grooming when a little breeze came up and her tail hit her leg. She kicked at it. I couldn't explain that, so she went down the road.

We never encouraged our students to buy mares, but once in a while a good buy comes along so you take the chance. Sometimes people brought mares for us to train. Sometimes they worked out and our last best school horses were mares. They were as kind and dependable as any gelding.

One mare that was brought to us was a Thoroughbred that one of our student's parents had bought from a friend for their daughter. The girl had been our student for years and was a very good rider, but her horse was a jumper, a half Morgan that had taken her over five-foot jumps. He had that wicked sense of humor that some Morgans have. It manifests itself into pulling pranks on the rider that result in loosening of the seat and occasionally the rider hitting the ground.

The mare was the equitation horse the girl had needed to show off her impeccable seat and hands. She rode the horse a couple of years and was well served in equitation classes. One day she was walking her mare out after schooling, when the mare stopped, backed up and rolled over backwards. I was on the rail watching and could not discern any reason for the behavior. I swear, she didn't rear; she just sat down and rolled over. It was such a shock to the rider she was always uncomfortable and fearful on the horse from that time on. She had no problem with riding her jumper with all his pranks, but she never again could be confident of what the mare might do. The horse had given no sign of what was to come.

When we moved to the racetrack to train, we owned a few mares. One I remember was so upset at the track that once we got her fit, we would keep her at home until a couple of days before her race. She ran well while we continued that routine and broke her maiden in Chicago. Most racetrack problems disappear after leaving the track. Racing is a tough life for people and horses.

Because of my admiration for the Thoroughbred, I wrote an article in my newspaper (The Illinois Horse Network) about their power, speed, beauty and athleticism. Joan Colby, editor of the Illinois Racing News, read it and called me to express her appreciation for the piece. She felt the same way and knew the breed needed friends. So many people think that Thoroughbreds are wild and crazy. They're just not used to being around horses that they have to pay attention to, and consequently they fail to notice things that horses do that could cause problems. I'm always amazed at how careless people are around horses. A Thoroughbred won't let you get careless.

Joan and I met at the Northern Illinois Horse Fest, and she told me about her friend who had a Thoroughbred that needed a new home. The owner had tried to sell the mare from a newspaper ad, but gave up when one prospective buyer asked if the mare was "an easy keeper." The owner felt if they asked a question like that, they wouldn't be the kind of owner she had in mind for the mare.

There was also the report from a veterinarian that the mare had arthritis in her hocks. This was a vet affiliated with a stable that claimed the horse was unsuitable for the present owner, but they had the perfect horse for her for only $20,000. Things like that happen too often. It can make a person very suspicious about vet pronouncements.

The mare had been trained up to second level dressage, but something had gone wrong and the mare knew she had gotten the upper hand. The owner had become leery of handling her. The owner put her in another stable and after a couple of days had been asked to remove her because of her behavior. Gee, sounded like a project to me! I said we'd be happy to give her a home, sight unseen and arrangements were made to bring her to us. I had a friend with a lovely stable and could turn the mare out in the daytime and provide a roomy box stall for nights.

We had a chance to meet the owner and her husband while they stretched their legs after the drive from Chicago. We were waiting for the horse to arrive when the huge six-horse warm blood trailer pulled in. We didn't get to see the horse there, but the trailer noises sounded big. A short time later we were at the rolling green hills of the mare's new home.

They opened the trailer and led out a big dark brown, dappled mare of such proportions that she had really did belong in a warm-blood trailer. She took my breath away. She had the head of a Canadian Thoroughbred, but her body was magnificent. I was amazed that this animal was going to be mine. We had trained horses that had gone to the Olympics with the Pentathlon Team and they were pretty special, but this mare was the highest quality horse we had ever owned.

The previous owner was holding the mare and we could see she was very uncomfortable doing so. Mel took the horse, to the previous owner's relief, and allowed the mare to pick a little grass. She was very pushy and clearly expected to be in charge. Being 16.3 didn't help her attitude. She was a bully! When you get a mare off the track and they have an attitude, they've probably been on steroids. This certainly wasn't the case here. She just had an overbearing attitude. We later put her in the stall and she seemed to settle in. We were expecting barn problems, but thankfully they didn't develop.

From the beginning I had to impress upon her the fact that I was the alpha mare. She wanted to flail her back feet around when I groomed. I'm afraid she felt the flat of the rubber currycomb along her bottom line more than once. She was sour and thought she could intimidate everyone or at least impress them.

She certainly impressed the first farrier we used. When she got tired of him holding her foot in the air she took it away from him and stomped it down with such force I think the barn shook. He got the point. He wasn't sharp enough to realize that he needed to put the foot down more often or keep it up for a shorter period of time. Like so many people working with horses, time is money and they do whatever is the quickest. That is not necessarily what is best for the horse and ultimately best for them.

I always kept a shank over the mare's nose whenever I handled her, as I do with every horse. A shank doesn't hurt a horse if you don't need to use it, but it's there if you do have to use it. We always taught our students to put a shank on their horses. Most were children with big horses, and because of that they didn't have any trouble handling them. There were no horses pulling away and getting loose in our barn. When we went to shows, no horses were ripping away as they departed the trailer. A shank is a great safety device and will keep a horse from developing a lot of bad habits.

I enlisted the help of a friend, who I thought had a steady seat and good hands, to ride the horse. The mare was about as aggressive under saddle as she was on the ground. She hated the feel of your leg on her side and over the years she taught a few people to ride with a light pressure and a quiet leg. If she felt your heel in her side she would kick at it.

Slowly ever so slowly she began to realize that it wasn't so bad to be ridden. We allowed her to use her head and neck and worked to stabilize her gaits.

That is, we asked her for the speed and balance we wanted and then let her alone as long as she stayed that way.

It was a long process. She had many riders, some of which didn't have good hands; but in the process she also learned patience. She had a name like Stardust when she came, but we always called her Big Mare or Biggo. Her show name was Sweet Georgia Brown, because the stable owner's husband called her Sweetie as we worked to cure the bad attitude. A misnomer if I ever heard one. Over time she did become a Sweetie. I loved to graze her on the best grass we could find. And I could gaze at her for hours. She was a true feast for my eyes.

After she settled on the flat, Mel started her over fences and still bold, she had great scope and courage. Some of Mel's students showed her, and she taught them a lot about being subtle with their aids. My son, David, drove 250 miles one way to show her and fell in love. My husband wanted me to sell her to David, who was getting back into the horse business. It was my son, but I didn't really want to sell her. I hated that I wouldn't see her anymore. I finally relented and David took her to Iowa. I did get to go see her a few times and she was jumping 4' to 4'6." What a thrill! We don't get to see horses going that high anymore.

A year or so later, David needed a different place to keep her and couldn't find anywhere that he thought was suitable in his area. She would do that to you. You always knew she was class and you wanted the best for her. She came back to live with us. It wasn't just the matter of bringing her; we had acquired three horses by then and it meant building a fourth stall practically overnight. It was worth it just to have her back in the barn.

About a year after that, David decided to sell her and her value was beyond my budget. He put pictures of her jumping on the internet and within a week he had a buyer coming from Florida. The potential buyer came and rode her and said he would buy her if she vetted sound.

What about those arthritic hocks? We had had her for years, jumped her over some big stuff and she had never taken a bad step. After 27 ex-rays of all legs, feet, ankles and yes, hocks, she was pronounced sound. The buyer paid the vet to examine the horse and he was well served. I personally have never seen such a complete exam.

The mare went on to compete in Grande Prix classes in Florida under a different name. Her owner thinks so highly of her that he had her picture tattooed on his arm. They say love hurts and I'll bet that did.

While I still don't recommend mares, she was one I was proud to own. Although we think we're too old now to handle horses, I'd take her back anytime. She has a good home now and fortunately they keep me apprised of her activities and they even send a picture once in a while. She's now a light bay because of the Florida sun, but she's still beautiful and a pleasure to behold.

Jenny McCormick-Friehs was born an "Air Force Brat" at Scott Air Force Base, Belleville, Illinois. She lived in Frankfort, Germany, for four years, and later settled in St. Louis, Missouri. She attended college as an art major, then studied hair design. She has been self employed for 23 years as a hair designer. Her passion is animals — all kinds of animals since she was two years old — but horses have been her "true love." As a young-ster, she was often in trouble at home when she sneaked various animals into her bedroom (including turtles, snakes, birds, cats, ferrets, hurt rabbits, even sick foxes she found in the woods!). Her parents began checking every possible hiding place in their house and on their land and sometimes gave out punishment. She says it was worth the trouble.

The Breeze and Me

By Jenny McCormick-Friehs

Early February of 2007 was a season of change in my life. I questioned and prayed for what was about to unfold. I felt an overwhelming desire to pursue a childhood dream.

I was officially horse crazy. I had ridden with friends as a kid, and occasionally a few kind souls who crossed my path invited me to ride with them. I had just turned 43 years old. I wanted a horse. Not someday, but now!

My search began, and because I wasn't very humble with a lot of horse savvy, I bought an eight-year-old Thoroughbred ex-race horse with jumping experience. He was a perfectly beautiful gelding with high spirit and much smarter than I was. I was in love and in a relationship I had longed for.

That relationship lasted three months. I called in a behaviorist to straighten him out, just to learn his problems were my own lack of confidence and ability. I finally submitted to my shortcomings and sold him to a wonderful man who was much more qualified.

I cried for weeks on and off, but people at my stable were very supportive and told me, "he was not good for you." But I knew I was just not good for him. I was crushed. I wondered why would God put this strong desire in me? I felt like such a failure! All the while, God was using horses to make me a better person, to make me humbly look at myself and let God take charge. All I needed to do was listen and respond.

I had always heard mares are awful horses. They are moody and stubborn. "Whatever you do, get a gelding," people told me. So I had everyone I knew looking for my new gelding, this time a quarter horse. I must have ridden 50 horses in a short time. My new criteria included: one, must be a gelding; two, preferably be a black gelding; three, four to twelve years old; and four, most important, must be bombproof! I didn't want to fall off again!

It's just amazing how we set perfect selections in life for ourselves and kick God's sovereign wisdom to the curb! Meanwhile a 23 year old mare named Reina became available at the barn, and the stable owner suggested I give her a try. I will always be thankful for this horse. I thought she was sweet, but she didn't fit any of my criteria. I leased her for a month to figure out what to do, and something magical happened. I regained my confidence with her maternal kindness. She was like a mother holding her baby, and I soared in my enjoyment of riding. I felt like I was back on my path, although she treated me like a toddler who needed to be held by her hand to cross a busy street. I still struggled with the connection of oneness. I fell in love with her, but more like a child with her mother, secure and safe. Again, I struggled, but this time I prayed that God would help me. I didn't want just anyone to have this mare. If I could have afforded two horses, I would have kept her. But I let her go and other wonderful girl purchased her at the stable.

I was so guilt-ridden that it was hard to look at her. She had given me so much and I passed her up. I must have been crazy, but my heart told me to hang on. A good match would arrive. "Be patient," kept coming to mind, along with "don't expect perfection from any horse…that doesn't exist! Just look for good qualities in a horse, and don't be so shy as to not pick a horse that will make you grow as a rider and overcome your personal fears." Those fears, by the way, are something of an embarrassment now. I want to grow as a rider and gain the respect of my horse.

I was on vacation in Florida with my family, and a friend of mine left a message on my cell phone. She said something like, "I have a horse, I feel you could be a match, call me soon." I called her back and she explained more about this horse. My mind was racing – "I hope it's a gelding, I hope he's black." My friend told me she was a six year old sorrel mare, exceptionally beautiful with three white socks and a blaze and built like a brick, very solid. She had been used for cutting and trail. I told her I would look at her. She told me another woman was to look at her the day before I would get back from vacation. I said, "That's fine, I'll call you when I get back if she is available."

I figured, why not? I hadn't liked any of my prospects yet. Fifty horses, and no connection! Then this little voice inside said, "This is your horse. Tell her to put this other woman off for a day." So I interrupted her and said, "Suzette, I have this silly feeling about her. As weird as this sounds, would it be possible to put this other woman off one day so I could have the first opportunity?"

I had a new friendship with Suzette and I had looked at another horse she had and it wasn't a fit at all. I would like to add that Suzette is not a horse broker. Every now and then a boarder or friend would find a good horse and she would help place them. She was an excellent trainer, gifted beyond words. She told me I had a good seat, and should trust myself more. Thank you, Suzette!

Suzette and I both knew at that strange moment Breeze could be the one. She laughed and said "OK, I'll put her off, if it means that much to you." By the way, I believe Suzette was a God send to me at that time. She totally understood me and what my experience had been. She said all in all she just wanted a good fit for horse and rider.

So I rushed to her ranch as soon as I returned from Florida, excited but cautious, because of being let down before. Again, God's voice whispered to me, "Be patient, be calm, and trust in Me." Those words have become part of my personal creed in all areas of my life.

I pulled up to Suzette's ranch and in my anticipation, the long gravel road seemed like forever. I slowly parked and walked to the barn, and Suzette's warm personality welcomed me. "There's Breezy," she said. I looked over at her and she looked at me. Wow. Her eyes were bright and full of life with a depth I hadn't expected from a young horse. Her conformation was exceptional...the barrel chest, striking head, alert ears. I could go on, but I felt the magic. Suzette said to go get acquainted, so I walked up to her. She was very attentive. I brushed her, touched her and hugged her.

Now the real test was to take her for a ride, first in the indoor arena, then the pasture, and finally a trail. We crossed roads with trucks and cars buzzing by (it was a breeze for her), then over a bridge 15 to 20 feet high (she passed again), then to a huge creek about four feet deep of rushing water. At first she was reluctant, then with encouragement she was splashing and wading. What a BLAST!

Needless to say, I put a deposit on her. Suzette said to call her if I changed my mind...and for the next three weeks, I rode her at Suzette's, waiting for her Coggins. Things were great! Then a few days before our transport date, I was riding her and she spooked at a scary monster in the night! She did a 180 degree turn with me lightning fast. Wow, she spooked! And guess what — I still wanted her! Oh, by the way, the scary monster was a donkey that the moonlight had transformed.

Now Breeze and I are having a great time. We've done many trails and adventures. I am learning more and more about her and she is learning about me. I look forward to becoming a better rider. She's been very forgiving of my shortcomings.

Her personality is amazing. Strong, aware, a little bossy, but only when in heat. But just like she forgives me, I forgive her. One of her most amazing qualities is, with my son, she is transformed into a good mother that would never hurt her child. After two weeks, my eight-year-old son took her out of her stall without my permission and led her all around by her halter and finally cross-tied her. I walked into the barn and freaked out, because she normally grabs hay and pushes the limits. But she kindly submitted to my pushy but daring eight-year-old. She is golden in so many ways. She has a kind and generous spirit. I don't think I could take any amount of money for her...she is priceless to me.

Breeze is also playful and fun. One day, I grabbed something out of my car trunk, and she grabbed shoes and jackets out of the trunk and tossed them up and played with them. I laughed so hard. Her curiosity never ends.

I feel mares are misjudged and they are truly intelligent and sensitive creatures. I think being too tough on her is a huge mistake, because she really gets her feelings hurt. I know all about being the Alpha; I have a 220 pound English Mastiff. But you can't push a mare unless she really respects you. You have to encourage and praise a mare. If you lose your patience, stop, thank her and call it a day.

Start over tomorrow. You'll get a lot further. She's not a gelding who can be pushed on and will forget it. She will remember if you aren't fair. I've made minor mistakes and she knows the difference. When it counts, a mare will give you her whole heart. Build her up, encourage her and she's loyal to you for life. That's true love.

Mary Wynn Craig says she cannot remember a time when she was not completely in love with horses. She got her first pony at age five and never looked back. She has served on the Board of South West Quarter Horse Association, and is currently a member of the Board of Alabama Quarter Horse Association. She is an associate professor at Thomas Goode Jones School of Law in Montgomery, Alabama, where she teaches legal writing and other courses, including Animal Law.

Lisa The Alpha

By Mary Wynn Craig

Before we ever looked at the weather report, we knew we were in for another hot Texas day. My husband took his morning coffee and wandered out onto the deck off our second-floor bedroom. "Just checking on things," he said. He came flying back into the bedroom, muttering "Nova's cast," as he headed down, taking the stairs two at a time.

Nova was a new acquisition. A big race-bred sorrel mare, she had firmly established her place at the bottom of the herd's pecking order. For days, she had lurked at the edge of the herd, nervously looking for who was going to harass her next. On that morning, she was really in trouble, though. She was cast in the catch pen close to the house. Made of oilfield pipe, the pen was immovable and dangerous to a horse like Nova who had two legs over and two legs under the bottom rail.

I don't know how long Nova had been in that position, but Lisa knew. Lisa, the alpha mare, who left no doubt who was in charge.   I wasn't there when Lisa was born, but I suspect she came out with ears pinned, teeth bared and nose wrinkled. She is all mare. More importantly, she is all alpha mare. Lisa ascribes to the notion that if you're going to do something, you should do it well. In fact, she loves her job.

When I first saw Lisa, she was a yearling filly, standing in a pile of sand and rocks outside a little town in New Mexico. We had gone to this place to look at a Quarter Horse gelding and two miniature mules for a friend who was starting a horse facility. He thought it might be fun to give wagon rides, and was interested in the gelding as a rental horse and the mini-mules as a draft team. The gelding had a club foot, and the mules were neither miniature nor mules. They were full-sized hinnies. We knew he would not be interested in any of the three equines.

We were dealing with a skinny cowboy with the ugliest hat I had ever seen. His face was dark from the sun, with deep wrinkles caused by squinting against that New Mexico sun for more years than I could count. We were trying to exit gracefully from his sales pitch when I looked into the back pen and saw a skinny, fuzzy buckskin filly. I had been in love with buckskins ever since Dale Evans rode Buttermilk into my living room when I was small.

I cleared my throat a little and asked, "Is your buckskin for sale?" His narrow eyes narrowed a little further, and he said, "She might be." We dickered for a little while until we had a price. I explained that I had a horse for sale, and until someone bought him, I wouldn't have money for another horse. I'd check back, and if she was still available, we would talk some more.

When we got back to El Paso that afternoon, we had a message that someone was coming to look at the horse we were selling. The woman came, rode the horse, and he bucked with her. I resigned myself to no sale when the woman started laughing, explained she liked a horse with spirit, and bought him without dickering over the price.

We went the next day and picked up the filly. She was wild as a deer. I couldn't touch her, and had a cowboy friend of ours put the halter on her. She dragged him all over the place, but he didn't let go. Over the next few months, Lisa and I became good friends. We stayed friends, even when she turned gray in her third year. By the time Nova came to live with us, Lisa was an 1100-pound flea bit gray Quarter Horse with a permanent scowl. She loved me and enjoyed spending time with me in the pasture or on trail rides, but she had little use for other horses.

Lisa had been Nova's worst enemy for the few weeks Nova had been there. She would leave food to chastise Nova. In fact, Nova walked around with bite marks and hoof marks for weeks courtesy of Lisa. That morning, though, Lisa was acting differently toward Nova because, while Nova lay cast in that pen, Lisa was standing guard like a mother over a foal.

My husband and I struggled to help, sweating and tugging and pulling on half a ton of dead weight to get Nova in a position where she could stand up and shake off the dust. First we would move her hind-quarters a little, then tug and pull on her front legs, moving her inch by inch out from under the railing and into the pen. Nova did not cooperate much. When we would pull or tug, Nova would fight. We would calm her down and start over. Always, Lisa stood out of the way, but watchful.

Finally, after what seemed like hours but was only about 15 or 20 minutes, Nova was free of the railing. She stood, shook hard, and breathed deeply. I supposed the trauma of being cast and pulled and tugged on made her take a few moments to collect herself. Maybe that is why she stood her ground when Lisa walked up to her and started smelling and nudging. We could see every bit of white in Nova's eyes, but she stood her ground.

Lisa checked her over. My husband and I got out of the way, not wanting to get tromped on when Lisa ordered everyone around in that little pen. For a minute or two, Lisa sniffed and smelled, poked and prodded. Finally, satisfied that Nova was fine, Lisa bit her hard on the rump. Life was back to normal in our little herd.

Lisa is part Two Eyed Jack, part Hard Twist, and a couple of other bloodlines thrown in. She's sure on the trail, bothered by little. If I don't ride Lisa for months, I can throw a saddle on her and she reacts like she's been ridden every day of her life. She takes everything in stride, but never loses sight of her responsibility as alpha mare.

I think often about Lisa standing over Nova, protecting her while she was in trouble, even though she did not like Nova and usually showed her no mercy. Then I think how much more Christ-like we would be if we treated everyone like we should treat our children, standing guard over our enemies, protecting them from evil.

My husband says that horses are much closer to God and understand Him much better than we do. I think he's right.

Mary Wynn Craig has written yet another story, this one about her husband's horse, Boss Lady. She and her husband live on twelve acres in Grady, Alabama, with their seven Quarter Horses and Paints, and a host of dogs, cats and fish. Mary has served on the Board of Directors for two separate therapeutic riding programs. She judged the equestrian competition for Special Olympics one year, and continues to support therapeutic riding.

The Lady Who Loved My Husband

By Mary Wynn Craig

My husband, Merve, grew up around horses, but he never liked them much. His dad's nickname was "Cowboy," partially because he would ride anything with four legs, including a cow, but mostly because he always had horses. Merve's brother liked horses and had a succession of his own growing up. My husband was much more interested in motorcycles and girls. His only contact with the horses was cleaning up after them, or "riding the rough off" when relatives would visit and want to ride. He never expressed an interest in owning a horse, and although he was polite and helpful when I bought a horse again after 20 or so horseless years, he seemed less than enthralled with equine ownership.

After about a year of carting me back and forth to the stable and declining offers from friends to ride one of their horses when I went out on the trails, he came home from work with a big announcement. He had sold a sizeable job and was getting a bonus. When I inquired about what he was going to do with the money, his response made my jaw drop open. "I think I'm gonna buy a horse," he said. "I've heard about one that's available. Wanna go look at her?"

Look at her we did, and what we saw made us heartsick. A beautiful chestnut mare was standing in a tiny pen with manure and muck almost to her knees, surrounded by literally thousands of flies. They were crawling all over her — up her nose, around her eyes, in her ears. The proud owner waded into the pen and brought her out where we could examine her.

"Her name's Boss Lady," he told us. "See that brand on her shoulder? She was a prison guard horse in Oklahoma." We saw an "O" and a star on her left shoulder. We also saw a "14" on her left hip. She was a genuine original Walter Merrick mare — a true find. Lady was a little sway-backed, and the owner said he thought she was about 20 years old. Her eyes were soft and kind, but she had a look of quiet resignation about her, as if her life was never going to be better. She was wrong.

After some negotiation, we bought the mare with accompanying tack, and a halter and lead rope for the queenly sum of $750 and a shotgun. My husband immediately saddled Lady and rode her about 5 miles to the stable where we kept our gelding. He was grinning all over by the time he got to the stable. "She moved right out," he told me. "Not one problem the whole way!" He was in love, and before long, Lady was in love with him, too.

Merve started going riding without me, spending hours out on the trails. He would return from those rides marveling at the sight of birds or the smell of the flowers along the trail. He became accustomed to the sound of creaking leather and the sweet odor of horse sweat. He found Lady liked to swim, and when he would ride her off into the Rio Grande, he would have trouble convincing her to get out of the water. Once, on a trail ride, we were assaulted by a pack of dogs. They circled us, barking and lunging and nipping at our horses. Merve turned Lady around and charged those dogs. They ran away, tails between their legs, yelping a little after she stepped on one. Lady was fearless. I suppose years of standing guard over convicts and the training that goes along with that gives a horse some confidence.

After awhile, we got our own place with enough property to support a horse or two, and Lady began living in our yard. Merve and Lady both liked that. In minutes, the two of them could be down the road and riding on the Rio Grande, or out on the mesas surrounding El Paso. I only rode Lady once. She gave me about one minute and then tried to buck me off. She didn't like me much. I was apparently a threat to her love affair with Merve. I got the message, and gave my blessing to the two of them and their relationship.

About three years into his partnership with Lady, Merve came home troubled one day. "Lady was stumbling a little on our ride," he told me. "I'm afraid she may be getting too old for what I'm doing with her." Admittedly, 23 isn't that old, but we could not really be certain of Lady's age. We had contacted Walter Merrick's ranch in an attempt to get information about Lady, but they produced lots of chestnut mares, and could not help us. After a few more months and a few more stumbles, Merve decided Lady needed a new career. We didn't have enough room or money to just let her stand in our paddock for the rest of her life. I was on the board of a therapeutic riding group in El Paso, and we contemplated lending Lady to them as a lesson horse. As much as we loved her, we could not bear the thought of just giving her to them and not retaining ownership. At least not then.

Our friend Joy came out to evaluate Lady. She and her assistant rode Lady backwards, threw their hats in her face, bounced up and down, climbed all over her, and did everything they could to make her spook or act in a way unsuitable for a therapy horse. Lady was unflappable. Once or twice she pricked her ears and wrinkled her eyes, as if she was wondering why those humans were acting so oddly, but we all knew she was exactly what those precious handicapped children needed.

When we delivered Lady to their stable, they already had her name plate hanging on her outside pen. We hugged her and cried and went home, asking ourselves over and over if we were doing the right thing, even though we knew the answer. We heard from Joy in a week. Lady was everyone's favorite and one of the best acquisitions they had ever made.

We gave Lady about two weeks to settle into her new routine, and then we went to see her. She was standing in her pen, munching on dinner when we opened the gate and walked in. She saw Merve, left her food, walked straight to him, and put her head in his chest. Then she sighed deeply, content to see him. She had obviously missed him. I started crying, and cried all the way home, wishing we had a place to keep her. But that was pure selfishness. She was doing a wonderful work, teaching earth-bound children to fly.

Therapeutic work is stressful for horses. They often have an unbalanced, incapable child in the saddle, one person leading, and another person on each side helping hold and balance the child in the saddle. Work can be slow and cumbersome. Lady handled it all with grace and style. The kids argued over who could ride her, and she never disappointed. Lady was often the horse Joy put brand new clients on, because she was steady as a rock.

When we could emotionally handle the donation, we gave Lady to the kids, thinking she would have a long life being petted and hugged and brushed by adoring riders. Unfortunately for Lady, that was not to be. In just a few weeks, Lady began to tire easily and grew lethargic. A vet examination confirmed that she had a pituitary tumor. She was too old to operate on, and the stress of therapeutic life would be too hard on her.

Merve and Joy and I talked about what to do. The vet had given us some good news and some bad news. Lady could no longer work for a living, but if her life could be relatively stress-free, we did not need to put her down. Joy found a woman with some property and a willingness to let Lady live out her life as a companion to other retired horses. Lady spent her last year as a pet of sorts, a designation she had most certainly earned.

Early one morning Joy called us crying. Lady had died the night before. Her caretakers saw no sign of a struggle. As near as anyone could tell, Lady had just gone to sleep and did not wake up.

If God allows me to, I'll work in the Heavenly stables. If He gives me that privilege, then I am certain of two things. I will see our wonderful chestnut mare there, and I will gratefully care for and minister to the Lady that loved my husband.

Jane Farmer was born loving horses. As a kid, she taught herself how to not fall off US Army rental horses. Her first riding lessons were at a day camp when she was eleven. At thirteen, she took serious hunt seat lessons, participating in a few shows. At fifteen, she inherited an unsound geriatric horse; a year later, she bought a "real" horse with babysitting money. While enrolled at the University of Tennessee, she rode with the Equestrian Club. After graduation, she became a park ranger at Great Smoky Mountains National Park. She rode in horseback rescues, taught park rangers to ride and frequently exercised park service horses on mountain trails. She met one of her life goals when she galloped across the fields in Cade's Cove. Now a Mississippi home school mom, she rides for pure pleasure but hopes to do a trail competition someday. She says, "My eternal goal is to work in God's barn in Heaven." She finds great comfort from Revelation 19:11, "I saw Heaven standing open and there before me was a white horse, whose rider is called Faithful and True…" Visit Jane's website at www.agapehands.com.

"Here, Kitty, Kitty"

By Jane Marie Allen Farmer

Recently, I heard that a horse with one blue eye and one brown eye is schizophrenic. That was many years after I had purchased Polly.

My horse ownership ordeals began when my parents purchased a weekend country retreat, complete with a gift horse who just happened to be unsound. I was fifteen and a blooming horsewoman with a year of rigorous huntseat training issued by Colonel Townsley, an authentic, bow-legged, retired cavalry officer. An unsound horse would not do for me, so I saved up my babysitting money and bought Polly.

Polly was close to perfect, a much more perfect and patient horse than I was a rider. A quarter-horse type bay with a big old blaze and one blue eye. I always thought her blue eye was really cool. Her personality became my measure for a good horse. Polly was six and only green broke. In a very short time I was jumping her 3' with no saddle and only a halter. A very giving mare, she was always forgiving of all of my immaturities.

Her traumatic death from colic two years later sent me into a tail spin. I was terrified of owning another horse. For the next thirty years I rode a lot but only other people's horses. I would not buy one for myself.

I finally tested the water by buying my son a pony. I boarded him, so I really did not have total responsibility for his care. After three years of owning Lucky, my confidence was a bit restored so I broke down and bought myself a rescue horse, Zack. What did Zack have to lose with me as his mom? Four years later, Zack colicked, foundered and was put down.

I did not have time to consider my future with horses because as soon as my non-horse-loving mother heard of Zack's death, she told me she was devastated for me and was buying me a new horse. A fifty-three-year-old little girl's dream come true.

I put hundreds of miles on my car as I searched and searched for the non-existent perfect horse. Smooth gait, sweet, bold color, good with kids, 15.2 hands, jumps, etc, etc. Maybe my high standard was my way of avoiding buying a horse.

Then a peripheral friend recommended that I contact a friend of his who lived only a couple of miles down the road from me. Wayne had been training some young Spotted Saddle Horses and was ready to sell one. Fat chance of that working out.

Unoptimistically, I went out to see my friend's friend's horse. I got out of my car and Wayne had the mare in the cross ties, I approached her from the rear and could see that she was a nicely built horse, 15.2 hands, a bay pinto, one of my favorite colorings. I eyeballed her as I walked closer, liking what I saw: 50/50 brown bay and white, cat paw spots, black polka dots on her legs, black coronets, dark hooves, very pretty. I walked up beside her and that is when she turned her head to look at me.

My mouth gaped open, my eyes flickered, and I got a lump in my throat. I must have looked odd. Wayne noted my stare and said almost apologetically, "She's got one blue eye." I don't even remember my response; I was trying to keep from crying. I almost bought her before I rode her.

My heart was saddened when Wayne delivered her to the barn where I board Lucky. As Wayne drove off, Miss Kitty ran across the pasture following his truck as far as she could. I hoped one day, she would honor me with that loyalty.

I have had Miss Kitty for a little over a year now. Miss Kitty has filled a hole in my heart that no other horse could have. She is my best bud. She is as sweet as Polly was, a faster learner although a bit more of an independent thinker. She jumps logs with enthusiasm. Her Spotted Saddle Horse gait is as smooth as silk. I can easily ride her with only a halter and rope. She has already helped a totally new rider earn a Boy Scout merit badge.

She is a character. She easily unties her rope. She turns and rests her chin on my foot when we stop for a trail break. She goes all soppy-horse when I spray her with the hose, pawing for more if I turn it off too soon. Scratch her on the chest and her nose points to the sky. Scratch her on the withers and she nods her big old head. She is madly in love with the aging, diminutive Mr. Lucky. If she sees my truck coming, she runs to great me. If she misses the truck she comes cantering to my call, "Here, Kitty, Kitty."

Miss Kitty has completed the circle. She has healed my cleft heart. She has eased the long festering hurt of the loss of my first horse-love, Polly. I can now think of Polly with fondness, not sorrow. Thanks, Mom!

"Hmmm…must be a mare!"

Instructor and trainer **Ron Meredith** has refined his "horse logical" methods for communicating with equines over 40 years as president of Meredith Manor International Equestrian Centre, an ACCET accredited equestrian educational institution. From its humble beginning with six students in 1963, Dr. Meredith has brought the school to its current world class level. He has held seven AHSA judges' cards and has trained top level horses and riders in the cutting and reining world. He has published over 75 articles in more than 150 equine magazines and journals and has been awarded numerous distinctive recognitions. In 1981, he received an Honorary Doctorate of Equestrian Studies Degree from Salem College.

Gender Differences: Training Mares

By Ronald W. Meredith, D.S.
President, Meredith Manor International Equestrian Centre

The first horse I ever bought for myself was a registered Arabian mare. Her name was Rafsu and after all these years I can still remember her registration number. She was one of my two favorite horses ever and she survived my early attempts at breaking her, which was how people perceived training back then. She just forgave all my mistakes and kept on being a nice mare despite everything I did wrong.

So I am a little prejudiced toward mares. Not everyone is. I know people who only want geldings because they believe they are more reliable. They point out that geldings do not have serious mood changes or interpret things differently from day to day because of hormone swings. So they have got a bit of logic to back up their prejudices.

Some people feel that mares are safer than stallions but I do not. You always know what a stallion is thinking about every few seconds so it is easy to predict his behavior and interrupt his thoughts every few seconds so you keep his attention focused on you. Mares are more unpredictable in that they do not necessarily allow you to interrupt whatever it is they are doing. First, they decide whether they are going to pay any attention to you at all. Mares train you to pay careful attention to what they are doing and to what you are doing at all times.

A lot of people say they do not like mares because they have more "attitude" than geldings. They do seem to have more definite attitudes but that does not necessarily mean worse attitudes. The key to working with mares is to understand what is behind their attitudes and to work with them from that understanding rather than fighting with them about who is right.

Mares are naturally protective of their individual territories. If they feel threatened, their first instinct is to get in position to fire both barrels. If a horse kicks in a show class, it is usually a mare objecting because she thinks someone has gotten too close and is coming into her territory uninvited.

When a mare turns her back to you when you open her stall door, she is telling you that this is her territory and you have no rights here. So you just wait at the door until she finally looks back and acknowledges you. Then you step back and acknowledge that this is her home, her space and you respect that. Then she says, "OK, you understand." And she will turn around and allow you to come in to get her.

If you flick a whip at her or try to force her to face you and come over to you, she will expect you to be rude whenever you come into her stall. You will get the cold shoulder every time. Her attitude is, "You're at my house and you have to behave politely if you want to come in." As I said, mares are very good trainers.

Mares, especially those raised in herds, also have higher awareness of pecking orders. If you start a mare and she is really submissive and nice, she will probably stay that way. If you start a mare that thinks she is at the top of the pecking order, you need to go along with her. You lead the dance without ever letting her become aware that she is not the one doing the directing. You accomplish that by never crossing the line that starts an argument.

When you first turn young horses loose in the arena to play, they often take off and leave like they are making a big escape. Geldings and colts will run and show off with a kind of "look at me" attitude. A mare with a strong personality is more likely to make a really big escape, do a lot of posturing, even kick out. She will look back to make sure you saw her display or her kick. Her attitude is, "Did you see that? Pay attention to what I can do."

Never argue with a mare. In her mind, she is right so if you cross the line that makes her mad, she will fight with you. So you just allow her displays and her kicking every time until she finally decides she wants to come up to you. Then you do a lot of grooming and making friends with her, using rhythmic grooming to establish relaxation and creating the feeling that you are a very nice place to be. If she feels she is at the top of the pecking order, she will think it is totally appropriate that you are grooming her and giving her attention.

As you start heeding her on a lead line, you introduce new pressures in the littlest bites possible so that she continues to feel that everything is her idea. If you stay just below the feeling that she is going to become resistant to the new pressure you are showing her, you will keep the situation under control without ever starting a fight. When you start her under saddle, you continue to show her each new pressure in the smallest possible bites. Never introduce something new that is more than two baby steps away from something she already knows and feels she owns.

A really bad mare may be as bad as it gets. But a really nice mare is as good as you will get. Years ago, we used to take extra horses to show and we would lease them to people for classes. One of the best we ever had was a quarter horse mare named WMD Aloha. We called her Mother. She knew the patterns for every contest. You could rope off her. You could put a little kid on Mother for a pleasure class, tell them to just sit there, and she would listen to the announcer and never miss gait change or change of direction. When the ringmaster stood in the middle with his arms out, Mother knew it was time to line up. Once while I was hauling her, the trailer came off the hitch. Thankfully, the trailer just rolled to a stop without incident. When I opened the door to check on Mother, she had broken a sweat but that was all. Mother was about as good as it gets.

Horses are patternistic but the different sexes seem to feel patterns differently. If a mare is used to a certain pattern of interaction with you, she gets to feeling you owe her that pattern whenever she sees you. Say, for example that you have gotten into the habit of stopping at her stall to give her some scratching and loving every time you walk by. Now if you walk by and do not stop, you will look back to see her frowning and fretting. She is indignant because you neglected your duty.

Geldings, on the other hand, see you coming and say, "Hi, good to see you. Are you planning to stop by today?" If you do not stop, they do not hold it against you. Stallions see you coming and immediately start wondering, "Is there going to be a party?" If you do not start the party routine, they just go back to eating.

Old time horse trainers know there are only two ways you can argue with a mare and neither one works.

Meredith Manor is an equestrian vocational school dedicated entirely to producing professional riders, trainers, instructors and farriers for the horse industry. All programs and courses are designed specifically to prepare students for a successful equine career. Students don't have to excel in academic, classroom based classes to be successful at Meredith

Manor, but they must have a passion for horses and a dedication to having a successful equestrian career.

Meredith Manor International Equestrian Centre, 147 Saddle Lane, Waverly, WV 26184. Phone: 1-304-679-3128. Or 1–800-679-2603 (in U.S. only) Website: www.meredithmanor.edu

Michelle Corvallis is 16 years old and lives in Collinsville, Illinois. She has been involved with horses since she was eight years old. Trained to ride and handle horses by Mary Skittino of Royale Ranch (O'Fallon, IL), she rides in several disciplines. In 2006, she qualified in Arabian Youth Nationals and Arabian Canadian Nationals. In 2007, she also qualified in Arabian Sport Horse Nationals. In addition to her 12 year old Mare, RRS Cheyenne, she has also trained from birth her now two-year-old Arabian Filly Mohktar Nasheeta and her five-year-old Arabian Gelding Royales Razmataz who is now beginning his Western Pleasure show career. Michelle rides five or six days a week and maintains a 4.0 average at Collinsville High School. She hopes to earn scholarships with her grades and her equestrian skills so she can pursue her dream of a career and owning an Arabian Horse Ranch.

A Mare, a Girl and God's Plan

By Michelle Corvallis

I remember the first time I saw my horse. I was a shy eight-year-old girl, having my very first riding lesson. I was so excited about riding! For as long as I could remember, I was in love with horses. I walked into this simple red and white barn and there were so many people and horses. The riding instructor, Mary, greeted me and said I would ride a horse named Cheyenne. I followed Mary into the back of the barn and in the very last stall stood this little grey Arabian mare. In much the same way I was looking at her, Cheyenne was staring right back at me as if to say "Yeah right, you think you are going to ride me?" To this day I still get the same look when she is in one of her mare moods.

Mary saddled and bridled her, which was not a easy task as Cheyenne held her head up as high as she could to make it difficult to put the bit in her mouth. Then Mary asked her niece Jessie to lead me around on Cheyenne.

As Jessie walked with Cheyenne, she told me Cheyenne's owner never came out to see her. In fact, her owner probably didn't even know what color she was, because when Cheyenne was a baby she was Chestnut with a white blaze and now at four years old she was dark gray. Jessie also told me that no one at the barn really liked Cheyenne because she had a bad attitude towards people especially on her bad mare days.

I felt sorry for Cheyenne and I told my Mom all about her after my lesson. I decided that I would give her the love that she needed. I had fallen in love with the little grey mare with the bad attitude.

I believe that Cheyenne and I were destined for each other and this was God's plan. As I was learning to ride, I was also gaining confidence in myself and in Cheyenne. By the time I was nine years old my mother was tracking down Cheyenne's owner so that she could buy her for my birthday. As much as I loved Cheyenne, this gray mare loved me. At times she would give me that certain nicker that a mare gives only to her foal. Dave, my riding instructor's husband, swears to this day that Cheyenne picked me.

This love connection between Cheyenne and I was not without its struggles. Some days both of us would be in a mood, and I would end up in tears and Mary (my trainer) would have to ride Cheyenne to straighten her out (Cheyenne would sometimes take advantage of my young age).

When my Mom finally was able to buy Cheyenne, she still did not tie or clip, she was hard to bridle and hated fly spray. My Mother and I soon found out that dealing with a mare required compromise and patience. Cheyenne is an intelligent Arabian mare with a lot of stamina; if I do not compromise, nobody wins. I wear out long before she does.

One occasion comes to mind. I was on a trail ride and there was a little creek that we had to cross. I said "Go" and she said "NO!" She was not going to get her feet wet. We fought over this stupid creek for five minutes. She would rear ever so carefully and turn around and go the other way. I would turn her back towards the creek and then as soon as we got close she would rear again and off we would go the other way. At one point we got really close to the creek and I thought finally we are going to go. No, she came to a dead stop and gave me a look as to say, "You have got to be kidding." So, I got off and was going to lead her across the creek. She decided to push me as if to say "You first." Then she jumped across the creek. She did not get her hoofs wet but my feet were soaked. Yes, she once again outsmarted me, and I let her have this one and everyone had a good laugh.

Even though she can be difficult, she is also loving. Every day when I go to her paddock and whistle, she whinnies and comes right to me. I love her more than any of my other horses, even though she has been a challenge. She does not like me riding other horses. Her paddock is right next to the riding arena, and if I am on another horse she will walk the rail following this horse with her ears pinned back as if to say "Why do you have my girl on your back... she is mine!"

Cheyenne has a dominate attitude and she wants to be the head mare in every respect. But with Cheyenne and me, we have come to an agreement that we are equal. I have found that when working with a mare you have to be willing to compromise and if you push too hard all that you will accomplish is getting more attitude from the mare and possibly ending up on the ground and not accomplishing anything.

I have taken this little gray mare from the back stall of a little red and white barn to showing in class A Arabian horse shows. I have shown her in Western, Hunt Seat, Dressage, Jumping, Speed Events and Native Costume. She has come a long way from being the horse nobody liked to the horse that all the other riding students now wish they had!

The one thing I want everyone to know is that even though we have days of attitude and struggle, we are a team and we work together. If I am having a bad day, Cheyenne can sense this and she tries to be as good as she can be. If she is having an especially bad mare day, I let her have a easy ride and just relax. We were meant for each other, and I thank God that he has brought us together. There is not enough money in the world that anyone could offer me, and I will never sell her. Even on our worst days, we know that we love each other more than anything else.

Oh, one more thing...Cheyenne had a foal named Nasheeta that is now a two year old filly. Cheyenne has taught her well. And here I go again.

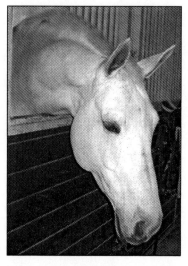

Laura Boyer and her husband Steve (an equine veterinarian) live in Northern California. They have a daughter, Kendra, and two sons. One son is a Green Beret currently serving our country; the other is a sophomore at the University of Pennsylvania. Laura grew up in suburban Denver without many opportunities to commune with horses, yet this was her consistent dream as a young girl. When Kendra began riding at the age of eleven, mother and daughter found they had a love in common. Although raising three children and working as an environmental engineering consultant kept her busy, Laura loved the moments she could spend getting to know these magnificent creatures up close and personal. After seeing Kendra off to college, Laura realized that if she didn't start riding consistently herself, she would lose contact with her past dream. At the age of 51, Laura purchased her first horse, Irena, a 14-year-old Belgian warmblood hunter mare, who passed away six months later from acute colic. After the loss of Irena, Laura searched for six months before she and Proster, a Russian Trakehner, found each other. So the dream continues.

Twenty Life Lessons from Irena

By Kendra Boyer

This piece was written by Laura's daughter based on remembered conversations during the time in which Irena was Laura's equine companion. "I received them within days after Irena's passing," says Laura. "What a tremendous comfort they were and continue to be."

1. Don't let anyone tell you what to do or how to do it; you obviously know what's best!
2. It's more fun to rebel through outsmarting someone, than getting in their face.
3. Listen to the ones who truly love you, even if you're scared.
4. If it's challenging, make it look easy; if it's boring, make it interesting.
5. It's okay to be sassy sometimes; everyone else will learn to deal with it.

6. Trust evolves with time, but once it's there, it's solid.
7. Listen to your instincts.
8. Never forget ANYTHING!
9. It's okay to wonder what's out there.
10. If you just stop and listen, you might understand what someone's trying to tell you!
11. It's smart to stay out of your special someone's way when they're having a bad day.
12. It's okay to be scared of something, even if it's always been there and you weren't scared of it before (especially if you're a mare).
13. Know your job and do it right the first time.
14. There's always time to hang out with the girls after work.
15. Never trust a man with steel shoes, no matter what!
16. It's fun to play mind games with those who think they can control you.
17. Work hard when you're young and a pleasant life will follow.
18. Those with a little spirit have no limits.
19. Look up to the hills – that's where you'll find your soul.
20. You don't need to speak the same language to tell someone you love them; it's one of those things they just know.

Kendra Boyer, 23, and Marilyn, six, currently reside in Northern California. Marilyn was just three years old when she and Kendra were fortunate to cross paths. One year earlier, Kendra had found another home for her first horse Joey, whom she'd had for about six years. She was missing that constant equine companionship. Although Dad, an equine veterinarian, thought being half-way through college was not a good time to be "saddled" with a horse, Kendra and Mom convinced him that there never really was a good time, just to humor him, and so why not now? Plus, Marilyn had stolen Kendra's heart at their first meeting. Since then, Kendra graduated from college with a Bachelor of Science degree in Animal/Equine Science, and Marilyn has been that constant refuge when post-graduate life gets stressful. Kendra is currently working as an accountant in the San Francisco Bay Area and continuing her education, striving to afford horse show expenses so she can occasionally show off that fancy hunter mare, Marilyn.

Don't Tell, Ask!

By Kendra Boyer

"Marilyn, let me put your halter on!" My three year old filly thought she would have a little fun today. Finally, after she spun her rear toward me the third time, I took the lead rope and gave her a smack. That was how I learned my first lesson about these absolutely divine animals called "mares."

She proceeded to go through the stall guard and head for the stairs. "No, Marilyn, not the stairs!" my fellow barn mates shouted as I ran around the side of the barn to catch her. If I ever was close to a heart attack, this was the time. I closed my eyes and prayed this wouldn't be the end. I can still vaguely hear the roar of excitement as I rushed around the corner, afraid of what I was to find. There she was, standing at the bottom of two flights of concrete stairs, calmly eyeing me like I was some kind of uptight freak. I immediately felt weak and had no control over my shaking hands. I heard someone tell me I could breathe now, so I did.

As I walked her back to her stall, I could hear people excitedly talking in the background about her amazing jump down one flight, her perfect stride, and leap down the next. Afterwards, she simply took a few trot steps and then just stood there ready for her halter. This is when I learned the lengths to which a mare will go just to prove a point. She may have given me the worst panic attack of my life, but it was then I understood: don't tell, ask (and nicely for that matter).

Mares seem to prefer to view us as their teammate and their friend, rather than their owner and authority. They teach us just as much as we teach them. Marilyn has taught me and many others similar lessons. I recall leaving a bossy braider with her at one of our shows. As I left to allow him to get to work, I was quickly turned around by a loud thump. The braider was picking himself off the ground outside of her stall very upset and calling her names I probably shouldn't repeat. When he saw me watching, he immediately changed his tune, put on a fake smile, and went back in the stall. When I checked on them, Marilyn, of course, was standing there perfectly relaxed looking like an angel. I did, however, recognize that upward tilt of her head and look in her eye. Yes, Marilyn, I'm sure he just fell on his own.

Another time on the show grounds, Marilyn decided she didn't really like this business-like, impersonal groom leading her to the mounting block and expecting her to stand still for him. Many times, as I would try to mount, she would resist the groom's strong hold attempting to either bolt forward or dance around, making a graceful mount impossible. Then, as soon as the groom released her bridle, she would walk ever-so-slowly to the warm up ring, as if everyone was making such a fuss over nothing. Later at the same show, the groom, with a rather sheepish look on his face, brought her out and she calmly endured the whole process. When my mom asked the groom what had changed, he reached into his chest pocket and pulled out a peppermint candy. Once again, Marilyn had trained someone in her life about how to appropriately ask her to do something.

It is amazing to me how mares teach us in ways that are not mean-spirited, but definitely firm and to the point. It is perhaps their motherly way of showing us how we should behave. "Motherly" is actually an excellent way to describe my mare. As I lead her various places, no matter where we are I can always feel her warm breath on my arm as she follows close behind. I can feel her compassion and love as she gently grasps my arm with her lips and stands perfectly still for a hug. If I'm standing nearby busily cleaning my tack or chatting to someone else, after a while I realize she is resting her head on my shoulder trying to catch some shut eye. Even when my little dog Louie starts playing too rough around her, she just stands there as he topples over between her front legs or she'll even carefully try to move out of the way. Not without a look on her face, of course, that says "Mom, are you kidding me? This dog is so immature."

I can also recall last summer when in her mind she adopted another mare's baby. This foal was turned out with her mother right next to Marilyn's pasture. After a few days, I realized I could not ride her in the arena without constant whinnying, and we could not move the mare and baby without upsetting Marilyn. Everyone told me she spent all day staring at this foal over the fence line. Although this baby had a perfectly fine mother, Marilyn still felt as if she needed to watch over her for some reason. It's as if she understands she is supposed to take care of little ones, even if they aren't hers. I honestly don't think I even know people that are that responsible and caring!

Recently I moved Marilyn to a barn where my mom keeps her horse. Although everyone was eagerly awaiting Marilyn's arrival, when she finally arrived, there were several days when it seemed the talk centered on which hormone regimen we should institute for her because she obviously was going to need something. I'd been through this before, in fact, pretty much in every barn we settled into. I knew it would just be a matter of time when both they and Marilyn would adjust to each other. When a lesson was going on in the lower barn area, Marilyn could be heard whinnying from the upper arena where we were riding. Perhaps she was supposed to be in the other lesson and everyone forgot? But make no mistake, everyone knows who Marilyn is. She is the palomino, the platinum blonde Swedish warmblood. She is the one who runs to her window as someone is walking past her barn, and whinnies to them in case they might want to come back and socialize for a bit.

Mares are truly amazing creatures, and Marilyn is no exception. I can only attempt to incorporate some of the lessons my mare has taught me in my dealings with others, especially when I have children of my own. Perhaps then I can use some of her teaching methods to raise them as she has raised me, remembering to ask and not tell.

Jennifer Appleton lives in Collinsville, Illinois, with her beagle-dachshund dog, Tiny, and eight cats. Her two geldings, Raja and Serengetty, and her mare, Chrissy, live at her mother's house about five miles away. Jennifer has a degree in Health Information Management and currently works for a Florida consulting company as a Medical Coder. She also works for Belleville Memorial Hospital. She has worked two jobs most of her life to pay for her horse habit and she has owned, loved and cared for horses for over 29 of her 40 years. She has a variety of interests, like riding horses, reading, gardening, fixing up her old house and hanging out with friends, but with three horses, her interests usually take a back seat and caring for the horses and working consumes her time. She still loves English Saddle Seat riding and Arabian and Saddlebred horses. "I believe in keeping my horses for life and I feel blessed that I can still keep and care for them. I'm forever grateful to Beau, Max, Hoss, Smokey and all the other equine friends who have graced my life…for teaching me how to ride, respect and love the almighty animal, the horse."

My Old Gray Mare (ain't what she used to be!)

By Jennifer Appleton

As a little girl, I loved all animals but horses were my passion. I just knew if I could have a horse of my very own, my life would be perfect. I am an only child that grew up with cats and dogs as my siblings. We lived in town, but our next door neighbor had a barn and a small fenced area and one day he brought home "Wizzer Boy," a race horse. Having a horse next door fueled my passion for horses even more and was a dream come true. I fed him carrots and apples daily.

I dreamt/talked/obsessed about horses. Horse pictures were iced onto my birthday cakes and appliquéd on my t-shirts and I had posters and calendars and Breyer horses throughout my bedroom. I still yearned for the real thing. My former babysitter lived across the street and had two ponies, Hoss and Smokey, that I brushed for hours and rode bareback and fell off of on a regular basis. I visited the emergency room several times with concussions, but that never stopped me from going back to the ponies. And my cousin had a mare named Flossie that I also loved dearly. It was becoming clear that my love for horses was not a passing fancy.

My Dad made the most wonderful mistake by giving me riding lessons on my ninth birthday. It was the best gift ever given to me and the biggest blessing in my life. It was a complete surprise when he said, "Let's take a drive," and we drove until we turned into a lane going to "Marion Brown Stables-American Saddlebred Horses." I saw a very long, white barn. My first riding lesson was English Saddle Seat on a big Saddlebred mare named Valentine, and I was in shorts and tennis shoes. The trainer, Marion, had Valentine on a long pole and although she listened to his every word, she got spooked by a noise outside the barn. She reared up at that point in the lesson — mares will do whatever they feel they need to at whatever time they feel they need to do it. It was completely unexpected and I was terrified, but the trainer said to keep going and so I did. It wasn't the same as falling off the ponies — this was the biggest horse I had ever ridden. I just naturally grabbed her mane and was able to maintain my position in the saddle. We continued with the lesson. I was asked to sit up and sit down and grasp the neck strap to help me do it, but I really didn't know what I was doing or why. It's called riding English Saddle Seat and posting to the diagonal, or riding English on an American Saddlebred Horse. I was thrilled.

I thought I was in heaven every week as I rode for those glorious 45 minutes, which never seemed to be long enough. I learned to post to the correct diagonals, and it seemed to take forever to learn my diagonals for the trot. I learned how to take the proper canter lead and to do serpentines down that long hallway. Thank God for Valentine, the mare, and Paulette, my instructor, who both had the patience of saints. I remember showing up for my lesson one day and instead of Valentine, they brought out Beau. I fell in love with Beau the first time I rode him. He had the smoothest trot and canter. He wanted to please and was such a sweet boy. I never knew who I would ride when I would get to my lesson, but I always wanted to ride Beau. I rode Natalie, Apache or Fancy, all great spirited Saddlebred mares. They were always very geared up and ready to perform and some more unpredictable than others, while Beau was always reliable and solid.

As a surprise, my Dad bought Beau for me on my 11th Birthday. I loved Beau so much! We boarded him across the street with Hoss and Smokey, the ponies, and then later moved him to a boarding stable. I wanted to show Saddlebreds, but Beau was not registered. He was a 17 year old, five-gaited Saddlebred gelding, and my Dad said I couldn't show him. I was allowed to take Beau to some small shows, which I enjoyed immensely but never won anything.

A year or two later, as my aspirations to have a show horse grew, I saw an ad in the paper for an Arab mare, for sale or trade. I thought if I had a naturally showy type horse, like this flashy Arabian mare, she would be great for English Saddle Seat, and then I could talk my parents into being able to show. I told them how Arabs have natural high energy and spirit with high head and tail carriage and natural high stepping without all the cost and upkeep of a Saddlebred. I remember telling my parents what I wanted to do and they were agreeable and supportive. I wanted to sell Beau, though it was a hard decision to make, and buy this Arab mare because I really wanted to develop her into a show horse.

We went to see the mare for sale — My Camirza (Christy, she was called) — and she was a yearling filly, very spirited and full of life! I wanted to train her from the ground up and I knew she was the one when I saw her. She was outside with a group of yearling sisters. They all ran into the barn, snorting with tails held high, very curious about this group of new onlookers checking them out. Christy was a beautiful chestnut with tiny white flecks in her coat, big brown eyes and a flowing black mane and tail. She had a natural floating trot and she lifted her tail over her back as she glided around the pasture. We traded Beau, the love of my life, for Christy and my parents paid some extra. The seller delivered her and picked up Beau. It was one of the worst days of my life, seeing Beau leave in that horse trailer. I thought this was how it had to be if I was going to have a future show horse.

So now I had this new yearling mare to work with. I changed her name to Chrissy and I thought life was wonderful, until that winter when my Dad got a call about Beau from a lady who had just bought him for her husband. She said she was worried that he might not make it through the winter. When I sold Beau, I told the buyer to please call me before reselling him and I would try to buy him back. I wanted to always know what happened to Beau and keep in touch with him. They said they wanted Beau for their young son, but instead, they sold him because he was getting fresh with their mares. Beau had been turned out with mares before without any problems.

This lady who had bought Beau was trying to trace his background and said she had somehow gotten my father's name. God does work in mysterious ways. Beau had been completely healthy, a beautiful shiny chestnut when we sold him at 18 years old. We didn't understand until we went to see him. My best friend, Beau, looked horrible! Only God knows what he went through before Margaret King bought him. She said he had several abusive owners and the last owner had tried to rope cattle from him and fell off and broke his leg.

Beau was depressed and he had welts on his back from being hit and his ribs were showing. His head hung down and he had lost the sparkle in his brown eyes. He looked at me sadly and I cried. I knew then that I would never again sell my friends.

I went to visit Beau for four years, often asking Margaret to sell him back to me. She finally agreed, and I paid her $20 a month for 10 months. I was 16 years old when Beau came back home to me. By this time, we had moved to rural O'Fallon, Illinois, and we had Chrissy and my mom's gelding, Max. When Beau arrived, Chrissy somehow knew instantly that

Beau and I had a deep bond from way back. After all, she had met him the day he left, that day she was delivered to me. Horses are very smart and they don't forget. Chrissy developed a special nurturing friendship with Beau and became very protective of him. As Beau became older and more fragile she was especially protective, always keeping him in her sight and standing between him and the others. She has always managed her pasture of geldings (and me) quite well, and has always been very structured and predictable with her behavior. I couldn't have kept the other two in line without her.

We lost Max in November of 1994 when he was 14 years old. One morning in late October, my mother found him down in his stall with severe colic. The vet came and worked on him in his stall. Chrissy was calling to Max, but he didn't respond. I took her out of her stall so that she could go and see him. She seemed calmer, as she made quiet, comforting and nurturing sounds like a mother with its foal. That night, we took Max to the University of Missouri-Columbia, where he was euthanized during surgery in the ICU nine days later. My mom and I were there at the time. We drove home in pouring down rain. It was still raining as we pulled into the driveway and I ran out to the barn. I let both horses out into the sloppy mud to get some exercise and the most amazing thing happened. The rain stopped briefly, and the change in weather created a double rainbow over the field. Twenty minutes later, the sun disappeared and the rain began again. I was in college during this time, taking a Death and Dying class at

SIU-Edwardsville. A fellow student had given me a poem about the "rainbow bridge," explaining when our pets die they cross over the rainbow bridge into a pleasant climate until we pass on and they run to greet us at the bridge. The very next week, a Belleville News Democrat columnist wrote about seeing the SAME double rainbow. He said a little girl in his neighborhood used to tell everyone when there was a rainbow, saying a double rainbow was magic. For me, it was a reassuring message from God, a sign that Max was at peace.

Chrissy, Beau and I settled into a new routine. It was a sad period and the empty stall was a daily reminder of our loss. By the end of November, we adopted Raja, a gelding from the Packwood/Longmeadow Hooved Animal Humane Society. Assuming her role, Chrissy quickly taught him what she expected from her pasture mates and also has taken good care of him.

Beau died when he was 37 years old. He had become swayback and arthritic and he would only get down and roll when the other horses were put in their stalls. I would sometimes find him down and unable to get up. I would put his halter on and yell "C'mon" and pull him up and we would walk around the pasture and life was back to normal for awhile. That night in 1997 when I found him down, I knew it was time. I tried and tried to help him but he couldn't get up. I literally dragged him toward the pasture so I could close the barn door. Dr. Russ Kinzinger came about 1:30 a.m. It was a peaceful passing and I knew in my heart it was right.

Chrissy was frantic because I had the barn door closed and she couldn't see Beau. I had lured her with grain into a stall so she wouldn't get in the way. After Beau was gone, I sobbed over him for hours while Chrissy kept up a frantic wail and ran in circles in her stall. Raja and Serengetty (a new pasture mate — an ex show horse/five-gaited Saddlebred gelding) remained in silence, probably more disturbed by her grief than anything. We finally opened the barn door and took her out. She sniffed Beau's body and stopped her screaming for him after that. But every morning, she would run outside and look for him.

Chrissy is my best girl, my sweet old gray mare. I have always loved her no matter what. She didn't become a top show horse, because I lost interest in attaining all of that, soon after I got her. I became involved with school and friends. It seems that she went from a one-year-old lanky chestnut filly with black mane and tail to a 26-year-old gray mare with red flecks and white mane and tail — in the blink of an eye. Chrissy and I have grown up together. She has been there for me through thick and thin – through all types of life issues, including the death of two of our geldings. I think she can read my mind and I can read hers. We get angry at one another at times and get frustrated with one another — but then life moves on. Sometimes she puts her ears back at me and shows her teeth but she knows not to cross the line. I have to get firm with her, but then it's over. I can usually predict what she will do in any given situation. I never trained her completely to ride, or to be shown and win ribbons. All of that became unimportant to me as I grew older. She has become my unconditional best friend and I have been her guardian since I was 14 years old. Now I am 40 and she is 26. I love Chrissy, and I will keep my mare no matter what happens in life. We have been through ear stitches, a hoof abscess with daily soaking (she wasn't co-operative then), and a cystoscopy at the University of Missouri, to discover she had an adhesion of her bladder to the abdominal wall. I've learned my Chris has unbelievable strength, stamina and courage in times of adversity. Of course, she is very intelligent.

I am usually lenient with misdemeanors, like at breakfast feeding time, for example. I put out three piles of hay and then lay a small amount of grain on top, for a morning boost. Chrissy travels each pile before the boys even get outside. They can all be eating at their piles and she will start the pecking order, heading over to one of the boy's piles. When I say "Chrissy, NO!" she puts her ears back at me and goes back to her own feed pile. She is clearly disgusted with me but she knows full well that when I turn my back, she will go right back to her former goal of stealing the others' food.

Every night I clean stalls and then when I want the horses to come in, we have this ritual. Chrissy was always first at the door with the two geldings standing behind her. She would never come in until they came in, and they wouldn't come in before she did. So I would say, "Chrissy, get the boys in…" The first time I said that to her, she went and rounded the geldings in and I was AMAZED! I swear she knows what words mean! It has been a nightly ritual for years now. She herds them into their stalls, one at a time! She isn't always pleased, but she needs to get the boys in so she knows where they are. Then life can continue.

Chris has always had an allergy to flies and fly spit. She develops sores on her front legs every summer. Fly spray helps but isn't enough. In the summer of 2007, she developed an ulcer on her back right fetlock. Very bad timing — I was changing jobs and completely stressed with very little free time. The vet had to make multiple visits and I had to dress her wound and wrap it daily. Chrissy had been poked, injected and prodded way too much and she began kicking and squealing at me. Just being a mare, she was telling me she had had enough.

It turned out to be a great bonding time for Chrissy and me. I had to take time out each evening and work on her leg. I would brush her each night while waiting for the medicated shampoo to soak into her wound for ten minutes before rinsing it off. The whole situation may have been God's way of intervening, using the horses in my life to help me slow down my own. I came to realize the most important things in my life are my horses and my mare, Chrissy. She is my touch stone.

Dianne Doll grew up in California and married her high school sweetheart. After 26 years in the Air Force (including many moves and two overseas tours) they decided to put down "roots" in metro east Illinois, near St. Louis, Missouri. Rex and Dianne have a son, Eric, and daughter, Crystal. They "bought the farm" for their 25th anniversary, naming it the Silver Rose Ranch in honor of the 25 long-stemmed silver-tipped red roses Rex had delivered to Dianne at her office (she is an office manager for a construction company). Her passion has always been horses. She shows her Tennessee Walker, Beauty, at local shows and has started training her Morgan mare, April, for future shows. Rex and Dianne love to trail ride. On their 34th anniversary they bought a horse trailer with living quarters and have enjoyed many overnight rides.

Beauty in the Midst of Sorrow

By Dianne Doll

When my husband asked me what I wanted for Christmas in December of 2001, I told him I wanted a trip to California to see my parents. They weren't getting any younger, and I really missed them. A few days after Rex had booked my flight, a friend called to say she had found the perfect horse for me.

I had donated my quarter horse to a handicapped-riding facility and missed riding in the shows with my daughter, Crystal. Peppy was a nice horse, but I never felt any connection with him. I did not enjoy riding him on the trails. He wanted to go, go, go, and I constantly had to hold him back. He was a pretty red dun quarter horse, but just not the horse for me. The riding facility could not believe we wanted to donate him. He was in perfect health and soon became their star horse. Peppy definitely went to a good home!

My friend, Sue, was sure that I needed a gaited horse, and she let me ride their gaited gelding on a trail ride. I loved the smooth gait! On the internet, Sue had found a 13-year-old Strawberry Roan Tennessee Walker mare with four white socks. I talked to Rex about it and he agreed to look, even though he had already gotten my Christmas gift. We made arrangements with the current owner to go see this mare the day after my return from California.

Rex, Crystal and I drove about an hour and a half to look at "Beauty." Her registered name is Gallant Roan Beauty. I fell in love with her immediately. I have heard that you can see a horse's soul in its eyes. Ah, what warm brown eyes she has! We brought her home. After a couple of days I found that she had some issues. She had never had her teeth floated and never had any shots. She threw her head really badly and it was apparent she was fighting the bit. When we had the equine dentist out, he braced her mouth open and told me to feel inside her mouth. It felt like raw hamburger meat! Her teeth all had sharp points that were digging into her check. She also had "ramps" on her front molars that were poking her tongue each time the reins were pulled back. Needless to say, the dentist took a while with her to sort out all her mouth problems. After giving her mouth a chance to heal, I rode her and noticed a huge difference. Beauty had a lovely head bob and no longer threw her head from side to side while we rode.

She does a quirky bob with her lip when she's nervous and it looks like she's talking. Her previous owner thought it was a flaw, but I find it endearing.

She did her "lip thing" a lot when she first came home. My family really enjoyed teasing me and imitating my new horse's habit. She soon became "Booty." I thought all of her quirks were cute and just imitated my husband and daughter right back. I felt totally at ease with my horse.

Beauty was definitely not an alpha mare. She was way down on the "horse pecking order." She was the oldest horse but intimidated by all the others. At that time we had a ten-year-old Morgan mare (Katy) that was definitely the alpha; Katy's son (Sonny), a three-year-old who was gelded at ten months but still thought he was a stallion; Katy's yearling daughter (Rosie) who was part Arabian; and a five-year-old quarter horse mare named Indy. I soon found myself feeding my new mare in her stall, or standing in the pasture with her to shoo off the other horses. Beauty was really good at listening and would come running to me to "save" her from the others. I could talk to her in a whisper and tell her to go around the barn, and then meet her over there with her food. We were quickly developing a bond.

Then I got the bad news from California. My mother was having problems breathing. The hospital determined she had a heart problem and did quadruple by-pass. My poor 75 year-old mother! I flew out to see her and spent a week reminiscing and doing what I could to make her more comfortable. Being so far away was so hard!

After returning from California, I spent a lot of time with my horse, brushing her and crying in her soft warm fur. Beauty would swing her head to me and just hold me with those warm brown eyes. She would listen to my stories and catch my tears. My husband was wonderful to give me the time I needed by myself. Beauty was my anchor. She never interrupted, never asked for anything in return. She was just there for me.

When I went back out to California, my father was on oxygen because he had developed problems breathing. We soon learned that he had lung cancer. I went out to see them again, and Dad died the day after I returned to Illinois. At least he had not suffered long. My Mother was loosing her battle. She had been suffering for months and her body was just shutting down. I went back out to California for my father's funeral and went to the nursing home to be with Mom after the funeral. My brother, Don, wanted me to take her the huge arrangement of roses because that was her favorite flower. She had stopped asking me how Dad was doing a few days back. Mom would drift between the present and the past. She would talk to a room full of relatives when I was the only one in her room. When I brought the flowers in for her, a tear slipped slowly down her cheek. She didn't ask, but she knew. They had been married over 50 years. She knew. When my last day with my mother came — too quickly — I kissed her good-bye knowing it would be the last time. Three days later I got the call that I was so dreading. The last trip to California was the hardest! She looked so peaceful, like an angel. Her suffering was finally over. I guess it just doesn't matter how old you are, losing your parents, especially both of them ten days apart, is just hard!

Crystal started giving me lessons on Beauty. My sweet Crystal! She so wanted to help ease the pain of loosing my parents! Soon Beauty and I were competing at the local shows and taking first place! I had some trophies to add to Crystal's trophies in our trophy case. Buying show outfits can be so expensive! I tried to cut corners where I could. I used an old vest as a pattern, took apart a clip-on tie, and bought some beautiful burgundy material with silver appliqués. They were so pretty and I had some material left over. I decided to make myself a headband to match my vest and tie. I looked pretty spiffy! I entered the class feeling like a million bucks! Beauty moved smoothly under me, and we had one of the best rides ever. Then the announcer called the judge to the stand. They were having a discussion and it involved Beauty and me. The rules required a hat in the class and my headband was not a hat. The judge told me we had been disqualified. How upsetting! Crystal met me at the gate and told me how well we did. She even told me that we were now the "standard" for the class. Beauty and I were the team to beat! She told me how proud she was of her mama and her horse! That truly made me feel like a winner! Ribbons and trophies collect dust, but a good impression left on your child, well, that lasts forever. Needless to say, I always wear my hat now.

Beauty has developed into the best trail horse. We were in the back of the trail on one ride, and the lead horse wouldn't go over a wooden bridge. The next horse saw the first one balk and was adamant there was a real horse-eating beast up there somewhere!

Rex saw what was going on and called for them to send Beauty and Dianne across the bridge. Beauty and I made our way to the front and she crossed right over, without another thought to it. Now if there is an area where a horse balks, Beauty and I will lead the way.

Crystal is now a married woman with a wonderful husband who shares her passion for horses. Mike bought himself a paint mare that he keeps at our place. Mike and Crystal decided to go on a trail ride with some of with my friends and me. I guess I forgot to tell them that it was a club ride. There just aren't that many people who usually show up for the trail rides. It turned out to be a great showing! Instead of the six of us, there were eighteen! Since Crystal and Mike had not taken their horses on a trail ride other than around our place at home, she was very concerned about being among so many horses. We decided to lag behind the rest and take it nice and slow. Crystal was on her gelding, Sonny, who is now a nine year-old, and Mike was on his seven-year-old paint mare, Jynx. Sonny was ready to go and Mike had his hands full with Jynx. My friend Lea was on my husband's horse, Angel, also a seven-year-old. It was a beautiful day in July, not too hot or humid.

The horses were feeling frisky on the ride through Pere Marquette's beautiful, hilly trails. We managed to branch off into a smaller group of eleven, still a lot of horses for our two green trail riders. Mike was trying to keep Jynx at a slow pace by going side to side on a steep incline. Jynx decided she wanted to go straight up the hill, and Mike held on and guided her as best he could. When Sonny saw his mare going up the hill, he also took off after his "woman." Crystal, who is an expert rider, let him go. She was going to follow her husband anyway, but her horse beat her to it! They all made it safely up to the top, but the only way down was to go back and follow the path. Lea and I rode back a little ways and waited for them to catch up. We let the group ahead know we were OK, and to just keep going, we'd catch up.

Beauty seemed to be really agitated with the slow pace. When Rex and I ride, we usually trot (for my horse it's called a gait) up the hills. It's a little easier on the horse to get some momentum going. I asked Crystal if she would mind if I gaited up the next hill and she said that would be fine. Beauty and I started off at a nice easy gait then she broke into a canter. I have not had the opportunity to canter Beauty much, and her canter is so smooth and easy going, it's like riding a rocking horse. We crested the hill and started down the other side. There in front of us was a small dried up creek and Beauty took it in stride with a beautiful jump! I had never ridden a jump before and let out a big "Yee Ha!"

Soon, I looked over and here was Angel coming up alongside us with NO LEA! I grabbed Angel's reins and stopped and Lea came walking up with spots of mud on her. It seems I started a chain reaction. Lea was keeping up with us until Beauty jumped the creek. At that point Angel bucked. Maybe it was the "Yee Ha" that spooked her. Lea lost her grip and slid off. Meanwhile, Mike was having problems of his own. His horse was right behind Lea and when she came off, he tried to steer clear and both he and Jynx went down. Mike landed on the rocks — definitely not fun for any of them! Crystal accused me of not being able to wipe the silly grin off my face when I apologized to everyone, but I really did feel bad. Hey, I'm 53 and to ride a jump for the first time in my life was a big thrill! I've got to admit, even writing this down I have a silly grin on my face.

I have found a relationship with my horse that I never dreamed could exist. I don't know how I would have kept my sanity without her. I am accused of babying her and pampering her, but she deserves it! She's nineteen now and still consistently taking first place in the local shows and just the best-darned trail horse anyone could ever want. I'm looking at retiring her from horse shows this year, but not from trail riding. We bought a 3-horse trailer with living quarters in 2006. Rex and I enjoy weekend trail rides. We even bought boots for our horses so we can ride them barefoot on the trails.

Lea only lives a couple of miles from our place. We rode over there one beautiful spring day and just hung out with her and Tom for a while. On the way back, Rex and I held hands while we rode off into the sunset. What more could any woman want?

Betsy Kelleher with her Arab mare, Syn-cere, after a Competitive Trail Ride. This was the event when Syn-cere's son competed on the same ride. Syn-cere was nineteen at the time, and she completed her first two competitive trail rides that same year.

Memories of Syn-cere

By Betsy Kelleher

Syn-cere was a 16 year old "flea-bitten" gray Arabian brood mare when I first saw her. She had been given to a young girl whose family was praying for the right place to keep her. I was praying for horses to board so I could afford my dream-come-true boarding stable.

At a competitive trail ride, I happened to mention my situation to a fellow distance rider who knew this family, and a month later they became my first boarders. Trying to help this family learn about horses developed into my giving riding lessons to each one of them, and then to another young girl, then to another and then another!

A military family, they had to move on only a few months later and decided not to take Syn-cere with them. As prospective buyers came, looked, rode and left, I fought a mixture of envy and desire, and a secret hope that no one would buy her! I had grown to love that mare myself.

Early one morning, the owners called me. Worried about what to do, they said if I wanted her and could tell them immediately, I could have her for $300! I said yes without hesitation, but even $300 was difficult for me then. Later that day, my mother paid an unexpected visit. As she got out of the car, Syn-cere was playing in the small paddock by the barn, just downhill from the house. I asked Mother if she wanted a half interest in a horse and a few minutes later she handed me a check for $150, which I used as a down payment. I still don't remember how I scraped up that other $150, but I managed!

Syn-cere was now mine — green broke and feisty. The first time I had ridden her for this family, I realized how green she was. Every movement of my body caused an immediate over-reaction. When I wiggled a toe in the stirrup, she startled. When I raised my hand, she jumped. I rode her that evening for an hour, gradually getting her used to my movements in the saddle. She was a handful!

Mares are complicated — like women. Each horse is different, as each person is different. We train horses with basic principles, but at the same time, we have to deal with an individual horse's unique behavior, breeding, experience and possible past trauma. Syn-ere was difficult to halter or bridle, but I learned the reason and depth of this problem after I bought her. She had been in a trailer accident and was fearful about any pressure on her head. I was told not to deal with it at her age and if I had to tie her, to use a bicycle tire or something stretchy. The tire would give and she wouldn't feel trapped.

A few years later, I tied her in stretchy crossties I had made from bicycle tires and twine with snaps. Something spooked her, and she pulled back so hard and so far that both ties snapped at the same time! She actually went rolling down the barn aisle, toward me, and I instinctively jumped into my tack room. She landed beside me, one leg extending into the tack room toward me and her head against one wall. She lay there, completely unmoving for at least 5 or 6 seconds before scrambling up and walking away with no apparent damage.

I owned her for four years. I can't say I was so knowledgeable and skillful that I retrained her to overcome all her resistance, but somehow along the way, I helped her and she figured it all out. At first, I accepted the way she was and I was careful not to test her fears too much. One day, a trainer friend worked with us and cautioned me, "You must deal with this. It's too dangerous not to." So I began slowly and inched my way along.

I started by lunging her with a rope laid over her back. That in itself raised her fear level immensely. Gradually, in time, I was able to tie plastic bags to the top of each leg and let them slide down and off as she moved. She wasn't afraid of plastic bags, but she reacted to anything that touched her anywhere.

Syn-cere visibly loved life. Turned out in a paddock, she put on quite a show. My mother had seen it the day I bought her. When I rode Syn-cere, I allowed her to run several laps around the arena for 10 or 15 minutes before getting down to serious work. Yes, I let her run, and I hung on for dear life (as my grandma used to say), as Syn-cere galloped around, bouncing much like a pogo stick under me. By the time she was ready to do serious work, I often had to take a moment to recover.

She kept herself fit. She even ran sometimes when I tried to catch her in the big pasture. I would get within a few feet of her and she would suddenly take off, run a circle around me and then go back to grazing. I didn't appreciate that game.

As a brood mare, she had maybe half a dozen babies, I was told, and some were involved in distance riding. She could have made a winning endurance or competitive horse herself. I later competed Syn-cere in a distance ride against one of her sons. At age 19, she gave her younger son a good race for the ribbons!

Syn-cere was a proud, feisty old gal. I clearly remember one day when she was being a bit stubborn, throwing her head around, and I used the palm of my hand quite forcefully once on the top of her head. There was a moment of silent stiffening. I could almost feel her response of indignity and hear her thinking, "How dare you treat me so!" But she tucked her head for me, and we went on with the ride.

She had a habit of sometimes putting her head down while ridden. And I do mean down. It was sometimes a challenge to hold on, and an unsuspecting rider could be pulled almost out of the saddle. When she spooked under saddle, it was like an elevator dropping. Suddenly she was crouched, still, as though ready to run, but she never did.

During the four years I owned her, I marveled at her love for life, and I watched her solve her greatest problem with only a little help from me. It was her own great intelligence that solved it. I had just dismounted after riding her in the outdoor arena. I was always very careful when taking the English reins off over her head; but this time, I can only say I must have looked at her wrong! Her head shot upwards and the rein caught over one ear. She went wild. She rushed backward, shaking her head from side to side, almost sitting down in her panic. We were in a large arena with the gate shut, so I just stood and watched it happen, waiting for the worst. Suddenly, she stopped, head high, eyes wide and nostrils flared, her body poised in fear. She looked at me and I saw something in her expression that I hadn't seen before. For a second, I felt I could read her mind. She seemed to be thinking, "Wait a minute, I'm not getting hurt by this. What's going on here?" I walked toward her, talking quietly. I stood beside her, but I did not touch her. She stood very still, as though she was waiting for me to remove the rein, but I didn't. After a moment, she lowered her head slightly and I quickly lifted the rein off her ear and rubbed her neck and praised her for being so smart. We stood there, together, for awhile, relaxing and soaking in what had just happened. I was amazed at this development. Syn-cere had started to figure it out, all by herself.

Next day, I rode again. After dismounting, I carefully took the rein and laid it over one ear, intentionally, just as it had been caught the day before. Syn-cere raised her head only slightly, her eyes widened a bit and she looked at me rather suspiciously. She was tense, but not moving. After standing there a few moments, she again lowered her head slightly and I removed the rein and rubbed her neck and told her once again how very smart she was. I could hardly believe she had figured it out that easily.

I remember another day when I was telling a friend about how Syn-cere had been so touchy about her ears. I was rubbing her ears and showing how she didn't seem to mind anymore. Syn-cere gently placed her nose against my cheek with a soft pressure, and I was touched by this expression of loving connection. A moment later, she pushed my face away abruptly with her nose as if to say "Phooey on you, girl!" I had to laugh. I actually think she was getting back at me for playing with her ear.

Later, in the spring of 1989, we were able to dissolve the last piece of her fearful past. I had put her back into her stall, and was taking off her halter. As I unfastened the buckle, I put too much pressure on her poll area and she suddenly zoomed backward, head up high, halter still fastened. OK, I decided, we will deal with this now. I led her back to the front of the stall, where we had started. I began to unfasten the halter again, but carefully used just the smallest amount of pressure. As she tensed up, but before she could react and move away, I released the pressure and rubbed her neck, quietly praising her. For fifteen minutes, I did this same thing over and over. I put a little pressure on the halter, as if to unfasten it, but stopped the pressure before she made any movement away. I tried to use just a little more pressure each time, building up to actually removing the buckle. At one point, instead of raising her head, she started to lower it just a little. I praised her and rubbed her neck, and I gave her a moment to think about it. I was able to unfasten her halter using normal pressure and she actually lowered her head for me instead of reacting. Syn-cere seemed to figure things out more quickly than any other horse I've ever owned. But for those who know Arabs, this breed often shows high intelligence and great personality and connection with someone who can keep up with their quick minds and proud spirits.

Three years after I bought Syn-cere, when she was 19, we entered two 30-mile competitive trail rides, her first experience with the sport. For each ride, she was tied to the trailer overnight while I slept in the back of the pickup truck on an old mattress under a camper top for cover. During the night, I would sometimes feel a tug. Looking up to check on her, I could see that she had reached the end of the rope and was moving to a better position.

I know in my heart that Syn-cere could have won both rides if I had handled things differently. One week before the first ride, I changed farriers and her new shoes apparently didn't fit. She was reluctant to move out on the second half of the ride, and I knew something was wrong, even when the veterinarian who checked her out said she was just needing encouragement. I went back to my old farrier after the ride, and he showed me the bloody corns on both front feet. On the second ride, which happened to fall on my birthday, I made a stupid decision to just enjoy the ride and not ride to win. I rode with a novice rider who didn't realize how quickly the half time ends! Instead of going back on the trail at the designated time, I waited for her to saddle up and join me. We lost valuable time and didn't realize our situation until the last vet check. The vet tech informed me that although my score was high, we had four miles to go in the remaining 40 minutes. We had to hurry to cross the finish line in time. Being pushed hard on a rocky path, Syn-cere tripped and went down to her knees. Walking for awhile, she seemed sound enough, and we hurried on, then she tripped again. We made it to the finish line in time, but during the vet check afterward, Syn-cere's stride was off. I could hardly see it, but the vet did. Those 18 points he took off knocked me down to fifth place.

During the four years I owned Syn-cere, she bucked twice, both times when I gave her too loose a rein. Once, the first time I jumped her, one of my boarders started it by laying a board over two tires in the outdoor arena. I had to join the fun. Needless to say, I was not an experienced jumper. I didn't want to hit her in the mouth, so I held the reins loosely. Syn-cere cleared the board enthusiastically, then gave three little bucks when she landed as if to say, wow that was fun! I laughed at the time, didn't even feel scared, because I sensed that Syn-cere was only expressing her joy at this new sport! From that day on, however, I kept a snug hold of the reins, except one other time.

It was a cool, beautiful day in November, 1988. There were eight of us, riding at Pyramid State Park, and we had been moving along pretty good for about two hours. I felt she might be tired and I gave her a little slack in the reins as we cantered up a long hill. My mistake. At the top of the hill, she gave a joyful buck. I was up in two point in my English saddle, leaning a bit forward, and when she bucked, I gave a surprised yell, "Hey!" At the sound of my voice, her head shot up and hit mine. When I yelled, the rider just in front of me turned in time to see me hit the ground. "I saw you bounce," he told me later. That hit knocked me unconscious for a few moments, and I fell from the saddle. It wasn't the bucking, it was the blow from her head that did it! Maybe if I hadn't yelled, things would have turned out very differently for Syn-cere and me. After I woke up, I was encouraged to get back on, but I remember wondering which horse I was riding and I didn't want to get back in the saddle until I knew! I finally figured it out, and we rode at least half an hour back to camp while I endured the pain. I went to the emergency room the next day and learned I had a slight concussion, bruised ribs, sprained hip and knee and a few other things I can't remember.

Before that, I had planned to take Syn-cere for more competitive trail rides. I knew she was perfect for it. But after my injury, I was hesitant to get back on her.

The next February, she developed a fistula on her withers, infected somehow from a blanket that rubbed during several days of very cold weather. I consulted with several vets, gave her medicine, and finally took her to the University of Illinois. Based on their prognosis, I donated her to be put down. I learned later that they kept her alive another ten years in their experimental program. One of her uses was to help students learn how to halter a horse. I was told that she also acted like a mother protector to many new horses that came to the facility.

I went back once to visit her. That experience again revealed the depth of feeling in Syn-cere's personality. When she first saw me, she turned her back and stood at the other side of her stall, refusing to come to me. I talked to her a long time, and told her how sorry I was for everything that had happened to her. After 15 or 20 minutes, she turned and came to me, reaching her nose through the stall bars toward me so I could rub on her. It touched me deeply, and hurt just as much. It was my only visit, although I did try to keep track of her and I did learn that she had been put down when she was about thirty years old.

If anyone would ask me about the "greatest" horse I ever owned, I would tell them it was Syn-cere. I loved Syn-cere for her expressive nature, her lively spirit, her ability and her personality. As mares go, she was one grand, feisty lady.

Julie Goodnight is a full-time equine professional with more than a quarter-century of experience. Her varied background ranges from dressage and jumping to racing, reining, colt-starting, and wilderness riding. Julie's extensive experience training horses and riders has earned her the moniker, "Communicating Clearly with Horses and Riders." She travels coast-to-coast and beyond much of the year to horse expos, conferences and clinics to teach horses and people about each other. Her training and teaching techniques are frequent features of *Western Horseman, Horse & Rider, Equus, The Instructor, Perfect Horse and America's Horse* and she has two syndicated columns in dozens of regional equine publications throughout North America and a world-wide presence on the internet. Julie Goodnight is International Spokesperson for the Certified Horsemanship Association, a non-profit organization dedicated to improving the safety and quality of riding programs. Her television debut in July 2007 rounds out her multi-media appearances. Julie Goodnight resides near Salida, Colorado, at her private horse ranch with her husband, Rich Moorhead, the CEO of Monarch Ski and Snowboard Area. Photo of Julie and her Morgan mare, Pepsea, by Elaine Klugman.

Territorial Mare Issues (Q & A)

by Julie Goodnight

Dear Julie,

I am a first time horse owner with a four-year-old paint mare. The woman I bought her from is training her and I can ride her but she is constantly testing me and backs up when she doesn't want to do something. That has improved as I ride her more (I am also inexperienced) but her worse behavior is around her stall. There, she pins her ears back and acts like she wants to bite when you approach her. She is much calmer with her halter on. I try to respond to any potential nips in a strong fashion, but I don't know how to teach her to stop being so protective of her stall. I would appreciate any advice you might have. Do you think this is a behavior she might outgrow, as her former owner believes (with consistent discipline)? She does seem to be getting a bit more cooperative in the ring. She is great on the trail and not very "spooky." My husband wants me to sell her and get a 10-year-old gelding. But they can test a new owner too, right? E.B.

Dear E.B.

From the sounds of it, you have a "hormonal" mare or what we fondly refer to as PMS (Pissy Mare Syndrome). Although not all mares fall into this category, many mares do and it seems to me to be a little worse when they are younger. Having trained quite a few mares that fall into this category, I'll tell you about my multi-faceted approach.

First, I would put the mare on a supplement to help stabilize her hormones. I have had great success with a supplement made by Figuerola Labs called "Relax-Saver," www. figuerola-labs.com. Before the days of great supplements like this, horseman commonly bred hormonal mares in order to stabilize their hormones. I have an exceptionally hormonal mare in training right now and I am happy to say she has made awesome progress, but not only did we put her on the supplement, we also bred her.

Secondly, you have to understand these mares and how territorial they are. They are especially defensive in their stalls or when a stranger approaches them. We are so used to trained and gregarious horses that we routinely barge into a horse's space- just walk right up unannounced and pat them on the neck or head or rump. You can't treat a hormonal mare this way. You need to approach her slowly and gently and make sure you introduce yourself before you barge right into her space. As you approach her, come only so close (however close that she notices) then stop, divert your eyes and reach out your hand, palm down, for her to approach you and smell your hand. Taking this little bit of extra time when you approach her will help a lot toward her defensiveness.

As she gets more comfortable and trusting of you, she will accept your closeness better. Along the same lines, these mares need a lot of space and do not do so well when you crowd them. Again, we are so used to horses that will tolerate us in their space that we tend to be too close to the horse all the time, hanging on his neck, smooching his face, etc. Give this mare lots of room, always ask before you enter her space and try to keep a comfortable distance from her as much as possible.

The third facet in dealing with hormonal mares is the training. This can be pretty tricky, especially if you do not have much experience (see other Q&As on green riders and green horses on my website). These mares need to learn obedience through lots of groundwork, but they tend to be very irritable and it is easy to escalate the irritability rather than instill obedience. You have to tread a fine line between discipline and correction and leaving them alone when they behave, with a very heavy dose of patience. As I do with all horses, I like to teach the horse some very basic rules of behavior and with consistent correction; the horse will learn the rules very quickly.

The first rule I like to work on is that the horse will stand absolutely still when I ask her to. I practice this with a rope halter and 12' lead (if you need one, I have the brand I prefer for sale on my website www.juliegoodnight.com), standing out in the open and asking the horse to stand by saying "whoa" and standing to the front and side of the horse with my toes facing the horse's shoulder.

The way you position yourself in relation to the horse is critical, as the horse will quickly learn to associate your toes facing toward her with her not moving. I will not try to stand close to the horse or choke up on the lead in attempt to hold the horse there, I want her to stand there on her own while I keep a fair distance from her. Every time she makes a mistake and moves, I will say "whoa" and pop the lead; if she has moved substantially I will put her feet back where I asked her to stand to begin with by backing her up. Horses are very aware of how and when they move their feet, and will typically be moving in a direction they want to go (like toward the barn), so it is important to put her back where you told her to stand.

I will also work on making the horse stand still at the hitching rail while I am grooming her. Often, these mares can be very fussy and fidgety, so usually I will attach a second lead to the halter and hang onto it as I groom. If the horse moves her feet at all, I will firmly say, "whoa," and give a sharp pop on the lead. Again, consistent correction will improve the horse very quickly. If she moves substantially, I will place her back where she was and tell her, "whoa." Keep in mind that often hormonal mares are quite sensitive, so be careful you are not putting too much physical pressure on her while you are grooming.

Now for the important part: don't hassle the mare, don't pick on her, just trust her to stand; leave her alone when she does and correct her when she doesn't. Most PMS mares do not care much for being rewarded by a rub on the neck or praise, but they do appreciate it when you leave them alone. Whichever reward your mare prefers, be sure to offer it when she makes the slightest attempt to obey.

The next basic rule of behavior I will work on is keeping her nose in front of her chest at all times when I am working around her on the ground or riding her. Again, to achieve this you only need consistent and gentle correction. Every time the nose moves away from me, I give a gentle bump of the halter rope until it comes back to center. When the nose moves toward me, it is a bigger infraction because the mare is moving into MY space, so I will twirl the end of the lead toward her nose to push it back where it was (in short order, all I will have to do is point at her nose to move it back).

There is much more groundwork to accomplish on the lead line and in the round pen, but the main thing with a mare like this is to insist on obedience without nit-picking and nagging the horse. Be patient and trust the horse to obey. If you aren't patient and don't have faith in her, you will start picking on her and getting irritable and quick yourself and since horses mirror our own emotions, this will escalate her irritability.

In answer to your final question, while some geldings can be a little challenging, on the whole they are much less challenging than mares. In the natural herd setting, a mare is generally at the top of the pecking order and the "boss mare" is responsible for keeping discipline in the herd and watching out for the safety of the herd. So by nature, mares tend to be more dominate and controlling than geldings. Another important factor is that geldings are neutered and mares are not, so the hormones become an issue. I would never suggest that you get rid of this mare without seeing you and her work together, but I would say that a well-trained older gelding would be much easier than a young hormonal mare for an inexperienced person to work with. Good luck and be safe!

Julie Goodnight, Clinician and Trainer
jgoodnight@ridingschool.com
www.juliegoodnight.com

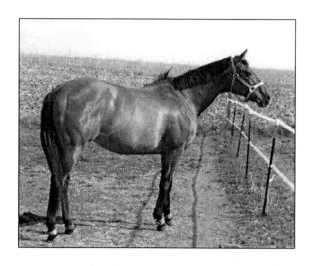

Kate Witas, 17, is a riding instructor, horse trainer and farrier with a special love for thoroughbreds and abused horses. She lives in Northern Illinois and is a volunteer at Wood End Farms in Barrington, a place that retrains OTTB's (that's off-the-track thoroughbreds). Kate calls herself a struggling young girl trying to find her way into the equine world. Her website is www.freewebs.com/belgianlover098.

Mid Summers Dream

By Kate Witas

When our eyes first met, we found a love connection that couldn't be broken. "It's A Likely Landing," whose name would soon become "Mid Summers Dream," was a stocky little thoroughbred at least 200 pounds underweight with a two year old colt still by her side. Her eyes were empty. No emotion, no sparkle, no real reason to keep them open.

A scrawny older woman came into the pasture and clipped a lead line onto an imbedded halter caked in mud. The mare walked with a heave in her chest and a slight limp on her left front leg, where you could see signs of old pin firing. As her colt called frantically, she didn't seem to have the energy to call back.

As soon as she walked into the concrete garage converted into a tack/feed room, a large western saddle was thrown upon her back. Immediately, her head went high in the air. She took the bit without much hassle and seemed almost too tired to fight all of these actions. Eight years she had been in a pasture bearing colts and fillies to go on and win the stake races, and then they decided she was broke.

Her rider mounted and she trotted off as she had done on the track, and she ran. As her rider tried to pull up, she bucked her heart out but even then, she could only manage a few baby cow hops. I took her home a week later.

She arrived covered in mud, looking even thinner than before, with a dull look to her blood bay coat. She was a good 15.3 hands but still short for a thoroughbred. No one wants a horse under 16 hands these days. Her mane was long but thin, damaged and matted in knots with burrs everywhere. She had the cutest little cow lick I've ever seen. It couldn't be considered a star on her forehead, but a few twirled scattered hairs that sat perfectly on her head. As I started to curry the mud off, I found other little scattered cow licks that aren't mentioned in her papers. There was the one on her withers and the circles on her neck. She seemed to enjoy the attention. Her head was high and proud, looking like the born-to-run gal she is. I'm a bigger girl so people didn't understand why I liked thoroughbreds as they are so thinly built. I retrain them and help others sell them, and that's what I planned for Summers. It's what I like to do. I knew she had never been in an indoor arena in her 15 years, so that was what I thought we should do on that very first day.

She took her surroundings in, not really scared, just needing reassurance. I gave that to her by walking bold and keeping her at a walk. I stopped to let her look at a few things, then finished walking the area by stopping at the mounting block. Now that was something to fear. Her head went up into the air as I sat down. I trusted her kind nature that she wouldn't act up, and I felt letting her be above me would be the best approach. It would let her know she had nothing to fear and I wouldn't hurt her. After she walked around the mounting block a few times, I could see her thinking and lowering her head in acceptance. I stood up, petting her freshly groomed neck and whispering how wonderful she was. At that point I stepped on the first stair of the block. She didn't care, so I went up one more. She lifted her head but stood still. I petted and talked to her and she started to lick her lips. When a horse is licking its lips, it is showing it understands, or it is thinking. When I got on the third step, she raised her head slightly above the level of her withers. She was so calm, so relaxed, it seemed to be fine for me to pet her spiny back as I stood above her. I sat back down on the block figuring out my plans for her. As I did, she put her head in my lap and sighed. She had made up my mind. She would be with me forever.

At that point in my life, I needed her as much as she needed me. I was fighting a depression that had followed me around since I was a young child in the open fields of Georgia. Now I was breaking up with a man I had known for years, and trying to figure out my life. Everything was confusing when I first got her. I didn't know what I wanted to be, and just a few months before getting Summers, I had retired my 31-year-old quarter horse and decided to give up horses all together. It was just too much heart break and extremely costly for board, vet care, farrier work and gas just to travel from the city to see them. I had refused to ever let my horse live in the city. Horses are turned out on concrete coated with sand — that is if they are allowed outside at all. When I went to see Summers, I wasn't looking for her for myself. I knew deep inside me I wanted to still be with horses, but I was looking at other thoroughbreds for other people I knew. But I found my way back into the crazy world of horse lovers with this mare. She was so willing to trust me, yet I couldn't walk outside my door and trust people I knew for years. She trusted anyone who cared.

Everyday I worked with her on the ground and slowly added weight onto her. On a vet's advice, I piled on the nutritional supplements. There was Weight Builder, and a thyroid medicine because her blood tested off the charts. She had brittle feet, so Bio Hoof should help there, and Source was a supplement for minerals I had always used. If a feeding was ever skipped it was easily seen. She also had MSM for her sore legs. Gradually, I noticed a new horse start to blossom. Her heath was regained and her spirit flew high.

From introducing the various items to desensitize her, she was never flighty but more of a thinker. Odd for a horse, they are normally flight or fight. The first time I placed a saddle on her back, I let her smell the pad and I messed around a good 15 minutes in the arena tossing it in the air, placing it everywhere on her body, tossing it on her back, on her neck, and her little butt. Then when I brought the saddle in, she had her head low and relaxed. I sat it on her gently so she'd know it will never hurt her. The one I normally used didn't fit her, unfortunately. It had fit most of the thoroughbreds I knew, but not her. My old quarter horse's western saddle did fit her. I took her for a walk with it on, girthed up loose. She didn't care. Tightened it a little, and still not a care in the world from her. I took her up to the mounting block. She knew stand means carrots so she didn't care at all. I put a little weight on the saddle leaning into it, nothing. She just stood. After that I got off and started flapping the leather. It made a loud sound by her side where my foot would go to get on. I swung the stirrup back and forth, still nothing from her. Just licking her lips. It's what she did all the time. I could talk to her and ask her something and she'd lick them.

Within a week it was time for her first ride. She was perfect and her head was low at the walk. Very relaxed and calm. She knew to just walk off. It was as if she had been under saddle for years. Within a month she was giving a two year old pony rides. Anything and everything I asked, she did with ease. I would let her run loose in the area late at night. One night a bucket was laying out, and she ran by, jumping over it again and again.

Soon afterward, she started to lose weight again. Later we found out the stable hands didn't care to feed her if she didn't come right in, because of the mud. She started tilting her head oddly and trying to move away at the mounting block. I knew something was wrong. I had taught her tricks, such as shake with her front leg. When I was tacking her up one night, she did that as I tightened the cinch. All of a sudden she fell on the concrete floor of the barn.

I learned that a friend of mine used a chiropractor for her horse, and I thought it would be worth it to have someone look at Summers. What Dr. Sherry found was a poll that was popped. It was easy to tell because one eye was lower than the other. Her back also needed several adjustments. Then we had an animal communicator help us. Summers had 2 ribs out of place. Not one but two. I learned that day that a lot of the things you see your horse do, could have a lot of underlying meanings. It's common for horses to have ribs out of place, but if it's left untreated it can be much worse. This can happen from anything, such as a too-tight cinch, or maybe saddled too far back. She has never been the same since then for mounting; I think she fears it will hurt.

With Summers' calm nature, I added her to my lesson program. She has a way of teaching riders if they are correct by whether or not her head is relaxed or slightly higher. She never misbehaves, but her response helps explain if the rider is doing something wrong. She takes care of her riders as if they were her foals. She is a mother, and it shows. She will always take care of you as long as you are kind to her.

Over the past few months she has started to show aging at 16 years, with arthritis in her hocks from being pushed so hard so young at the track. Her heart is still young, and always will be. She has had to deal with EPM, sesamoiditis, hock injections, slipping on concrete floors, neglect, and too much time in the breeding shed...and yet she is still willing to give all her love to anyone who gives her a rub on her face and a crunchy carrot as a treat. She is a true mare, one that gives her all no matter what. She will try to please even when in pain, and will always let you wrap your arms around her so she can cradle you with her head.

ADDED NOTE: EPM or Equine Parasitic Myloencephalitis is a disease in which a parasite infects the central nervous system and can cause irreparable damage if not caught quickly. Symptoms include unsteady movement.

Sesamoiditis is when damage occurs to the bones from repeated concussion, as on a race track, and the bone can develop micro fractures that calcify and cause inflammation and pain in walking.

Debbie Antognoli resides in Granite City, Illinois, and is married to an attorney. Her daughter plays ice hockey for Ohio State University, and her son is a video game designer in Australia. She is a licensed massage therapist in Missouri and Illinois, and also practices equine massage through her business, Hands-On Equine Health, Inc. You can learn more about equine massage on her website: www.Hands-onequine.com.

More Than Blue Ribbons

By Debbie Antognoli

This story begins in February of 1997. Purely on
the advice of my trainer, I purchased a ten-year-
old, half-Arabian mare, Karedin KandyKiss+/, sight
unseen. Kandy came from a well-known Arabian
trainer in Wisconsin. My goal was to have a national
quality horse to compete in the 1998 U. S. Arabian
Nationals. Kandy seemed to fit the bill. She was a
spirited chestnut with a flaxen mane and tail and
she possessed a ton of talent. She was the picture of
wild beauty when she pranced and snorted. She had
that "look at me" attitude needed to compete on the
national level. One thing we quickly discovered was
that Kandy was not showable when she was in heat.
We kept her on Regumate and that seemed to solve
the problem.

I had never competed on the national level,
and I wanted to prove to myself that I could do it.
Kandy and I accomplished that and she gave me the

unexpected gift of a new career. We made quite a successful team and racked up an impressive show record in Huntseat and Dressage: 1998 National Top Ten, five Regional Championships, three Regional Reserve Championships, six Regional Top Fives, and 32 1st place ribbons. The 1998 National Horse of the Year Awards, sponsored by AHSA, ranked Kandy third in half-Arabian Huntseat *and* Dressage. We had accomplished more than I had ever dreamed of.

Anyone who shows horses will recognize that achieving this show record involved many, many hours of practice, weeks on the road traveling from one show to the next, and deep pockets! I look back on this period of my life and wonder how on earth I had the time to devote to this. I had a family to take care of and a house to run. Somehow everything just worked out. I guess it was our time to shine. Kandy was a star. In 1998, I turned down an offer of $40,000 for her. I knew we had a good chance of winning Nationals and I wanted to be the one riding her.

It was at Nationals that our problems began. Kandy started to develop tendon problems in her left front leg. We rested her a few days and her leg looked pretty good. I made the decision to go ahead and enter our classes because we were there and this was my goal. We made our cuts and rode in the finals. Kandy won National Top Ten but this proved to be too much for her tendon. She tore the fibers in the left front flexor tendon during our final's ride. We were looking at a minimum of six months rehab.

After a successful rehab of her torn tendon we continued showing. I had my sights set on winning the 2000 Nationals and it seemed within my grasp. We had both improved and our winning streak was continuing. This was not to be God's plan for us. Kandy developed tendon problems in the same left front leg three weeks prior to Nationals. Having been down this road before, I decided to scratch from Nationals and retire from the show circuit. I gave her a couple of months of stall rest and then we quietly started to study dressage with Thomas Ritter and Simon Battram. I wasn't sure how I'd adjust to not traveling around the show circuit with my friends and winning those blue ribbons. Surprisingly, I found I didn't really miss it. My daughter plays ice hockey and her dream was to play Division I. For the next five years, she and I traveled most weekends to Chicago or Wisconsin for hockey games. She now plays for Ohio State University.

Kandy's front leg problems resurfaced in April 2003. No one could give me a definite diagnosis to her lameness. There wasn't any swelling or heat in her leg. In fact, sometimes it seemed the problem might be in her left shoulder. I didn't ride her for 2 ½ years searching for a diagnosis to her lameness.

Here's a synopsis of her veterinary diary:

June 2003-nerve block of left heel and fetlock, no change

July 2003-Radiographs negative for the knee on down

September 2003-ultrasound of left knee showed joint capsule had scar tissue, treated with ultrasound, photon laser and massage; slight improvement

December 2003- ultrasound showed scar tissue reduced by more than half but she was still lame

February 2004- series of five Adaquan IM injections, lameness improved and was 90% better, this lasted only 3 weeks

September 2004- more x-rays of knee were negative and I was advised to take her to the University of Illinois for diagnostic testing.

September of 2004- she also developed mastitis of the right cranial half of her udder and was treated. However, the swelling never went away and she would drip a milky fluid from her udder.

November 2004- I took her to the U of I where she had nuclear scintigraphy. No areas of significant uptake were seen. A needle aspirate was taken from the right mammary gland. This was nondiagnostic and a biopsy was recommended. One unexpected finding was an inability to hear heart sounds in the cranial thorax bilaterally. To identify the cause for the decreased heart sounds the thorax was radiographed and the heart ultra sounded. These tests were within normal limits. The bottom line was no one knew why she was lame and I was $1200 poorer!

February 2005- I got lucky and a vet that worked on the horses at the local racetrack came to look at Kandy. He blocked the left carpal cannel and she was sound! The official diagnosis was Carpal Tunnel Syndrome. We tried various therapies to treat this but nothing worked 100%.

June 2005- Kandy had Carpal Tunnel surgery. I started riding her again in September of 2005. It had now been about 2 ½ years since I had ridden her.

During this 2 ½ year period of Kandy's lameness, I met Suzy Franz of Indian Creek Rehab. Suzy, a human physical therapist, taught equine massage. This was amazing stuff! I enrolled in the nine-day course and became certified in Equine Massage in 2003. I started my own business, Hands-On Equine Health. Equine massage became my passion. I love helping horses become useful again. To further my massage skills and knowledge, I enrolled in a 600-hour human massage curriculum at the Healing Arts Center, St. Louis, MO. I graduated in 2007 and am a licensed massage therapist.

Every day I could ride Kandy was a gift. I had about five months of riding when Kandy became extremely uncooperative. She didn't want me to touch her and would pin her ears back. She became the typical "bitchy" mare when in heat, but this behavior lasted continuously for a couple of months! The vet said she was stuck in PMS and not ovulating. Another challenge! In February of 2006, the vet recommended a prostaglandin IM injection. This improved her behavior for about one week! We tried herbs but that didn't help much. In May of 2006, the vet implanted a cattle growth hormone to stop her cycling completely. This lasted two months and then she came into heat again. During this six-month period, Kandy didn't want me to touch her or ride her. In fact she had become down right dangerous to ride. I had no idea what to do with her.

In July of 2006, I moved Kandy to a new barn where she was turned out everyday. We changed her feed from sweet feed to Strategy. The change in Kandy was miraculous. Within one week she was her old self again! I was back in the saddle and enjoying every ride.

She was looking so good we resumed riding lessons. The owners of this new barn were Arabian owners and went to the shows. They encouraged me to show Kandy in halter the fall of 2006. She looked great! You would never guess she was 19 years old. This encouraged me to consider showing her again in huntseat. Our debut show was scheduled for the following spring. Kandy looked awesome. The old girl still had that special "look" that turned the judges' heads.

Tragedy struck again in February 2007. This time Kandy tore her left hind suspensory ligament. I have no idea how this injury occurred, but I suspect she did it during turnout. We were looking at 6-12 months rehab and the prognosis for riding was guarded. I was heart broken that she would have to go through stall rest again. Her other lameness issues had taught me that patience and time were the keys to successful rehab. I had learned to be an equine healer and would use these skills on Kandy. I was getting pretty good at this rehab and after the initial shock of the diagnosis, we started in on the long road of recovery. We had beaten the other injuries and we could do it again. I knew this devastating injury meant the final end to her show career. I could accept this. I just wanted her to be able to be turned out and maybe ride her lightly.

Kandy was 20 years old. She had been my friend and teacher for ten years. When I look back on this period of my life with Kandy, her legacy is not all the blue ribbons and awards we won. She taught me confidence and courage, and she led me to a new career as a massage therapist. She taught me acceptance, win or lose, and how to turn my problems over to God. She was my "forever" horse. I owed her so much and I would not abandon her. Little did I know there was one more path for Kandy to take and this path would not include me (A footnote to this story is…I did buy another horse. You guessed it…another mare!).

The story continues…

My name is Jim Hayes and this is my part of the story of KandyKiss. The first time I saw Kandy was on an early April afternoon. I went out to visit a friend of mine, Jeff Heinzl, at his Shepherd Hills Arabian Farm. I was not there to buy anything. I already had nine horses of my own, quarter horses being my preference. I was visiting with other boarders and moseyed over to the stalls looking at the horses, just killing time. That was when I saw her, a beautiful Arabian with a bandaged leg. I didn't think much about it and went on. Then something drew me back to her stall. She came to the door and I scratched her neck and face. She tried to nuzzle me through the stall door. I guess you might say it was love at first sight, for both of us.

Even though she was lame with an uncertain future, 20 years old, and could possibly never be ridden again, I knew that I would enjoy our time together. Watching her prance, she had a style all her own. She held her head and tail high with grace and pride. I got a hold of Jeff and jokingly asked if she was for sale, thinking that no way someone would sell such a magnificent animal at a price I could afford. Jeff said yes, she might be for sale and introduced me to her owner. Debbie said she would let me know on the price after she came to visit my farm and facilities to make sure Kandy would have a proper home for her retirement. After Debbie's inspection and spending some time with me, she agreed this would be the ideal place for her mare to spend her remaining years. Two days later, Jeff and Debbie brought me my KandyKiss.

For the next two months, several times a day, we would massage, bandage and unbandage her injury. The healing process gave us some of our best times together. She had a 12' by 12' stall and a 60' run for exercise, with all the hay and fresh water she wanted. She was taken on walks every day for 30 minutes to an hour to graze and be free. When I had time, I would sit in my chair in her run or in the arena and just watch her. Kandy would eat hay and I would rub her head. She would nuzzle and nicker to me.

Kandy made a fast recovery. In mid-June, we put a saddle on her for the first time. My daughter Dawn took her for her first ride in the arena. You could tell

Kandy really enjoyed it the way she glided around the arena. Dawn said it was the smoothest ride she had ever enjoyed. This meant a lot since she had a lot of experience with Tennessee Walkers and other breeds. Kandy was truly the Rolls Royce of our stable, beautiful, gentle and loving. On occasion, Dawn would put the grandchildren on her for a ride. Everybody loved her from day one. Anytime you went into the barn, she would greet you with nickering and whinnying as you entered. When we were through riding her we would walk her and turn her into the pasture where she could graze on fresh grass.

Kandy experienced everything in life that she had missed as a show horse. We thought it was all down hill from here with her injury being healed and the expectations of her recovery being higher than we had anticipated. In July, she was stricken with an unknown illness. In spite of our efforts with the vet, myself and two experienced trainers by her side, Kandy went down and we could not get her back up. She fought to rise and would get anxious. I would lie down next to her and talk to her, which seemed to calm her. On a July morning around 4:30, surrounded by me, two trainers and family members, KandyKiss passed and galloped her way to heaven.

Even though it's five months later, I didn't want to write this story because of the pain it brings me. I wrote it as a tribute to Kandy because of Debbie's persistence. I am glad that I did. For my 65th birthday on October 11th, my children presented me with a water color portrait of Kandy. Now that she is gone, all I have are memories. Though our time was short, and I have a beautiful Paint that I am attached to, I don't think I'll ever have the same interest or bond with a horse again. KandyKiss was my one true love.

Although she is gone, there are still tests being done to find out what took my KandyKiss from me.

In Loving Memory of KandyKiss
5/9/87 - 7/14/07

Jim Hayes is a real estate investor but his love and hobby is animals. He is the owner and caretaker of 80 head of buffalo, 11 llamas, nine horses and one Sicilian miniature donkey.

Monica Gay has written three stories about the mares in her family of five humans and five horses. Their equine collection began with her own mare, Kaley. Incredibly, each horse has matched in personality the family member who rides that horse! Once Magic, a ten-year-old 15-hand black registered Quarter horse, worked through some of his issues, his easy going personality was a perfect match for her husband, Mike. Their teenage son, Sam, was more drawn to four wheelers, snowmobiles, cars and friends. He rode three times. Sunny, a ten-year-old 15-hand Palomino Quarter horse gelding, was purchased as a spare horse for Monica, but Sunny's and Sam's personalities were a match. Both are friendly, eager and likeable. The rest of the stories are about the mares!

Flame Rekindled

By Monica Gay

At the age of 32, I became the proud owner of my first horse…a three-year-old, half Arab/ half Paint mare named Kaley. As a young girl, I had ridden briefly for a couple summers on our neighbor's horse. I remember flying through the fields bareback and free, with no fear, in complete ignorance of the potential danger. I know now that God was watching and protecting, keeping me safe and it wouldn't be the only time.

My family moved, and I didn't ride again until my husband took me on a trail ride for my 30th birthday. The moment my seat hit the saddle, the memories flooded back and I had to have a horse of my own. My poor husband. He had no idea what he started. Later I told him I'd be happy when I had a horse of every color and he promptly retorted, "You already have more horses than I ever promised!" We *only* had two then, and now we *only* have five.

Our chiropractor owned horses and at an appointment he informed me that he had a mare for sale. He said she was brown and very nice. I reluctantly agreed to look at her. In my mind I pictured my first horse to be big and black. Standing at 14.2 hands, chestnut with a flaxen mane, white star and snipe, Kaley was nothing like what I had dreamed about. But I fell in love with her and my husband agreed to buy her for me.

So, now I owned this beautiful animal and knew next to nothing about her. This is not a scenario that often goes well. She's three years old, green, and knows that I don't know much. Had I received some direction and counseling from **anyone** who knew something about horses, things might have gone differently. This would be the second time God covered my ignorance with regard to horses, and by His grace things have turned out really well. Funny thing is, He picked a horse for me that is a mirror image of myself.

Kaley was and still can be strong willed (me too) but for the most part she has a desire to please and a really great heart (more so than me...I'm still getting there). Up until a couple years ago she was the alpha of our heard, ruling with benevolence. When a new horse was introduced to the herd she would watch as it fought for its place with the other horses and she would be the first to allow the newcomer to eat off her hay pile. She is confident, aloof and not often given to expressive behavior or affection. Getting her to let me in has been a big part of my fascination with her. Although sometimes frustrating, it is a challenge I enjoy pursuing.

Kaley's internal qualities are ones I have come to appreciate more and more as I look back on our first years together. With her being so young and me so inexperienced, I could easily have gotten bucked off, run away with, kicked or bitten. But none of those things ever happened. My biggest difficulty was one day trying to get her to take the bit. It was a struggle that lasted for about an hour. I was determined not to give up and she eventually did take it. We never fought about that again. She continued to test me like any good alpha does and I'm sure she won battles that I was completely oblivious to. Someone once said, "A horse knows what you don't know even when you don't know what you don't know." Our biggest challenge was and still is in moving together harmoniously when I'm on her back. My thirty-something body forgot how to ride and her three-year-old body didn't know how to carry a rider. I ended up sore and frustrated after our rides, longing for the graceful, flowing freedom that I had experienced as a girl.

Our outings became sporadic as I dove into educating myself about horses and took some riding lessons. I spent a couple years making very little progress and becoming increasingly frustrated. Then I decided to take Kaley to a clinic. What a huge turning point in our relationship! I learned you could have a relationship with a horse…that a horse wasn't just something to get on and make do what you want. I learned the basics of how to communicate with a horse on its level and how to establish myself as the alpha horse.

One of the first things I learned at the clinic was to drive the horse with my body in different directions. The task given was to have her face me and drive her backward. I spent 15-20 minutes trying to get her to stand still and face me. She just wouldn't do it. Now, I wasn't particularly fond of the idea that I had paid good money to look ridiculous in front of a bunch of people, so I called the instructor over. I did get a certain amount of satisfaction when she wouldn't stand still for the instructor either. When Kaley would prance off to the right, the instructor made life unpleasant for her by waving her training stick up and down. Bang, she ran into it. It's not safe over there! So Kaley tried going left and, oops, ran into it again. Not safe over there either! Kaley experimented, going back and forth and running into the stick every time. After a few minutes she suddenly stopped directly in front of the instructor and faced her. Well, at least with her body. She immediately turned her head and looked at her tail! You could just see her thinking, "You got my feet to stop but I'm NOT going to look at you!" This brought immediate laughter from the auditors and everyone in the clinic including the clinician. Someone yelled out, "Is she an alpha?" And I'm thinking, "Gee, you picked that up?" It didn't take long and the clinician "persuaded" Kaley that giving her two eyes was in her best interest. Then she handed the lead rope back to me and I was also able to get two eyes and still feet. That was the turning point. I made a step up in her estimation, the first to **earning** my position as alpha. The most significant part of that whole exercise was that Kaley still had her spirit and her dignity.

We went home and I began to apply daily what I'd learned at the clinic. Sometimes we would practice specific skills in the round pen; sometimes I would just practice them on her in the barn as I was grooming or feeding her. I learned that it's important to use the concepts as a matter of routine. As she saw changes in me she began to come to me when I'd go to get her in the pasture. Today, at liberty (no lead rope and halter), I can put her in the trailer and she stands for a bath in the middle of the driveway.

The spring following that first clinic on a beautiful, perfect day, I took her to the round pen. It had been a long cold winter and we hadn't done much. I asked her to circle around me. She trotted off briskly, but the fun hadn't yet begun. I asked her to turn and face me and she responded with such exuberance and energy that I was caught off guard and could only stand there looking dumbfounded. As I looked at her standing in rapt attention, with my jaw hanging open (remember I said she is usually very unexpressive), she proceeded to launch herself straight up into the air three times in a row, kaboing, kaboing, kaboing. She was suddenly possessed by Tigger! She landed in the same stance of rapt attention. With me still looking dumbfounded she closed the 12 foot gap between us with a sassy trot and stopped abruptly with her nose a hair's width from mine. With as much force as she could muster up she blew through her nose and showered me with horse snot! It was okay, I'd missed my morning facial. I fell to the ground and howled with laughter. I had never seen that side of her before and she has not shown it since. I wished she knew how much I loved that! I wonder why she doesn't show me that side of her more often and can't help but think that maybe it's me. Maybe I bore her. Maybe I'm too serious.

Kaley and I are members of the Carlton County Mounted Posse, a division of the sheriff's department. We do search and rescue when people go missing, patrol public events, and ride in parades. Each spring we attend a mounted patrol clinic. This spring our first class of the clinic was Formation Riding and Crowd Control. Well, Kaley and I got in front of a snorting, fire breathing monster of a gelding who was so close to Kaley's rear that he was dripping and flinging snot all over her. Let me just say that his rider was not much better. I was distracted by the instructor and trying to pay attention to what he was saying, and so Kaley of course had been putting up with this beast quite some time before I realized there was a problem. By the time I was just beginning to get annoyed, she'd had enough. Then it happened. SMACK. She kicked him. I was torn between concern for anyone getting hurt and thinking, "You go girl!" Is that mare behavior or is it a horse protecting herself? I don't shoe my horses and that's one of the reasons. No one was hurt. However, she did to that horse what I felt like doing to the rider! If I had been a better alpha I would have done something about the situation earlier. As protector of our two horse/person herd, I should never have put her in a position where she had to defend herself. I've learned to be careful of what I blame my mares for and of the labels I put on them.

Although our riding has improved by leaps and bounds, I still struggle on her back. Often I feel like I am riding a granite horse (maybe she is wondering why I am a granite rider!), and then when I think I'm ready to give it up, she gives me a moment or two of soft suspension and suppleness.

One evening my husband and I headed out to our fields with Kaley and Magic, the recovering nut case (notice I have no problem slapping that label on a gelding). Those rides are some of the most enjoyable. If two horses can be in love they are. So, it's couple's night out and everyone's happy with the company. We were riding the eastern perimeter of one field, and Kaley picked up a fairly soft slow-medium trot. As I looked over my right shoulder I saw Magic pick up a really slow, soft beautiful lope to catch up. He's a dream to ride anyway, but this time everything about the softness, slowness and suppleness of his movement was exaggerated. He drew up next to Kaley and an amazing, strange thing happened. She matched his stride perfectly. Then it seemed like we were in a dream sequence of a movie. Everything was in slow motion, surreal and softly blurred. It lasted maybe a minute until we came to the corner of the field and stopped. We picked up a lope again and it was very nice but the magic moment had passed. Even so, I was thrilled! She has it in her somewhere (I have it in me somewhere) to move with the grace and elegance I have always dreamed about and hoped for. It was a gift from God to tell me to have patience and continue to seek those things that are deeper within her, just as He pursues me and coaxes out the beauty that is deeply hidden there, hidden in all His children.

Amanda Gay and Cinders, after their first county fair, with all the winnings...six blue ribbons and three trophies plus the high point trophy! It surely was a "Cinderella" day! Cinders and Amanda were both ten years old at the time.

A Cinderella Story

By Monica Gay

Cinders, our bodacious 16 year old 14-hand Arab, had one owner prior to us. She had been named Cinderella by the five-year-old girl who owned her but when Anna turned 15 she decided she had out grown her little Cinderella and put her up for sale.

When my daughter, Amanda, was ten, we decided she could have a horse. My husband, Mike, had planned a weekend away for us in Minneapolis and I had found a pony for sale. We stopped to have a look at it on the way but decided it was not a match for Amanda. Shortly after getting back in the car I let out what my husband describes as a blood-curdling scream. He nearly went off the road! I had glanced down at my left hand and the entire setting of my wedding ring was gone! I began to cry and he quickly tried to console me saying, "Don't worry, it's insured...it's insured." Then a seed began to germinate in my mind. "How much is it insured for?" I sobbed. When he told me, my tears subsided quite rapidly as I realized that would be enough money to get Amanda a **nice** horse. I frantically began to search my mind for a way to tell Mike that I would rather have a horse than a wedding ring. Before I could get a word out he said, "You know...I've never been much into diamonds and jewelry, I'd rather get you a horse." Impossible! Was I hearing things? Nope. I was elated!

I began to comb the classified ads and surf the web with zeal...and I came across Cinder's ad. The Lord nudged my spirit to call but when I saw that she was four hours away I put it aside, wanting to find something closer to home. Besides that, she was a bay and I had my heart set on a palomino for my blonde-haired little girl. The prompting to pick up the phone wouldn't go away, so I finally made the call. After talking with Anna's mother for about 15 seconds, I knew this was the horse for Amanda. Color didn't matter anymore and bay was Mike's favorite anyway.

Amanda and Cinders were both ten then and dispositionally a perfect match. They are both cautious, pensive, thinkers and ponderers. They both like to take their time making a decision and you can't hurry them, but once decided they're sure. Neither likes to be surprised and they're both somewhat moody, constantly mirroring each other's mood. If one is up so is the other; if one is down so is the other! I'll never forget the day I saw them in the round pen in a stare down. Feet and shoulders squared, neither was budging!

Even though she had only a handful of riding lessons, Amanda was eager to ride Cinders in the county fair. It would be her first year, but Cinders had been competing at the county fair level for five years with Anna. She had even been to the state fair three times and completed in the top nine all three times. The county fair came and it was a roller coaster day emotionally. As parents we had never done the fair thing before and didn't know anything about anything. Even at ten, Amanda was a perfectionist and when she didn't place in the first couple events the tears flowed. By the end of the day, however, Amanda and Cinders had acquired six blue ribbons and three trophies. Although Amanda really couldn't take any of the credit, she was thrilled and smiles replaced the tears. I think it took Cinders a couple events to realize she was going to have to do it all herself. One of the experienced 4-H moms approached us and said that we should stick around until all the scores had been tallied. We didn't think it was possible for the day to get any better, but as it turned out they received another HUGE trophy for high point earner!

Fifth graders are not eligible for the state fair but that didn't matter to us. It was a Cinderella day! They competed for the next three years but their performance was average while Amanda learned to handle disappointment. Last year's performance was an exact repeat of their first year together and they earned a trip to the state fair where they placed in the top nine! Since then, we discovered that Cinder's thyroid was nearly non-functioning, which explained her extreme mellowness and her rotund figure! After only a week on medication her whole countenance changed and Amanda reported that Cinders was running faster than ever and she is looking forward to the county fair (2007).

At sixteen, Amanda has outgrown her little bay friend and we have encouraged her to switch to one of our larger Quarter Horses, but she won't hear of it! She wants to get a first at state on Cinders so they can take the victory lap around the Coliseum. Their story is not over yet but no matter how it ends, Cinders will always be our little diamond and we'll always have our Cinderella story.

Joe Gay on Rosie, his Arab mare. This is the photo mentioned in the story, a picture of "yielded and trusting" on a windy day, and a picture of true connection of horse and rider. Freestyle riding of this type is a Level Four skill in the Parelli program, and Joe and Rosie have only passed Level One.

Two Hearts United

By Monica Gay

Joe and Amanda are two years apart and have been best friends since they were toddlers. After ten-year-old Amanda got her horse I knew Joe would soon follow. We bought Rosie for Joe when he was ten also.

An internet ad pictured Rosie as a dapple grey mare, so when we went to look at her we were a little disappointed that she was, by then, flea-bitten, at 13 years old. Leslie, her owner, informed us that Rosie was very experienced but she was hard put to show us her "stuff" that day as the area we had to ride her in was icy and snowy and it was extremely cold... sub-zero, in fact, as often is the case in northern Minnesota in the winter. I was hesitant to buy her but Joe wasn't. They had connected and he knew. He wanted Rosie, so she came home with us.

Years later I bumped into Leslie's mom at a local horse expo and she told me that when they bought

Rosie she had been soured by too much gaming and she struck, kicked and lunged at anyone who came into her stall. Leslie was the first human she'd let in. Since we've had her, Joe has gamed her in 4-H every year and she's been a dream. We've **never** seen anything but a pleasing and gentle disposition. How often do horses get blamed when the real issues are about the human? It is only by God's grace that she ended up with Leslie and then us.

Rosie is a registered full Arab, great-grand-daughter of Bask. When we got her home she was a little excited and nervous, being in a new place. Joe was eager to ride as soon as we came home, so I decided to put him on bareback and lead him around, even though she seemed nervous. The second he touched her, she calmed down and began to baby-sit him. So I put the bridle on and let him ride unas-sisted. She put herself in a perfect frame as she gently walked and trotted him around the yard looking proud to carry him. She's loved him ever since.

When he wants to ride, sometimes Joe will go out to get her and she'll be lying down in the pasture… so he'll climb on (no reins or training stick) and she trots him up to the barn, pushes open the gate with her nose, trots over to her stall and pushes that gate open then stands and waits for him to tack her up.

The photo of Joe riding Rosie is a gift. On the day I took the picture, we had two young girls visiting from St. Paul. They had never been on a farm or even to the country before and all they wanted to do was ride the horses. It was extremely windy that day, with gusts 25-30 mph. I was a little hesitant to let them ride, but decided to put them on Rosie and Cinders, the two Arabs and our most reliable mounts. The south side of the arena is bordered by tall grass and trees and when the wind blows they avoid that side like the plague, which was fine. I didn't need them spooking with inexperienced riders! They walked and trotted happily up and down the north side for a couple hours! I had watched Joe riding bareback and bridle-less earlier that morning before the wind had picked up and I was enthralled. I couldn't take my eyes off them and wished I had a picture. So when the girls were done riding, I got my camera and asked him to get back on again. I am not a skilled photographer and only snapped one shot! It was a gift from the Lord, I believe, to show what being yielded and trusting looks like. Even on that scary side with the trees and tall grass in the wind, she was not afraid because she was completely trusting in Joe and relying on his guidance oblivious to the scary surroundings.

Rosie and Joe, now 17 and 14, are two of the sweetest and most gentle souls to grace our presence. In the beginning he relied on her to teach him because she'd done it all: gaming, Western, English, Hunt Seat, schooling and five-time mom. Rosie's sixth pregnancy was with twins. She was still with Leslie then and when she foaled the first was still-born but the second was alive. In her efforts to revive the stillborn foal she neglected the live twin and by the time it was discovered it was too late. Both were gone. Now despite our best efforts to breed her she will not take.

Joe and Rosie won their first trip to the MN State 4-H horse show (2007) in gaming. Cinders and Amanda also went on their second gaming trip. As much as I harp on them to practice the games all year, they don't do a lot of it compared to some of the other kids who put in hours and hours and compete all year round. I believe their success is a testimony to their relationships with their horses and it serves as an example. As desirable performance and behavior is a natural outcome of a strong relationship between horse and human, so also is our "good" behavior as Christians a natural outcome of a strong relationship to our Lord. We see each of our horses as a gift from God, teaching us many things about ourselves and our relationships with Him. He has blessed us exceedingly and abundantly in this area of our lives, and we are thrilled and grateful.

Betsy McGee Rice rode a horse before she could walk. She has trained and shown professionally, exhibiting Arabians and American Saddlebreds. She is a graduate of Morehead State University (Kentucky) under the tutelage of Liz McBride Jones, and she did graduate work at the University of Kentucky. Marriage and children gave horses a temporary back seat, but Betsy stayed connected by working with a friend at Cedar Horse Farm in South Carolina. She is currently studying Level Two Parelli while also learning from Leslie Desmond and Brent Graef. An EAGALA and OK Corral certified horse specialist, she helps people learn about themselves and others through the eyes of the horse. Working with Catherine Poland and Trinity Horse Farm LLC, they offer Equine Assisted learning and psychotherapy to youth and adults. Betsy is president of the Hancock County (Ohio) 4-H Horse Council and advisor for Freedom Reins 4-H Club. She is a board member of Hancock County Family First Council and Challenged Champions, a NARHA Premier Facility. She owns In His Hands Stables where she trains and instructs horses and riders. She is also the proud mother of three wonderful, supportive sons.

Cindy is a Survivor

By Betsy McGee Rice

Mares! If given the choice between a mare and a gelding (or even a stallion), there is no doubt I would take anything over a mare! Who hasn't heard of the CMS (Chestnut Mare Syndrome)? Why would anyone want one? That is how I felt for many years. It took a special little mare to break through my mental wall of stubbornness to show me that in many ways mares are like women. No, did I just say that?

I have been "blessed" with the tolerance of several memorable mares in my past. What that really means is that they didn't kill me for not liking them simply because they were mares and "different." Ok, what I really mean is that I considered them difficult because of their sex. To Sophisticated Lady, who didn't want to be "Sophisticated" and certainly did not act like a "Lady" anytime I was riding her, I am sorry for taking you from a trail horse to a Saddle Seat Equitation horse. Mt. Joy's Rose of Sharon tried

185

very hard to teach me some lessons on understanding mares; but again, I am so sorry I didn't learn. Beverly had emotional scars that needed healing, whereas Peggy's mare needed emotional support, but all I saw was "CMS!" Lorafic almost made me like mares, but I was too busy with my twins to notice. The lesson I should have learned is how much mares are like women. They like to have fun, just want to be understood and above all, loved for who they are. Can any of us ask for more?

Cindy came into my life as I was struggling to save my beloved thoroughbred, Major Havoc, from founder. She was Major's best friend and for the life of me, I wasn't sure what he saw in her. Cindy was known as Strawberry in her previous life as a school horse because of her strawberry roan coloring and the kids liked that name. I saw her as a different Strawberry — kind of seedy and cheap. There I said it. I had no respect for her. She served a purpose as a kind school horse.

The first time I rode her to see why the kids were having a hard time cantering her, I discovered she didn't respect me either. She loved the little ones but had no tolerance for an experienced rider who just wanted to see what she could do. She was a total nutcase, jigging around, acting like she had no brains inside that head of hers. I rode her briefly and then stepped back to take a better look – and saw something more. This was the first of many "ah-ha" moments she was to show me.

Once I started looking for the "real" Strawberry, I saw a horse with a past. As I wiped her down after a particularly sweaty ride, I noticed a change in her look. Her eyes softened and a deep sigh led me to appreciate her big, bright eyes and little fox ears. She gave me the impression that there was a time in her life when she had indeed "been something to take care of." Was she a show horse turned into a school horse?

Strawberry had the habit of sticking her tongue out of the side of her mouth. Everyone made fun of it. Thinking of it as her way of telling people what she really thought of her position in life, we were humored by it. The vet pointed out that the reason she did that was because her tongue had a huge scar across it and she had no sensation or control of it on one side. Ugh! I hadn't even taken the effort to figure out why she was funny about her mouth. I guess I would be too if something that bad had happened to it!

She also had the cutest way to hold her nose, sort of over to one side. Isn't that interesting, I thought. It gave her an expression as if to say "yeah, whatever." I swear if she could roll her eyes up in her head, she would! I did not find the scar covering the facial nerve for a couple of years. I think I found that about the same time as I found the scar going under her left eye and across her cheek. Her past was becoming clear to me. With those findings, I began to search for the horse she kept so well hidden.

When Strawberry was given to me, the first thing I did was to change her name. Somehow this mare was more than a "Strawberry." When I look at her big eyes that I now see as filled with amusement, I

187

thought of Cindy Lou Who from the movie, "How the Grinch Stole Christmas." She had that inquisitive look of innocence that belies the story the scars have kept hidden. So Cindy she became.

I'm not sure when she stopped being a "CMS." It was a gradual process, and yet – I can hardly remember thinking she was a pain. I think it came about as I sought to understand what she had kept hidden. She even began to snake her neck on occasion! This time I found it funny that the "real mare" was finding her voice again.

Her previous owner gave me her registration papers which held another clue to her past. Her registered name is Skips Sweet Dream. Wow! What a wonderful name! Her papers read like a "Who's Who" of Foundation Bred Quarter Horses. I remember reading about these great horses in the old Western Horseman magazines of my youth. I've seen pictures of Skipper W, Blondy's Dude, Joe M Moore, Poco Pine, and Darin's Skip in the advertisements. And there stands Cindy with all the greats behind her looking at me as if to say "I tried to tell you!" What took her down the road she has walked is still unknown to me, but I know the road she has helped me walk and it is a road just as tough.

I've learned a great deal from this old mare. Initially, she asked me to look beyond her name, beyond her "fate" in life, to see who she really is. I started looking at people the same way, wondering what brought them to where they are in life. If they could choose, would they be where they are? The question I continue to ponder is: do we succumb to our circumstances or are we called to be more than our circumstances? I think mares are greater than their circumstances! We are survivors.

AN UPDATE: I recently kept Cindy's 15-year-old daughter (Rosie) for a brief stay during the weaning of her foal. Rosie and her mother have the same face, similar markings, same thoughtfulness about things and situations and the same "voice." Like mother, like daughter! I am thinking there must be a way to someday own Rosie myself.

Cindy's story by Betsy McGee Rice continues in another chapter, this one including another mare named Suzie. This beautiful story of two old mares has a sad ending, after the story was written. Suzie was laid to rest in October of 2007. Cindy seemed to know the night before and she was frantic. The connection between these two mares is unbelievable...like two old women who have been there for each other through life's trials.

The Old Girls

By Betsy McGee Rice

"The Old Girls" is the expression everyone uses when talking about Cindy and Suzie. At ages 23 and 25 respectively, they are the matriarchs of the barn. They didn't choose to be with each other but rather the circumstances of life led them to this relationship.

I've heard it said that a horse's life is full of goodbyes. Their herd mates change on the whim of their owners — who sell, change boarding barns, or simply decide the horse should be in another pasture. There are a hundred reasons for horses to have to say good bye to their friends. And it isn't only the horse friends that come and go in their lives but also their owners and caretakers. By the time a horse reaches the ages of these old mares, they have seen their share of comings and goings.

Much like two older women who get together by circumstances out of their control, Cindy and Suzie were thrown together. Neither was particularly fond of one another initially. They are quite opposites! Suzie, aka "The Princess" is a tall, athletic mare who hides her age well and can still jump a four foot fence with ease and grace (explanation later). Her preferred companion is a tall, elegant Thoroughbred gelding named Rain...but he went to another barn when his owner changed colleges. Cindy, on the other hand, is a short, foundation-bred Quarter Horse. The years have not been kind to her as her body wears the scars of unknown events.

Now, about Suzie's jumping abilities. I once put Cindy in an adjoining field with a horse that needed a friend. Suzie jumped the fence, apparently so dependent on Cindy that she to be with her. She preferred Cindy's companionship, perhaps, to the other horses with their unfriendly, ears-back attitudes. No one saw her jump and we were convinced at first that the fence must be down. But no, Suzie's need for safety and comfort meant being with Cindy.

The biggest difference between the two horses is the very thing that brought them together. Suzie doesn't like other horses whereas Cindy is the friend to all. Suzie lives to be safe and comfortable, not too hot or too cold and certainly not wet! This is where Cindy stepped into Suzie's life. Cindy became Suzie's life guard as she kept other horses from picking on Suzie. Cindy must have sensed Suzie's fragilities at that time and took care of her. The tables turned when Cindy was seriously kicked and Suzie took on the job of protecting Cindy. Suzie would pin her ears at any horse who dared to look at them. The funniest part was that she could only do that from the far side of Cindy or while trotting protective circles around Cindy.

Just as the proverbial two old ladies don't always get along, Cindy and Suzie have their disagreements too. Cindy does not like horses looking at her, whether real or imagined when she eats. She will attack the stall wall with her ears flattened, teeth barred and heels up. Initially, Suzie would cower in the opposite corner of her stall but as the years have passed, she now stands just out the reach of Cindy's teeth as if taunting her and calling her bluff. Out in the field, being the more athletic, Suzie races to the gate to come in for dinner quickly outstriding Cindy with her long legs. Not to be outdone, Cindy just drives Suzie away from the gate with "that look" when she finally catches up. Mid morning you will find the two old girls napping in the corners of their respective stalls closest to each other, heads together if not for the stall wall. If they were people you could picture them sitting in their recliners napping while in the background the TV blares with The Price Is Right!

Life brings to all of us relationships that aren't always of our choice. People are forced together by life events in work and in leisure. Wouldn't it be great if we choose to make the best of all situations and take life as it comes as these "old girls" have done?

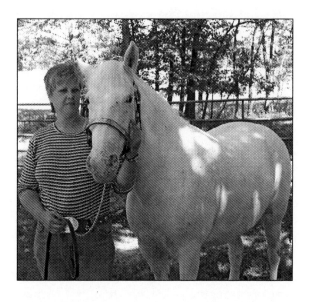

Pamela Erb and her husband David live in rural south-west Missouri along the banks of the beautiful Pomme De Terre River. Pamela is a Registered Nurse and practices as a Certified Legal Nurse Consultant from her home office. She has had a deep love for animals since she was a toddler, and her passion has only grown with the years. Owning a horse was never an option until she and her husband moved to the country. They now own horses, donkeys, cats, birds and a dog. A pet rooster, rabbits and goats were a past part of her animal family during the seven years she has lived in rural Missouri.

It Only Took a Split Second

By Pamela Erb

It only took a split second to find myself at one with Mother Nature in the round pen dirt, after Little Star threw me into the corral panel. That was the beginning — or the end — of one more chapter of the detailed history of our relationship in the four short years she has been with me.

Little Star's life, as soon as it began, was destined for hardship. A white and grey Appaloosa/Missouri Fox trotter, she was the product of an irresponsible man who always left his mares and stallions together with full knowledge he would not have homes for the babies. He used the sale barns to sell his horses to the killers, whose only desire was to buy unwanted horses at low prices, and transport them (inhumanely) to slaughter houses to await their demise. I outbid the killer for Little Star and it was the best $155.00 I have ever spent. She is worth her weight in gold to me.

Taking her home was not what I had expected. Little Star gladly loaded into the trailer and unloaded easily as well. That was to be the only "easy" experience with Little Star for a very long time. She is five now, but she was just a yearling when I brought her home. She needed to be handled with extreme care then; she was emaciated, full of worms and fearful of humans. They told us Little Star had never seen a human until her capture in the field the day before she was brought to the sale barn. My husband got angry with me and said that I bit off more than I could chew, that this horse would never calm down and would kill me in the process.

I knew Little Star had a softer side but I had to prove to her that I was not there to harm her. Several weeks went by with both of us testing the waters. She would come closer to me, a little at a time, but she was always apprehensive. When the time came for her to trust me to touch her, she trembled as I stroked her beautiful neck. She would look at me shakily as if she were going to be punished. Knowing how afraid she was made me cry. I was told she had had no human contact but I was beginning to wonder. Was she abused as well as neglected? Or was there something the seller was not telling me?

This leads me back to the beginning of my story when I found myself on the ground after colliding with a steel corral panel. Little Star and I were in the round pen after she had gone for some Horse Basics 101 at a local trainer. She and I did the round pen exercises, then I put the saddle on and did a little more longeing. Then it was time to get into the saddle. Slowly, I came up to her left side and stroked her neck while talking quietly to her. No shaking this time, no fearful eyes. She turned her head to me as if to say "It's okay mom. I'm okay." As I praised her softly, I gently placed my left foot in the stirrup and with even pressure I gently lifted my body up and my right leg over. Within a split second, she swung her head and neck to the right and her eyes got wide. Before I could get my right foot into the stirrup, she bolted off, started bucking and threw me into the steel corral panel. Bam. Thud. Everything occurred so fast that I hardly knew what happened. Little Star was racing around the 50 foot round pen snorting, ears alert and eyes flashing with fear. She quickly came back to me and stared down at me in shock as if to say "Mom? I don't know what happened! Can you please forgive me?" I sat there and cried, hearing myself say that I was too old for this stuff. I just can't do this anymore.

I sat there for a few minutes while Little Star stood over me. I cried and said, "I am sorry, Star, and it's not your fault. Mommy is not mad at you." I have tears in my eyes now as I write this story because I vividly remember the whole incident. My left side from under my arm to my thigh was already badly bruised from being thrown only minutes prior and I had a difficult time getting to my feet. Luckily, I did not strike my head. My doctor told me this incident knocked my pelvis out of place and injured my ankle, and that I was lucky she didn't kill me. "You ARE going to sell her for this stunt she pulled, aren't you?" was a common question asked by my friends, coworkers and my doctor. Every one got the same answer: "No. She has put her trust in me and I am not going to fail her." This was not her fault I got hurt. It was mine. I didn't understand her and her fears and give her enough time to work things through before getting in the saddle. After all, it was not I who trained her in horse basics but someone who would never see her again. I was not going to give up on her, ever.

Although I have not ridden Little Star much since that incident two years ago, we have bonded in another special way. She would never let me touch her ears or really any part of her body without skittishly moving away. She showed the yearning to be loved and stroked, but her fears of the unknown kept her away. She now allows me to gently scratch her ears and she even finds pleasure in it. That feat took more than one year to accomplish, but with patience and love, anything is possible.

Little Star has a difficult time with horse flies. My other horses and donkeys will rub up against a tree, bite at the horse fly or roll on the ground if a human is not there to swat it off. But Little Star seems to always get one on her rump and is unable to rid herself of its painful stings. All my others will let me swat the flies but with that comes the loud noise of the swat and the feeling they are getting spanked. They all are happy that I do this for them and will quickly trot over to me to have me rid them of the pest. Swat! Until recently, the loud noise always frightened Little Star and she would run around crazily trying to get the horse fly to stop biting her. For several weeks this year, I desensitized her by gently slapping her rump when the horse flies were not around. This she stood for, although she still seemed a little frightened by the spank and the sound. Soon after the horse flies were in full force, one landed on her rump and she started to gallop away through the fields. Taking my life in my own hands, I stepped near her path and as she ran by I swatted the horse fly as hard as I could. Smack! She stopped abruptly, swung her massive body around and looked at me crazily with those Appaloosa whites of her eyes. And before she realized what had happened, I started praising her. "Good girl, that's a good girl," and started stroking her rump. After a few more times of my chasing her down to swat the horse flies, she no longer runs away, but quickly looks for where I am by the stalls and comes to me at a trot. She now trusts me to help rid her of those painful pests. We have worked through this for a long time and she must be reassured regularly.

She is more like a human than a horse to me, with the whites of her eyes resembling ours. The softness in her eyes has made me cry on more than one occasion. She has come such a long way in the four short years she has been with me, and we continue to learn from each other. It is like grasping and understanding the subtle nuances of a new language. Little Star and I have worked hard together to bond and trust each other. She has come so far.

More recently Little Star became very agitated when I would attempt to scratch her belly or come anywhere near her flanks. Premenstrual Syndrome maybe? Not so far fetched as some may think. As I went to give her some loving strokes and scratches, her ears pinned back, her teeth showed and she swung her head towards me in warning. I quickly came up by her face and started gently stroking her chin, and her eyes seemed to soften. I remember only too well when I was in the midst of my own menstrual period. I was definitely not a fun person to be around. Little Star was having "her time," and I tried to respect her space, her quick to react attitude, and her swift turning of her head as she attempted to warn me that she wasn't feeling well. All she wanted was to be stroked and loved in certain places during that time. Loving scratches to her ears, neck and face were all she would allow. Any deviation from those areas, even if only a few inches, and her ears would quickly flatten and her eyes warn of an impending bite. I respected her wishes, and within a few days the symptoms subsided and all-over body scratches were again gratefully allowed. Does this somehow remind you of your own bad "time of the month" when all you wanted was to be left alone except for receiving food, water, and medicine…the essentials? Little Star is the same way.

My last story of this grand creature happened last night when all of my horses and donkeys got their hooves trimmed and two mares received their shoes. Little Star was highly agitated and kept sniffing around the farrier and his son, licking their truck, running off into the fields and then trotting back up to see what the stir was all about. Little Star must be contained in a 10x10 corral to get her feet trimmed, as she feels more secure and so does the farrier. Because she had been very sensitive the last few days with her cycle, I was fearful she would try to shove the farrier out of the way in anxiety. I entered the corral as I always did and held the lead line, placing her head almost to my chest. I kept telling her what a good girl she was, over and over. I kept stroking her face and gently over her eyes as the farrier did his work. She went into somewhat of a trance as I cooed to her, and she acted very much a grown lady. I was so proud of her! When I opened the corral gate, she slowly walked out, then looked back at me as if to say, "Mom said it was okay and it was." She seemed to thank me. It was a Kodak moment.

To those who are not in tune with your mare, you surely are missing an amazing opportunity. They are like children showing us new and amazing things they are capable of every day. Mares have a language all their own. They converse with their eyes, their body language and their voices. They are willing to allow us to learn about them and spend time with them. Keep your mind open for they offer us endless opportunities.

Hold your horses near, as they love you more than any one person could. Seek solace in them, as they truly understand and want to ease your suffering. Their soft eyes knowingly lower as they nudge you with their soft muzzle. "I love you mom," they nicker. "I will love you forever too, my dearest friend," I reply. "Forever."

Linda Zavada had a thirty year career in public education, teaching third grade children. She gave "first rides" to many of her students and used her horses as part of an incentive program for the three R's...Respect, Responsibility and Reasoning. Linda and her husband, Dave, have one grown son, Ryan, and live on a four-acre ranchette with one dog, two cats, a lovebird and four horses. She and a friend attended an informational seminar at Crystal Peaks Youth Ranch near Bend, Oregon, in May of 2007, and they hope to become involved in using rescued horses to help children. Linda has been a village trustee for more than twenty-five years and has been Mayor of Long Point, Illinois, since April of 2005.

This Mayor Rides a Mare

By Linda Zavada

Ah, mares! My first horse was a mare. Three of my four current horses are mares, which makes ten mares that I've had in my 34 years of owning horses. But which one stands out and is worthy of having an essay written about her?

Would it be Cinnamon, my very first horse? A girl's first horse is always special, even though this "girl" had to wait for her first horse until she was a married adult with a teaching career. But age didn't lessen that unique place in my heart that a first horse touches. Because of an injury (before I bought her) which caused a permanent split in her right front hoof, I learned to trim her hooves and even nail shoes on her front feet! We won trophies in several local parades, and she gave countless "first rides" to many of my third grade students.

Maybe I should write about Candy, the American Saddlebred, my third mare. After all, I've had her for the longest of any of my horses. She is still going strong at age 23 after being with me for nearly 22 years. She turned out well considering her owner/ trainer had no experience or knowledge about starting a young horse. Aside from having slight claustro- phobia on a narrow trail, she has been a true friend and wonderful companion.

Maybe the mare I should write about is Amber, a sorrel grade mare with a gorgeous head and a jack- hammer trot. Why would she be a contender? Well, she let me realize my dream of raising a foal...but only for seven months. Her sweet baby, Misty, was that age when she broke a leg and had to be eutha- nized. It still gives me shivers when I remember how that mare mourned the loss of her filly. The memory of that empty, far-away look in her eyes can still bring tears to my eyes after ten years.

I wouldn't even consider writing about Emmy, the Saddlebred filly I bought on the rebound from Misty's death. I want to forget about her. She was the only horse I've ever known with a sinister, mean streak in her personality. The timing wasn't the best, either, since she was here during the time my mother was battling terminal colon cancer. Most of my horses have been my partners for their entire lives, but this little maverick was here for less than a year.

My youngest mare, and most recent, is Dazzle, a Missouri Fox Trotter/Spotted Mountain horse. She is a flashy tobiano with great conformation. I wanted a gaited horse because my Baby-Boomer bones are beginning to demand less jostling and smoother, gliding gaits. There is one minor problem. She is not gaiting yet! She is only four, and the rest of her training is coming along fine. I know the "light bulb moment" will occur soon, and she will make a great trail horse. But, no, I'm not going to write about Dazzle.

So, you ask, what mare is she going to write about? The mare called Sierra. Sierra is a Pryor Mountain Mustang. She had two years of wild freedom before she was rounded up. Sierra, and about a dozen other Mustangs, eventually found their way to the Hooved Animal Humane Society in Woodstock, Illinois. She and her best buddy were given the names Thelma and Louise and had lived at HAHS for several years before I began my adoption proceedings. I was looking for a horse on the rebound from the untimely colic death of my 16-year-old Arab, Liberty (Misty had been put down three days before my birthday, and Liberty died three days before Thanksgiving). Since I had resigned from my teaching job to advocate full time for our son who had ADHD and bipolar disorder, I couldn't afford to pay much for a horse. I thought that adopting a horse from HAHS would be helping an animal in need of a good home.

After two trips to Woodstock and much deliberation, I chose "Thelma." They delivered her, as the single-digit temperatures would have made for a very chilly ride in my open stock trailer. Thus, my Mustang adventure began on a frigid January day... and what an adventure it has been. I have learned more from this one horse than all of the other ones put together. Renamed Sierra, this mare has clearly taught me more than I've taught her. Sierra is very intelligent in her own primal way. Her lessons (I was the student) in body language opened up a whole new method of communication with my horses that I didn't know existed. Her stubborn streak tries my patience, and the "wild" air about her fascinates me. She loves to be groomed and wants to be included in everything I do with the domestic horses. I love to watch her trot in the round pen. She simply floats. Her personality included a heaping dose of playfulness which sometimes includes some awesome dressage movements (at liberty) that I've only seen done by Lipizzaner stallions.

So, we are living happily ever after. End of story, right? Not quite. Her ground training and under-saddle work were going well when I fell off and broke my arm during one of her 180-degree, half-second turns. I blamed my poor riding ability, not her. After a summer of healing, I got back on her only to be catapulted into the air from her fearful explosion at the sound of a cracking stick. Unhurt and undaunted, I rode again, only to bite the dust after a "feeling good" bucking episode. Although I landed in a plowed field, the fall caused major damage to my back. Again, I blamed myself for getting on without first working her in the round pen and for not being able to sit out the bucks. None-the-less, I had vowed that if I had a third mishap, she would be returned to HAAS. I couldn't transport her for several weeks because I was hurting too much. When I felt physically able, the cold winter weather had closed in, making travel in a stock trailer unacceptable.

I did a lot of soul-searching that winter, and I decided to keep Sierra and give her a forever home even if I couldn't ride her. Sometimes our children, spouses, friends and animals don't or can't live up to our expectations. Wishing they were different doesn't make it so, but accepting their quirks and limitations and loving them anyway is an option that makes a win/win situation. Over the past couple of years this mare and I have grown close. The reactive, Mustang behavior has mellowed, although I have not ridden her since that fateful day in the plowed field. I believe events in our lives happen for a reason. I think this mare is meant to be here; I'm just not supposed to ride her right now. I do feel that Sierra could excel in nearly any discipline, especially dressage. She is very athletic and carries herself regally. I would love to find the right person to bring her to her full potential, but if I don't that's O.K. She will live out her life as part of my equine family, knowing love and security and receiving quality care. I feel honored being loved, respected and accepted by this living piece of American history. I know we will continue to grow and learn from each other as we communicate in the Equus language. The bond with this mare is one that no domestic horse could duplicate. Thank you, Sierra, for coming into my life and for being you.

And about the title: I really am the mayor/president of our small, central-Illinois village!

Donna Vogt and her husband Dennis have resided at Jerseyville, Illinois, on their 400 family acres since 1972. The name Trinity Hill Farm evolved from their Christian beliefs and representing three family farms situated together. They are the parents of Ben (Los Angeles) and Christyn, married to Brian Bond (St Louis). Brian and Christyn are the parents of Joshua, Ashlyn, and Alexander. Another grandchild is due in April of 2008. Dennis's experience with farm work horses and mules and training his own first horse helped to develop his natural abilities. As a design engineer, he is able to formulate ideas and strategies for effective training. Dennis has trained for others for over 20 years. Dennis currently trains any breed of horse, concentrating on those used for families and trail. Donna teaches English and western riding to kids and adults. Donna has studied English pleasure, dressage, saddleseat, and western pleasure and has participated in local shows. Her main interest is equitation and developing a balanced, elegant rider. Trinity Hill Farm offers lessons, training, clinics, and other special events in their indoor arena and meeting room. They feel blessed to have this opportunity to serve the horse community.

Mares We Have Known (and not always appreciated)

By Donna Vogt

While we have always loved, on various levels, all the horses we've owned, we've not always appreciated all their behaviors or characteristics. Some have been crabby, some have actually hurt us, and some have caused frustration. But, all of them have given us joy of some kind. That is the world of horses. It enables you to experience every realm of emotion: elation to despair, energy to exhaustion, love to hate, and joy to sadness. If you decide to involve yourself in horses, you have to be willing to open yourself up to every emotion.

Dennis and I started our horse adventures with a quarter gelding and a thoroughbred gelding. As geldings, Smokey and Moon had their issues but almost everything was dependent upon their training and education. Nothing seemed to change with the day or weather or the time of the month. Since we were young and enthusiastic, their challenges were exciting. But, the day came when Smokey died and we began our search for another riding horse.

While Dennis had grown up riding work horses and mules on his grandparent's farm, I was a city girl who never thought seriously about farms and horses. There was nothing in my lifestyle remotely connected to farm life other than a yearly visit to great grandparents in Arkansas. There, I felt like Annie Oakley. When I returned to my urban home, I was able to ride at a local stable once a year but never dreamed someday of actually owning and living with horses (or a cowboy for that matter). Little did I know what God was planning for my life.

Our horse education level, in 1978, was very basic and our training techniques common to many others. We had little exposure outside our 120 acres. Our search for a new horse was simple: look in the paper and answer an ad! The first ad was for an Arabian mare due to foal in several months. Good! 2 for the price! We didn't know anything about Arabians, mares, or raising a baby, but how difficult could it be? I see those grins!

After being rounded up in the hills of Fieldon by a motorcycle, Shakira came sailing down over the hill, tail flagging and her pure white body glowing in the sun. We were sold. They said she could be ridden? I don't think we even did a test drive! Surely there would be no problem? Shakira was a beautiful desert-bred small Arabian. Even with both of us being tall, her size was outweighed by her beauty and personality. Arabians are known for their love of humans and she captured our hearts. Her baby was born on October 22, not the usual time for babies. Shahani, named for dam Shakira and sire Ahani, became Dennis's next student. Looking back, we wish we knew then what we know now. Shahani was smart and quick to learn and today, at 27, is still gentle for ground handling. We attribute good ground manners to lots of discipline and respect and years of treating leg injuries. She was not, unfortunately, an easy ride. Because of raising our kids as well as taking care of the farm, Shahani did not receive the calm emotional control training she needed. Soon we found our life busy, and Shahani, being a very small horse, seemed to fit the need of the neighbors and their family. She spent several years with them, getting lots of riding but little reassurance and calming for her emotions. When a fire struck their home, Shahani reacted to the trucks, noise, fire and smoke by crawling under the wire fence, not displacing a single wire, and running back to our barn. She came home and here she remains.

Both mom and daughter were blessed with great hearts and gentle personalities. They say if you want to know how a horse will be, watch its mama. We now have a gelding who was only with his mom until weaned, who grinds his teeth just like her when nervous. Shakira and Shahani had very similar personalities and spirit. Both are kind toward humans but full of themselves when saddled.

Shakira was known for her very fancy rear end action at the trot, sort of a cross between the tango and the rhumba. When she cycled each month, she would dance against the stall walls to a point where we eventually had to replace them. As with many Arabians, known for their endurance qualities, she had plenty of "go." We were not concerned; we loved her fancy dance movements.

Because the Arab market was good and since we had enjoyed Shahani so much, we decided to rebreed Shakira. A well bred Arabian stallion was standing at stud in the St Louis area. Once again, we had very little method with our madness — just boy meets girl and then 11 months later baby. Shakira, on the other hand, neglected to tell us she was not an easy breeder — although very fond of the boys. Maybe her October baby should have given us a clue. So, off to the stallion we went, and went, and went. Many dollars and drugs later, Shakira was in foal. It was a long 11 months, then 12 with the final result being a false pregnancy. Another valuable and expensive lesson. We did rebreed locally and her resulting foal was Sheer Joy. Shakira lived a wonderful life, never sick or lame or even crabby. This mare started with joy and ended in peace. One beautiful winter day in February 2004, I stood with her in the pasture and remarked how wonderful she was doing for 34. The next morning we found her lying near where we had spent time the day before. Maybe she just needed to hear "you did good ol'girl. Thank you!"

As with most horse owners, it becomes an accumulation game. We had a couple; why not add another? A neighbor had a 10 month old paint filly with no white markings and wanted to sell her for $150. She was quite wooly and very stocky but seemed like a nice horse. Again, why not? KoKo, as we named her, changed from a woolly mammoth at 10 months to a beautiful dark palomino three months later. Now, we were "so much more experienced," we thought we would do an extraordinary job of training. What we know now and didn't then: there is a great deal of difference in handling an Arabian and a stock type horse. Arabians are quick to respond and don't like to be in trouble. Everything with Koko was an argument and slow. While she didn't offer any help, we also don't blame her — she was just being a horse. If you wanted a big, pretty, and somewhat sluggish ride she was great. Therefore, we decided she might be a good breeding candidate? Yep, adding more and on a roll.

Again, there was a wonderful Arabian stallion in the area. We were still impressed with the beauty and character of the Arab horse and thought combining Arab with the stock breed was a wise choice. This was the beginning of a very good decision. The Arab-stock cross is generally very successful. Koko provided us with a beautiful bay colt in April of 1983. Kollende was my personal trail, English, western, pole, dressage, and all around friend for many years. He is now teaching many others how to ride and think! I could go on and on about him but since this is all about the girls, I'll move on. Koko had a second filly, a solid bay, sold to a friend at an early age. Her third and final baby by a friend's Arabian stallion was Firedancer, born in April of 1985. Dancer was raised along with Shakira's second and last, Sheer Joy. "Dancer" quickly became Dennis's next project.

By this time, our education and training skills were beginning to improve. Dennis has many times been called a "whisperer," having a natural ability to calm a horse, getting submission and respect, and making it look very easy. Dancer was not an easy mare to train. At the beginning of her training we had begun studying John Lyons. We were not familiar with "giving to the bit," only "make them do it." The first time Dennis sat on Dancer and asked her to "give" it took 45 minutes. Thankfully, the skills and abilities have changed and improved through trial and error and thousands of hours of practice. Dancer quickly became his favorite student and riding partner.

Although Dennis is the trainer and major rider, I do ground work and daily handling. Sometimes the handling can be just as dangerous as the riding. Dancer, as a two year old, presented me with my first major injury. We were having an ice storm and horses needed to be moved. I handled and rode, but my years of experience didn't and couldn't prepare me for every situation. When I went into her stall and asked her to move around, she presented her backside and then her feet in my chest. As I flew back against the door, I could not breathe and I could feel the pain. The many layers of clothes protected against additional damage but cracked ribs take a long time to heal. Dancer and I are still not close buddies! I had made an error in horse communication. This was another lesson on speaking and understanding their language. Even to this day "when Dancer speaks, I listen."

Dancer learned to ride fence and go down the trail. She was not spooky and loved being with her partner, Dennis. He truly loved and enjoyed her. That partnership lasted for many years until Dennis moved on to an Arab gelding named Sabrin. Dancer is now 22 and serving faithfully as a lesson horse. She has fluid movement so riders can easily learn sitting and rising trot. She is known for her frequent "potty" stops which seem to draw her as soon as she hits the sand arena. She is more than happy to go over the small jumps and is willing, whether riders are accomplished or struggling. When her final day comes she will take her place alongside the others in the pasture.

Sheer Joy was Shakira's second and last baby with us. Because she had a false pregnancy and the stallion was no longer in the area, we decided to breed with a Saddlebred standing at a local farm. We thought this cross would give us additional size and "flair." This might be a good place in which to interject a caution about breeding. Sometimes it is much more complicated than boy meets girl. The implications can be expensive and certainly life long. Because of her complications, it involved a great deal of time and energy. Breeding is a huge commitment. There are so many unwanted horses — the decision should come only after consideration for the foal as well as the ability of the owner to maintain proper care.

Sheer Joy was a beautiful red, sorrel type bay, very feminine and dainty. Her name became her personality. Her frizzy red hair gave her the nickname "frizzy lizzy." She was animated and vocal and there was not a chance of sneaking into the barn without her warning everyone. Feed times were greeted with her joyful, exuberant neigh. She and sister Shahani certainly have our "vocal" awards. Once when Shahani was having surgery at a clinic in Chatham, they commented they had never had a more vocal patient. Joy and Dancer, both born in April of 1985, grew up together and were recipients of each current training insight. Joy was quiet even when the rider was nervous. Every beginner rider rode Joy and she carried them with patience. Her way of going was like her moms, confident with a bit of flair. In November of 2006, Joy suffered a severe case of colic. After pain medicine would not work, the decision was made to put her down. Dr. Rebecca Schuff from Equine Medical cried with us. We buried her next to her mom. It would not have been fair to allow such a wonderful friend and partner to suffer. Sheer Joy had become an intricate part of Trinity Hill, to live in our hearts and memories forever.

The last mare acquired and currently residing at Trinity Hill Farm is Sierra. Dennis calls her his "airwalker" because of her probable Arab-Tennessee Walker breeding. She has a lovely Arab type head with large soft eyes, a 14'3 well proportioned body, and a beautiful red coat. Sierra was part of a small rescue group. Dennis purchased her while attending and riding in the National Field Dog Trials in Mississippi. She was quiet and pretty, but had a hesitancy which is common in horses with little socialization. We didn't know then the lessons that would follow. Early interaction is very important to a horse's concept of human relationship.

When Sierra stepped off the trailer, we immediately were pleased. Her sweet, kind eyes drew us to her. Sierra had no experience in trusting, so yielding herself to us was a huge step for her. It took many months before she allowed one of us to be close unless haltered. She was cautious and protective of her food. All these issues would eventually surface in situations.

In August, after being with us for about six months of being ridden and handled, she came home on a beautiful evening without a rider. Dennis had taken her for a sunset ride in back of the house. Within a half hour, Dennis was in the kitchen, obviously had fallen and partially incoherent. Something had spooked Sierra to a point where a seemingly quiet riding horse had thrown the rider. The end result was a stay in the hospital with a collapsed lung and multiple fractures. It was months before he would be training or riding again.

Many comments and conversations surface when there's an accident. We certainly heard "maybe you're too old." Well, our answer is that it takes a lifetime to do horses and to always make the right decision. We are wiser now and hope to learn from every experience. Some questioned the safety. Horses can be dangerous and it pays to continually train your horse as well as continue your education. Through the years, we have made it a practice to study all the training available. We have attended fairs, clinics, classes, participated in shows, read, and watched

RFD and any other venue possible. We have studied, listened and watched but have also worked hard to use the information. It is critical to use training techniques you can actually do yourself. You can watch a roping technique all day but if you can't rope, it won't work for you. Our final answer is "we love them and it's worth the challenge and risk."

Dennis continued his work with Sierra. She was still protective, but Dennis grew to love her quiet willingness. She has a desire to please but with very meager coping skills. She is gaited as well as a walk, trot, canter horse. Gradually, she would come to us and seemed eager for the attention. She now lives in a pasture with Shahani and a quiet quarter gelding named Ramsey. Each day it's a joy watching them from my computer, as they run and play in the pasture. Eventually, we began to use her for some lessons in the arena. Dennis has the ability to get a horse to be willing and light in the bridle. Sierra is not an exception.

As I sit here with a broken arm, I wish I could say Sierra has caused no other situations, but it's not the truth. Education with horses never ends. What I've learned this time has been a good spiritual reminder. Dennis and I are Christians and God has blessed us with many wonderful people and horse relationships. Knowing God completely is impossible. Knowing horses completely is also impossible. Their thinking is just as different from ours as ours is different from God's thinking. Our challenge is to want to know both the horse and our God more each day. Each day gives another opportunity.

On a Saturday morning, one day before leaving for our annual camping trip to Land Between the Lakes in Kentucky, I went to feed as usual. My thought was "it's going to be simple; I have one less horse to feed." Daisy, a boarded horse had already gone to the campground, and she had been the #2 horse with Sierra being #1. We were feeding three horses, using ground feeders in this lot and had been doing so for several months without incident. Because I was thinking as a human, I did not consider the changed horse-dynamics. I fed Sierra, skipped bowl #2 and fed Ramsey at position #3. Sierra immediately grabbed a bite of her food then ran to claim her extended territory. Ordinarily, she would have moved Daisy from her bowl, but with Daisy absent, I found myself in her feeding position. Sierra's reaction was to swing her rear end around and throw her hind legs at me in protest and disrespect. Her legs connected with my arm and the rest, as we say, is "history." As if this wasn't enough for one year, Dennis had a broken right arm from a spooked training horse in May. Thankfully, he could resume feeding and the barn chores.

So what's the lesson learned? Get rid of the horse? In some cases, that is the correct answer. If you don't have the ability yourself or the money for professional training, it will save you much frustration. Second, never quit thinking. Thinking is a valuable lesson that must be taught to the horse, so he thinks instead of reacts. The same goes for us as horsemen. The more we study horses, their natural instincts, and how to train them effectively, the more we can enjoy them in our lives.

Are you asking if Sierra is still a resident of Trinity Hill? Yes, she is, and likely to stay. Since we have experienced God's forgiveness, we try to extend that to our horses. Each time there has been an incident, we became aware of something incomplete in their training. We simply had more work to do. Dennis said "she was remorseful." As with our children and friends, you don't get rid of them just because they made a mistake. It is, perhaps, a thought sometimes!

As I've written this with my left hand wondering how long I'll have a cast, or watch Dennis train horses now riding with his helmet, there are a few thoughts about whether it is worth it. The answer is yes. The benefits far outweigh the deficits. What they teach us about life and who we are is far less painful than some of the alternatives.

Do we prefer mares over geldings? Probably not. We've been very fortunate to have wonderful mares who have not been affected by disposition or hormonal issues. We attribute that to their ability to live as horses, running pastures, receiving good hay and grain, as well as good training and good old fashioned work. Because God's favorite animal is the horse, they have been given to us as a gift. May you always enjoy the gift!

Dianne Doll has written two stories, this one about a Morgan mare that belonged to her daughter, Crystal. Her first story was about her walker mare, Beauty. Dianne and her husband own the Silver Rose Ranch at St. Jacob, Illinois, and she is an office manager for a construction company. Readers may quickly see that Dianne is a doting Mom, and Crystal is a special horse-loving daughter.

Precious Katy

By Dianne Doll

It was 6 A.M. on a frigid November morning and my twelve-year-old daughter was slipping out the door to go work a horse before waiting for the school bus. That's dedication. Crystal has always been passionate about horses. Sammy Jo was a grade mare at the barn down the road from our house. She had injured her leg in the field and Crystal wanted to make sure she suffered no long term damage, so she lunged her every morning and then again after school. She wasn't asked to do it and she wasn't getting paid to do it. It was for the love of the horse that she continued to do it for two weeks. Crystal is a natural when it comes to horses and she has a ton of common sense that simply amazes me. She got excellent grades in school and always did her chores at home before heading off down the street to the farm. Everyone should have a child like that!

Crystal started working racehorses off the track, training them as Hunter/Jumper prospects. She had permission to use "Perky" for showing, and a neighbor would trailer us to a local show. Crystal soon had ribbons lining the ceiling of her bedroom and showing was part of our schedule. She laughs now at those early videos.

Our friends, Sue and Jeff, heard about a special deal on a Morgan mare. Their friend named Katy was offered the horse first and declined, so Jeff had the option of buying her at a really good price, sight unseen. She was a six-year-old, very green and never yet saddled. Jeff decided to take the risk. When his friend pulled up with his horse trailer, he gave Jeff one last chance to back out. "No, go ahead, I want to see what I bought," Jeff told him. Out of the trailer came a gorgeous, stocky, dark chestnut mare with a flaxen mane and red tail, standing at 14.2 hands.

Jeff and Sue were starting a herd of American Bashkir Curly horses, but they sent off to register this new mare with the American Morgan Horse Registry. As a joke, their first choice for a name was UB No Curly with a second choice of Precious Katy's Mistake (because Precious was her barn name and Katy lost out on a beautiful mare!). The paperwork came back, of course, with their mare registered as UB No Curly! Sue and Jeff had a good laugh, then sent the papers back and requested the second choice.

Then came the job of breaking Katy to ride. Jeff put his western saddle on her and got out his spurs. When the spurs touched her, she proceeded to lay down with Jeff on her back! He didn't wear spurs after that when riding Katy. Crystal helped Jeff work with Katy and they soon had her under saddle. Katy had quite an attitude. She was built like a tank, very barrel chested. Sue watched her from her kitchen window one day, moving along the back edge of the pasture fence, pushing the boards with her chest, popping them off the poles, munching grass, then moving on to the next panel. We went over that weekend and helped them put a hot wire along the top of the fence.

Jeff and Sue were getting their American Bashkir Curly horses ready for a demonstration at the Illinois Horse Fair, and they decided to take Katy to the fair's Sale Barn, hoping to find a good home for her. They asked Crystal to join them as a rider and Rex and I went along as ground crew.

The Curly demonstration was a huge success! Many people had questions about Curly horses and we spent a lot of time showing people the horses and explaining about the breed. I looked around for Crystal and couldn't find her. Sue said she had gone over to the Sale Barn, so Rex and I walked over and saw Crystal leading Katy into the Coliseum to ride. There was something about watching the two of them that really struck Rex. He liked Katy. Sue and Jeff received no serious offers for Katy and decided she was a good horse for Crystal. Sue made us an offer we couldn't refuse and we became the proud owners of Precious Katy's Mistake.

Katy came with a breeding to the Davis' Curly stallion, UB Basil, a beautiful strawberry roan with a flaxen mane and tail. They wanted to see if he would throw curls off a straight mare and we were going to be the proud owners of a part Curly! The American Bashkir Curly horse was first thought to originate in Russia, but someone has determined that it is an original American breed from American Indians. The horses actually have curly coats similar to poodles.

We kept Katy at the Davis' farm and started looking for a place of our own. Soon we had found the perfect place, and we signed the papers on our twenty fifth anniversary. I was working for a contractor at the time and my romantic husband had twenty-five long stemmed red roses dipped in silver delivered to my office. What a sweet surprise! When we signed the papers that night, I told him I had the perfect name for our ranch — The Silver Rose Ranch. Of course, he liked it. We now had a place to keep our two horses — Katy and Sammy Jo's filly (Indy) we had bought earlier for Crystal.

That's another interesting story: our neighbors hadn't even known that Sammy Jo was pregnant until a couple of days before the filly was born. Meanwhile, Crystal had flown out to California to spend some time with relatives. During a baseball game she started crying. "There's something wrong with Sammy Jo!" she told her Aunt Judy and Cousin Kathy. It was at that moment that Sammy Jo was giving birth to her little filly! Crystal called home and we told her the good news. That was in July of 1996, and the filly's name became Crystal's Independence (Indy) in Crystal's honor and because she was born right after Independence Day. We bought the filly for Crystal that Christmas.

The previous owners of our ranch had used portable pens inside the barn, but Katy was really good at bending and breaking things that weren't stout enough to keep her from wherever she wanted to go. Rex went to work on new stalls. With the help of friends and his father, he soon had five stalls and a tack room inside the barn. Our friend Dave came by and Rex proudly showed them his completed project. He had allowed eight feet for the aisle so he could get a vehicle in if necessary. The barns were constructed of old barn wood, seasoned and very sturdy. He had bought a "kit" with the dividing bars and sliding gates installed on top of the barn wood. He even had a swinging wall on one stall that would open up for the two stalls to become one large "birthing stall" for Katy when her foal was due. Dave complimented Rex on his planning and said they looked great. But why five stalls for only two horses? Rex said he just wanted to utilize all the space he had. "Well," Dave said, "If you build them, they will come." And he was right. We now have five horses.

Crystal worked a lot with Katy and wanted to ride Saddle Seat. That's an English form of riding where you wear a long fitted coat that flares at the waist, a top hat, and either a vest and tie (for daytime) or cummerbund and bowtie (for evening). She wanted to take Katy to the Illinois State Fair in Springfield, Illinois. Crystal took Katy for help in fine-tuning their natural abilities. Katy was now lifting her feet really high at the trot, presenting an awesome road trot and parking out and she seemed to put her heart and soul into every ride. Crystal and Katy became the standard for the local horse shows. Crystal soon had many ribbons with Katy, including a lot of first and second place ribbons. Crystal rode her beautiful liver chestnut mare in an emerald green long coat and they were spectacular together! I'll never forget the first time Crystal and Katy went to State Fair. She rode Katy into the coliseum, making a grand entrance, and we all erupted into whoops and applause. Crystal was winning high point awards and earning money in the State Fairs. I remembered that night Rex and I had watched Crystal walk Katy into the Coliseum to ride when Katy was for sale…and now we owned this magnificent animal and Crystal was riding her in this same beautiful building!

The Illinois State Fair lasts several days. In between classes, Katy was in her stall with the door open and just a rope across the entrance. Katy loved people. She was always looking out with her head over the rope and I think she got as much enjoyment out of the parade of people as they enjoyed looking at the "pretty horses." We were all relaxing in our chairs in the aisle and a man with a baby stroller walked over to Katy. She put her head down into the stroller and we jumped! Oh my gosh! Before we could get to the stall, Katy had given the baby a huge lick across her face and the baby was giggling! Katy was nuzzling around the baby and the baby put her chubby little hands on our horse's jaws. We pulled the stroller away from Katy, who had put one hoof on the concrete aisle. She pulled the stroller back once with her head, and then we got it away and told the man this was not a good idea. When I think of what could have happened, especially as people are so quick to sue about anything these days. Katy just loved being around people.

One brisk October night we had a bonfire at our ranch. Katy was standing by the fence with her head over the top watching everyone. Crystal went out into the pasture and brought Katy into the back yard, where she proceeded to walk around sticking her head in laps or pushing backs to get some attention. Crystal climbed up on Katy's back, dangling her legs over her shoulders and resting her head on her rump. Katy just stood there watching everyone and enjoying being a part of our bonfire. Then we started roasting marshmallows for "some mores." It turned out that Katy loved marshmallows. When an 1100-pound horse wants your marshmallow, there is no stopping her! Time to put her back in the pasture!

For my birthday (in September) we decided to go on a trail ride to Pere Marquette State Park, near Godfrey, Illinois. I was going to ride my horse Peppy, and Rex decided to ride Katy. Katy was pregnant with her first foal, so Rex wanted to take it easy and just do a short ride, only an hour or two. The fall colors were already starting to come out and the scenery was fantastic. We came to the top of a hill that overlooked the convergence of the Mississippi, Missouri, and Illinois Rivers. There were seven of us on the ride that day. Crystal was riding Indy, and Sue and Jeff and their two children, Andy and Jenny, were riding their horses. Heading back, we somehow lost our bearings. The weather was turning bad and it looked like we were in for a storm. It was getting dark and the wind was picking up. What started out as a two-hour ride turned into an eight-hour ordeal. A previous storm had damaged parts of the trail and we couldn't find the trail markers. Rex got off Katy first, very concerned about his pregnant mare. Then we all dismounted and started walking because the horses were getting very tired from the hilly terrain. To keep everyone's mind off our plight, Jeff started singing silly songs. Soon we were laughing as we trudged up another hill, looking for a way back to our trailer. When we crested the hill we came to a corn-field. Was that a road in the distance? We mounted our horses and followed the edge of the field to the road. Rex and Jeff flagged down a pickup and the driver was happy to take the guys back to our trailers. We held the horses and waited. Once the horses were tied, we offered water…and the horses were all very thirsty! I gave Katy some then went to give some to Peppy, but she swung around to kick him. OK, Katy wanted more. I gave it to her and then gave some to Peppy and Indy. We can look back on that trail ride now and laugh. We compared it to Gilligan's Island – going out for a two-hour tour!

That trail ride started a close relationship between Rex and Katy. When it came time for Katy to foal, Rex had to go on a business trip. When he returned, I was out in the barn but he went straight over to Katy's stall and I didn't even get a "hello!" He opened her stall gate, she put her head out the opening and over Rex's shoulder and pulled him close to her. He wrapped his arms around her massive neck and gave her a big hug. She was bagging up and looked like the foal was coming soon. Rex sprang into action opening the dividing gate between the two stalls and hauled in a bale of straw. He cut the string and started spreading the straw and Katy pawed and helped move the straw around. Crystal came out and braided her tail to get it out of the way. Down went our mare. The time had come!

Crystal called the Davis' and the whole family came out. Katy was definitely having her baby right now! We got out the video camera. Crystal and I stayed in the barn while everyone else went into the house to watch the Oscars on TV (the big winner that year was Titanic). We kept everyone posted over the intercom while Crystal videotaped the big event. We saw a hoof! Everyone came back out to see the progress. Katy would get up then fall back down. The hoof went back in. It seemed like it was taking forever. Then two hooves and with the next push the nose! One of the feet moved. Then the foal's head emerged. A full blaze! Soon we had a foal on the ground...and we got the entire event on video! Katy nuzzled her new foal. It's a colt! Jeff thought Titanic would be a good name for him. When Katy ran she thundered, and we all agreed Thundering Silver Son would be a better name.

Our small town was having its homecoming parade in July. Sue & Jeff thought it would be fun to participate, so Rex and I agreed to go along. Rex rode Katy and I rode my gelding Peppy. We got all dressed up with our cowboy hats, but Rex went further and got his rifle sheath out, pistol, saddlebags, and his spurs. He put his rifle on the saddle, along with the saddlebags, fastened his pistol around his waist and tied it to his leg, then put his spurs on his boots and mounted Katy. She stood perfectly still for him. The last time she had an experience with spurs it wasn't pretty. But this was Rex. He sat tall and proud in the saddle and they looked great together! Katy is small of stature, but she really strutted her stuff out on the parade route. Her neck was arched and she lifted her feet high. What a sight! Rex did something around her flank that would make her leap straight up, like a Lipizzaner. The crowd loved it! Rex would take Katy over for the children to pet. She loved the attention. And Rex was enjoying the attention over his beautiful horse, too. After the parade we tied the horses to the trailers and relaxed before heading home. Sue's horse, Baby, tied at their trailer across from us, decided to kick Katy. Katy just looked at her, swung around and let her have it with both barrels! She plastered Baby against her trailer…and that was the last time Baby kicked anyone. I guess Katy showed her she chose the wrong horse to mess with. That was the only time we saw Katy intentionally kick a horse, except over food. All the horses knew that Katy got as much as she wanted and gave her a wide berth. I started feeding her under the overhang around the barn so they could all eat in peace.

Crystal sometimes got upset over her mare's hormonal actions. I can remember one of her very first shows with Katy. Her mare was "in heat" and not listening to her at all! When I asked what was up, she said her darned mare was just too horny! But the same hormones that made her so obstinate were also responsible for her incredible drive. I rode her once in our front pasture and it was like sitting on top of a volcano. I could feel the power beneath my seat. When she moved out it was incredible! Her trot was like floating on air, and her canter was like riding a rocking horse. She was as cool to ride as she was to watch!

We decided to breed Katy again to an Arabian stallion owned by our friends, Dave & Mary. That would give us a Morab (half Morgan, half Arabian). Crystal and I were hoping for a filly this time. We were pretty sure when Katy was due. I had checked her at 4:30 a.m. that morning and she was bagged up and dripping milk. I fed the horses, then went in to get ready for work while Crystal got ready for school. We stopped at the barn on the way out, about 6:20 a.m., and Katy had a pretty little **filly** already nursing and running around the stall. Crystal stayed home from school that day to make sure everything was going well, to imprint the new filly, and use the video camera. We decided to name her Precious Desert Rose after her mama **Precious** Katy and the stallion **Desert** Liberty plus being born on the Silver **Rose** Ranch. Rosie was a pretty little chestnut with a long narrow white blaze, flaxen mane and tail and two white socks. She was running and jumping, definitely enjoying a healthy, active start in life and Crystal was thrilled! Katy strutted her new little foal out into the pasture. The other horses came up to the fence and Katy charged at them, letting them know they should "back off" from her precious little filly. Rosie did a little hop in front of the horses and frolicked off with her mama.

Our neighbor, Madison, who lives across the road from our ranch, loves horses. When her parents bought the lot, she made sure her window overlooked the pastures. At six years old, Madison could tell you whatever you wanted to know about the horses. She would come over and help with chores whenever she was asked. She was always so helpful and her passion reminded me of Crystal when she was young.

Crystal would put Madison up on Katy and lead her around and Madison had a really good seat. She was totally serious any time she got on Katy. Whatever Crystal would instruct, she obeyed immediately. Crystal decided to use Katy for lead line with Madison, with her parent's permission. We could not find a matching coat, so I made one for her. Soon Crystal, Madison and Katy were making the rounds at the local shows and taking the blue with every class! Madison was adorable in her matching green coat, vest and tie. She looked like a mini Crystal with her long blonde hair and blue eyes. Madison's posture was perfect; she held the reins correctly and would answer the judge's questions with a crisp "yes ma'am," or "no sir." Her parents were so proud! Now Madison had ribbons and awards in her bedroom from our Precious Katy. One day when Crystal and Madison were working Katy, Crystal decided Madison was ready to start riding on her own. She unclipped the lead line and told Madison to walk Katy. I was standing on the side, like I usually do, and you should have seen the smile on Madison's face! Madison was riding Katy! Her father Scott was across the street working in their yard and looked over. His jaw dropped and he stood there for a minute then walked across to watch, olding his arms over the top of the fence. Katy was perfect for Madison. Rex walked over to the fence and stood by Scott. And that was Katy...she would accommodate Crystal in the show ring, was also the best trail and parade horse he could ask for, and now she was as gentle as could be for little Madison.

Then came the fateful day. Rex and I were getting ready to leave for California. Rex had a business trip, and I was taking him to the airport and would follow two days later. While we were on the way to the airport, Crystal called Rex's cell phone. She was out doing the morning feeding and something was wrong with Katy. She wasn't eating her grain and had her head down with foam around her lips. Rex told her to call the vet. Later when she called my office, Crystal said Katy had yellowed gums and the whites of her eyes were yellow. My heart sank. Jaundice — liver failure was all I could think. I prayed earnestly that the Lord would spare our horse. The vet made numerous trips to our farm over the next two days. He tried IV's and different medications, but he warned me it didn't look good. Crystal and I slept on the couch and checked on Katy all through the night. We were losing her. Our vet said if love were enough, she'd be cured. The last time I held her head in my hands and looked into her soft brown eyes, they were vacant. She went down the next day and couldn't get back up. Even with the help of friends and neighbors, we could not get her back on her feet. I had to tell the vet it was time to end her suffering. And I had to tell Rex over the phone that his horse was gone.

We had enjoyed many parades and trail rides with Katy. Crystal had showed her for seven years earning many ribbons, trophies, and high point awards. There will never be another horse like our Precious Katy. We kept a lock of her hair and I found someone who would do horse hair jewelry. I had a key chain made for Rex and a bracelet for Crystal. We have her picture in the living room with Rex's key chain beneath it. When we went to the Morab Nationals this year with Rosie, she reminded us a lot of the "old days" when we showed Katy. Rosie is a lot like her mother. Our beautiful mare is gone, but her many precious memories and the two horses she gave us are still here. Crystal shows Sonny in Dressage and we sold Rosie to a friend and Crystal is now her trainer. I thank God for all the good times and the many good years we had!

THERE'S MORE TO THE STORY...When it came time, I advertised Precious Desert Rose (Rosie) for sale as "the ultimate Christmas gift." I got a call from Wade, who was looking for a horse for his wife, Jean. She had always wanted a horse and Wade decided that Rosie was the one. This was the end of November. Wade brought Jean's daughter, Stacy, and other family members to see Rosie, and amazingly they all managed to keep it a secret until Christmas day. I was amused when Jean called that morning, "Dianne, this is Jean. Can I come out and see my horse?" Jean, her son, daughter, husband, mother-in-law, and father-in-law all piled into their van to come out and see Rosie. All the way out Jean just kept repeating, "I own a horse, I own a horse!"

When they pulled up, all the horses came up to the gate and Rosie came right over to Jean. We had a big red velvet bow on the stall, with a sign that said, "Merry Christmas, you are now the proud owner of a Morab filly – Precious Desert Rose." The cameras were rolling and the moment was pure magic!

I feel so blessed to have someone as special as Jean as the new owner of our precious little filly. The love between them is so heartwarming. Not only did Rosie get a wonderful new "momma," but I got a good friend out of the deal! On Jean's first birthday after becoming a horse owner, I had bought a card, painted Rosie's hoof and stamped the card with it. As Jean walked Rosie out of her stall, Rosie picked up the card off the bridle hook and "handed" it to Jean! Floored us both!

(Parts of this story were taken from an article, The Ultimate Christmas Gift, previously published in The Morab Horse magazine) And the rest of the story comes next!

Jean Reinhardt describes herself as a married "middle-aged woman" with four children, two horses, and two granddaughters. Her love of horses started when she was eight, but she got her first horse when she was 43 years old. She and her husband own a building and roofing company in Illinois which has, for the past seven years, given Jean the money and time to follow her natural horsemanship journey. She is currently studying Level Two with the Parelli Natural Horsemanship program, and she also enjoys learning from Brent Graef of Rafter G Farms in Canyon, Texas.

Rosie, My Ultimate Christmas Gift

By Jean Reinhardt

Have you ever wanted something so badly but never in your wildest dreams thought it would ever be possible? That was me from as far back as I can remember, wanting a horse. I took riding lessons as a youngster and a friend owned a horse for a while, but that's as close as it got.

My friend's horse was a bay quarter horse mare named Prancer. I adored that horse. You could ride her bareback and she would walk right up to you out of the pasture. When I was eighteen, I moved out of the area and the dream faded as I got older, but my love for horses never changed, even in 25 years. Every time I would drive by a pasture with horses I would exclaim "Look at the horses!" It always amazed me that no one else was as excited as I was.

Then came the Christmas of 2000, when we sat around watching each other open gifts, and it seemed to me that everyone's attention was focused on me and my gifts more than usual. They were telling me which gifts to open and which one to leave for last. When I opened that last gift, all eyes were on me, and out of the wrapper came a picture of a horse.

"Oh, that's awesome," I said. "What a great picture of a horse! Thank you." And they all exclaimed at once, "It's YOUR horse!" I was in a state of shock for the next few minutes. Staring at the picture, I began to cry. My dream had finally come true. My husband, Wade, had surprised me with my very own horse. How they all kept it a secret, I'll never know.

Her name is Precious Desert Rose, and she was ten months old at the time. She is a Morab (Morgan/ Arabian), the color of a shiny copper penny. Some call it chestnut and some say sorrel. Rosie, as I like to call her, and I have been on quite the journey ever since. Thankfully, I have had the support of many friends to help me. At 43, my feelings and emotions around horses were quite different than at 18. As excited as I was, I was also intimidated by this 500 pound young animal, and spending any time alone with her was scary for me. Picking up her back feet was another hurdle. I was determined to have a relationship with this horse, and so for the next few years I read every book and bought every piece of tack you could imagine to help me communicate with her. Rosie put up with all my tactics and tried very hard to work with me.

My fears hurt our relationship more than anything. She read me like a book. I tried everything

I knew to hide the fear from her but nothing worked. With each success, however, confidence grew in both of us. Thank God for groundwork. Rosie and I began to dance on the ground together and my fear was diminishing. Then came the time to ride her. My good friend Crystal Doll (now Crystal Welsh) helped me to start Rosie. I didn't want to ride Rosie until she was three; I am not a petite person and I wanted to give her bones time to mature. Rosie started under saddle with Crystal just like a pro. She never offered any defensiveness towards the saddle or rider.

When it came time for me to ride her, the fear began to once again well up inside me. It was a catch 22. Rosie felt the fear in me, which caused her to be nervous, which in turn made me more fearful. Rosie was always looking for what was causing my fear, and I was always looking for things that would scare Rosie. The first two years that I rode her, I spent more time out of the saddle then in it, and the more I fell off the more scared I got. I purchased a more seasoned horse, Phantom, a now 11 year old quarter horse gelding, who gave me the time in the saddle I needed to build my confidence while riding. With the help of my good friends and the Parelli home study program plus the Rider Recovery program managed by Boo Titchenal, I slowly but surely overcame my fears with Rosie.

For the past three years, Rosie and I have over-come many thresholds together, resulting in her being more confident in me and me being more confident in her. She has taught me that patience, love and under-standing go a long way with horses as well as with people. I no longer go at things head on like a bull dozer. With Rosie's help I have learned to take whatever time it takes, accept the slightest try, and reward the smallest of efforts in order to reap the highest benefits. I wouldn't trade in my mare and what I have learned from her for anything.

While my relationship is good with my gelding, my mare and I have a bond that is much deeper and more rewarding then any other I have ever had. With Rosie, I am constantly learning how to deal with many diverse situations. She keeps me in check and helps me to be prepared to handle all that the world has to offer.

Sarah Bower is a twenty-something Southern Illinois native. Sarah's experience with horses has been short and sweet, only a year and a half so far, but horses will be a lifetime love for her from here on out. She is a graduate of Southern Illinois University and is currently a Special Education teacher in Roxana, Illinois. Sarah lives in an apartment with her fabulous cat, Bingley, who used to live at the barn where Reina boards.

Reina, Queen of My Healing Heart

By Sarah Bower

I haven't always loved horses. In fact, I had only been on one pony ride in my whole life until about a year and a half ago. I was never enchanted or even interested in horses like my friends were. These friends of mine got their own horses and would let me ride sometimes. I went through the same things most new horse riders feel…nervous, excited, fearful and in awe. I never clicked with or felt comfortable riding horses, until I met Reina.

Reina is my 22 year old, beautiful chestnut mare with two white stockings and a white blaze on her forehead. Her mane and tail are the most beautiful flaxen color I have ever seen. Her eyes are intelligent and deep; I often wonder what she is thinking. Reina is so spunky, she loves to run! If she could canter every day, all day, I think she would. Her personality is very sweet, nurturing, independent, and opinionated! She is never afraid to let you know what she wants or thinks.

When Reina doesn't like something, such as brushing and loving on her too long or trimming her whiskers, or when she wants to go eat, she does something very humorous. She curls her top lip up in the air and holds it up, shaking her head around. It looks so funny! People at the barn will stop to check it out and laugh along with me. It usually happens if she doesn't like the way something tastes or she has to do something she doesn't want to do. She was due for wormer, and we all know horses hate the taste of it, but Reina knew it was coming. She did her best to fight it off, but of course still had to get it. As soon as a little bit got in her mouth, she made her "yucky face," as we lovingly call it, and her teeth were coated with the white cream. The whole time we were giving her the wormer, the face got worse and worse and she held it longer and longer. Poor thing! She makes sure we know when she is not quite fond of whatever is happening to her.

This girl *loves* to run! Being an inexperienced rider, I was scared to canter or gallop. I had no idea if I could stay on and steer at the same time, and it seemed a little bit overwhelming. The first time I cantered Reina, I felt like she was saying "finally!" I knew she had been waiting for me to let her loose and canter through the field. Words cannot describe the feeling of cantering on my horse. Every time I smooch and give her a little kick, she gives me a little nicker and takes off. She loves it so much that when we are done running, she starts prancing around like a circus horse. Everyone around takes note, she literally prances around for five minutes or more after we have finished. When we head in the direction of the field we canter in, her ears start to perk up and she looks back at me like she is waiting for me to give her the signal.

It has always been hard for me to trust horses, but I have always been able to trust Reina. She is the most steady, trustworthy horse I have met. She seems to be comfortable in situations when other horses would be tense or nervous. Reina is not the most social horse in the world, but she seems to be an anchor or strength for other horses out in the pasture. She is a very confident girl; I will often find her in the pasture away from the other horses that are eating together. Her confidence is part of the reason why I think I can trust Reina.

Reina has brought healing to my heart in a way that I never thought a horse could. About six months ago, a friend of mine passed away. Her name was Rhana. When I first considered buying Reina, I was sure I would change her name; it would be too difficult to have a horse with a name so close to my dear friend's name. Rhana held a special place in my heart and we shared a special bond. When she died, I felt a void inside. Even since the day I bought her, Reina has slowly started to fill that void.

I think God also used me to help Reina feel whole and loved again. When she came to the barn, she seemed to have some sadness about her. Over time, she has perked up and seems so much happier. Now, she nickers when she sees me and seems to enjoy riding out in the arena and on trails. People have told me that it seems as if Reina and I were made for each other. What is interesting is that her name means queen in Spanish and my name means princess. It is one of those God coincidences; I believe He planned for us to be together.

The past few months that I have had Reina have been such a blessing. Toni Robinson said, "Horses change lives. They give our young people confidence and self-esteem. They provide peace and tranquility to troubled souls. They give us hope!" This quote embodies the relationship that Reina and I have. She has helped me have more confidence and self-esteem, and she absolutely has provided some measure of peace to my troubled soul. I am sure that God uses horses to heal and minister to people. I am positive that God planned for me to have Reina for such a time as this...at a time when my heart, and Reina's too, needs healing.

Erin Landers is a 15 year old who comes from a big family in Georgia. She has four brothers and another whole family of pets. Erin is homeschooled and has been playing the piano for ten years. She has been riding horses since she was seven, but crazy about them since birth. She started out doing vaulting, tried a little dressage, then spent many years riding and showing in hunters. Since the tragic ending for Duchess, Erin has decided on a different path in riding and is now trying reining. Her new mare Hannah Rose is beautiful and sweet, but her attitude has been a challenge at times. Hannah will never be Duchess, but maybe someday she can be a close second, if the problems can be resolved.

For the Love of Duchess

By Erin Landers

There she was. Standing there on the driveway, in the dark, under a garage spotlight. Her name was Duchess, and she was like something out of a magazine. Well at least in the 12 year old eyes of a girl who had dreamt day and night of owning a horse. I think my only real requirements were that it had to have four legs, a tail, and say "neigh", and the tail probably would have been optional. In reality she was more like a 14.3 hand, five year old, mystery breed, downhill and long as a greyhound bus, skinny, shaggy little sorrel mare, and to complete the perfect picture she was *covered* in hives.

It had taken a number of small miracles including talking her owners down several hundred dollars on the price, a nine hour trip crammed into a truck that couldn't get above 50 miles per hour pulling a borrowed trailer, and talking my parents, who due to our financial state couldn't and had no intention whatsoever of buying me a horse, into my crazy plan. I know God was really pulling for me that day. He must have known how important this was.

I found Duchess online while searching for a fancy hunter prospect, and her ad just popped out at me. Don't ask me why, it didn't have a picture or anything, it just said that her name was Duchess and she was a sweet child safe horse that loved riding around in the pasture. I never looked at the ads without pictures but for some reason hers just said "pick me!" So there I was a couple days later nine hours from home, seeing for the first time the horse who would soon become my world.

I think I had pretty much decided before we even set out from home that this horse was coming home with me. Upon arrival I was told that she was in fact gaited, which pretty much squished all of my oh-so-realistic dreams of a blue ribbon hunter horse. I was not the least bit deterred though and was still determined that this was the one. So after a couple hours of riding the next day and a couple more hours attempting to get her into the trailer, she was mine! I was the *very* proud brand new owner of a horse that basically had no potential for anything, had virtually no training under saddle, and I was the scardy cat responsible for training her. I had been tossed a couple of times recently and my confidence level was pretty much zip.

With her experiences she had much more reason to be nervous than I. She had been bred and raised at a farm with about 30-40 horses on two acres with no grass. She was very underweight, wormy, covered in rain rot, and down on life when she was rescued by the nice folks from whom I bought her. She also had had a foal at age three, and I don't know how she survived in the malnourished state she was in.

So we got her home that night, got her all settled in at the stable we were boarding her at, and went home to bed eagerly awaiting our first day together. So for the next couple months I spent many hours bonding with my new best friend, and being the expert trainer I was at age 12, riding her around bareback in a halter. Our biggest obstacle to being a part of the hunter world was our lack of a trot. She had never been made to trot and didn't become solid at the trot until about a year into our partnership. It also took about a year and a half to get her to consistently take her right lead! The huge plus side to this horse was her personality. She was the single sweetest most forgiving horse I had ever met. She had to have been to not have injured me with my lack of patience and skill.

In the next year I moved her quite a few times for various reasons. She always took it in stride and was the same sweet, energetic, happy, wonderful horse every day of the week. Our bond as well as my confidence grew by the second and soon we were racing down dirt roads, riding bareback on trails and through neighborhoods, and surprisingly enough, entering a couple of local hunter shows where we actually didn't do terribly!

Our next challenge to tackle was the Georgia State 4-H Show in which I had entered hunter classes as well as a couple timed event classes just for fun. We spent many hours practicing, I wanted to be ready! Soon after arriving I found out that I was competing against 60+ horses, and I'd be willing to bet that they all had trainers. I entered my hunter under saddle class with the hopes for a great ride and nothing else. She delivered and I was delighted with her performance. I was in complete shock when I heard our number announced to come back for the call back class! She again gave a flawless performance and I experienced one of the, or probably *the* single proudest moment of my life when I heard the show name I had chosen for her, Morning Glory, announced in fifth place. I busted out in tears and gave her a big bear hug around her neck, professional I know. I could not have been prouder of her.

Fast forwarding to December, I moved her yet again to a new barn where shortly after I met my soon to be trainer and mentor, Mary-Ruth Taylor. She was the first person to think that Duchess might have some potential to be something other than a sweet trail horse. Under Mary-Ruth's guidance and training, Duchess seemed to blossom. All of a sudden people started noticing her for her floaty trot, flat kneed canter, and her willingness to learn. We started bringing home the occasional blue ribbon and soon became quite the contenders in local hunter shows! We also started jumping and she just took to it like she had been doing it all her life. Her sorrel coat took on a shine, she put on a bit of muscle, and her blonde mane and tail made her stand out in a crowd. My favorite thing about her though would have to be her precious face. She had a perfect little blaze, the cutest blonde forelock, and the biggest sweetest eyes that made you feel like you were looking straight into her heart. People would come up to me and tell me that what made her stand out in the ring so much is that she just looked so happy. She *was* happy, all the time. Not once did I see that mare lay her ears back.

Not only did Duchess become a great show partner, but also my best friend and constant companion. Some of my most cherished memories were created then. One of our favorite activities was galloping across the pasture bareback with the wind whipping my hair, dropping the reins, throwing my hands up and yelling "WOO-HOO" at the top of my lungs. That's a feeling not easily forgotten. We also spent many hours swimming across the lake next to the barn. Duchess LOVED it and half the time I would fall off and she would end up swimming across with me hanging on to her mane for dear life! She was also the horse that I could put my little brothers on and let her go without a single fear in my mind. She seemed to know the difference between the people that knew how to ride and the ones that would be easily intimidated. With a beginner in tow, she was suddenly as slow and dead headed as some of the pleasure horses you see at the Paint shows.

In what seemed like a month, but was actually more like a year, the State Show was coming up again, and this year we were going to be at our best! We were going to show them all what a mixed breed, self trained, little mare, with more heart than any of them, could really do. We trained twice a day six days a week, and by the time we got to the competition we were both in the best shape of our lives. This time we were up against 66 horses, of which she was the shortest as we missed the pony class by a little less than an inch. She rode in the class just like we had been practicing and made the final heat! This time my hopes were to place, which I didn't see as being too unreasonable. She was perfect in the final heat. The judge threw in a couple curveball gait changes but she took it with her usual style and didn't miss a beat. They lined us up and started calling the placings from 10th up. There were ten horses so each time a number was called that wasn't yours you knew you had placed a little higher! My heart pounded faster with each announcement and after what seemed like a lifetime it was down to me and one other girl on a quite large intimidating looking quarter horse. The judge announced second place and it wasn't my number. We had won. I was elated. I again busted out in tears and hugged my partner around her neck, so glad that I got to share this precious moment with my best friend in the world.

Upon returning to the barn I was walking around somewhere on cloud nine and we were working more on jumping stuff. She was so trusting and just seemed to love it. There didn't seem to be anything that she wouldn't jump and the higher we went the better her form got. I felt invincible, until July 18th when I got a phone call telling me that Duchess had gotten kicked on the hock in the pasture and we needed to have the vet out immediately. I wasn't really too worried. I thought it's just a cut, right? The vet came out and said that I should stay off of her for two weeks and keep it wrapped. At the time, my biggest concern was our upcoming show! We were in first for our division and missing the show would mean forfeiting being champion in the division! Two weeks came and went and after following the doctors orders the cut looked exactly the same and was now dripping something yellow. We had the vet out several more times over the next few weeks always with the same answer that they didn't know why this wasn't healing or what was dripping out of it. During this time she was never lame a step, but wasn't her usual spunky self I expected with her being on stall rest. Finally after seven weeks we decided it was time to take more drastic action. We took her up to the University vet school where I was shocked to hear their prognosis of "she might make a full recovery, and she might not make a recovery." The protective sack around her hock joint, also known as the calcanial bursa had been pierced when she was kicked, and was now infected. The yellow fluid coming out of her leg was joint fluid. In the three weeks she spent up there I was there every other day bringing her homemade horse cookies. I spent hours up at night just praying that she would be ok. She underwent two major surgeries and we almost lost her at one point when she seemed to just give up. I was determined though that she was going to come home and she didn't let me down.

She came home with strict doctors orders that she was to be on stall rest for at least 8 weeks in which I was there every single day to doctor her leg. She finally got to feeling better and started to become quite the handful to take out! It was tough, but I was glad she was feeling better. The first time she got to go out in the pasture again we were both so happy that I went out there and ran with her. Playing was her favorite pastime so because I was a bit too slow she would run circles around me or double back so I could keep up. We had a blast! She started going out regularly again and one of those days she did something I will never forget. She was out with the girls running as fast as her legs could take her and she decided to make a sharp turn, her feet came out from under her and she was laid out flat on the ground. She just laid there for a minute and my heart was beating a mile a minute. Just as I was about to panic, her head shoots up and she stares straight at me with a look that plainly said "MOM! Did you see what I did? That was AWESOME!" And she jumped straight up in the air and took off again like a firecracker. I also started riding her again. I was so excited to have my buddy back! She had lost a lot of muscle and strength, so riding wasn't easy on her; but we were getting there slowly and steadily. Everything was coming back together.

Christmas day came and I was so excited to get brand new pink Sports Medicine Boots for her, a professional shot from the state show my mom had ordered as a surprise, among other Duchess related gifts. I had planned to make a quick stop by the barn to say Merry Christmas to her but I ended up not having time. I promised I would go spend time with her the next day, but it was not to be. The morning of the 26th I was showered and ready to go when my mom came and found me. She was crying hysterically and I knew something was really wrong. She said "I don't know how to tell you this, but Duchess broke her leg in the pasture this morning and they can't save her." I was speechless, heartbroken, I can't even put into words what I felt. I can say that I now know the true meaning of the word heartbroken, and that's not an easy lesson to learn. I decided I wanted to go say goodbye to her, but got the call halfway there that it was too late. The next day I went out there and stood by the place my best friend now rested, under her favorite tree and said what I didn't get the chance to say the day before.

I don't know why this happened and I don't think I ever will. Why did such a young, beautiful, precious, loving, pure hearted being that found so much joy in life have to die? I do believe that animals go to Heaven no matter what I'm told and I know that if any horse deserves to go there it's her. I plan to plant morning glories on her grave this year, and I still feel lost without her, but life goes on. Whether or not I choose to live it to its fullest, is a choice I have to make. Sometimes God has other plans for you and you just have to trust that He knows what He's doing. I know that I will never forget Duchess and I hope that someday when I think of her I will smile and think of the beautiful memories we made.

Lisa Dennis was first exposed to horses in the summer of her eighth grade year when she was invited to attend National Center West by the Girl Scouts. She spent two glorious weeks riding a horse named Confucious and taking care of him. In high school she took Horse Handling and Care which further fueled her love for horses and taught her anatomy, physiology, training, and basic care. Although she worked at stables on and off to feed her horse craving, it wasn't until she was married with four children that she was finally able to realize her dream of being a horse owner. Their small herd consists of three Paint horses with a foal due in early March 2008. Her son Adam, whose story you will read, is currently training young and green horses. Come visit their website at www.starlightstablesnc.com.

One Mare That Saved a Life

By Lisa Dennis

My son, Adam (whose permission I obtained to tell his story), has lived in the city with his father since he was ten years old. Last year, Adam's grades bottomed out and he began breaking all the rules. They tried counseling and put him on medication to help him concentrate in school. Nothing seemed to help. When he got caught carrying gang colors at school, it became a police matter. The police scared him some but after all, in a gang, getting arrested is a status symbol. I can't begin to describe the amount of tears that flowed or the heartache I felt.

We picked Adam up for a long weekend shortly thereafter. His father and I met at a spot ten minutes from my horse trainer's ranch. I had business there that day. As we stood in the barn overlooking the pastures containing more than fifty horses, Adam pointed out a loud chestnut and white Paint and started out to the last pasture to check her out. While my trainer and I continued our conversation, we started slowly after him. She explained the horse was there to be sold. Being hard to catch, liking to buck, and having more issues than her current owner was willing to pay to fix, she had been standing for a while. Approaching the mare, Adam reached for her forelock and rubbed slowly as she lowered her head. He rubbed and scratched his way across her back. As we entered the field, he leaned against the horse as if he were leaning against a wall. Cheyenne just continued to nibble from a round bale. The trainer was very surprised and it showed on her face. Adam then said something I will never forget. "I want this one. She is beautiful, she's smart, and she is built. This is the one I want!" My son wanted a horse? I hadn't considered it! What could this shabbily dressed, hat on backwards, baggy pants boy want with a horse? We had a few horses at home, but I hadn't seen much interest in them from my son.

My friend gave me a sly smile and spoke directly to Adam. "Owning a horse is a very big responsibility, but I'll make you a deal. You come up for the whole summer, help your mom around the house, take care of Cheyenne everyday, and I will let her come live with you for as long as you are there. If you stop doing any of those things, she comes back. This is not your mother's deal; it's yours and mine and she should not have to lift a hand to take care of this horse. If you have any questions or need help, you will know where to find me and I will help you." She left no room for negotiation in her statement.

With a huge smile, a hand shake, and a promise, the deal was done.

Cheyenne came to stay with me two weeks later and Adam a week after that. Things got very interesting. My son (who normally wouldn't be seen before noon) was up every morning no later than 7 A.M.! He spent hours getting to know Cheyenne, grooming and working with her. He would talk to that trainer and her friends that are trainers, people at the local tack shop and the farmer we get hay from. He learned all he could about every aspect of his new friend. He cleaned the house and stalls while we were at work, took care of his younger brother and sister and became the first to move when I said I needed help. The change was amazing.

Six weeks after his introduction to Cheyenne, a local girl convinced him he should enter Cheyenne in a show. She schooled him on the proper technique to show halter. None of my children or Cheyenne had ever seen a horse show! I hadn't shown in 20 years; I wasn't sure what to expect or if we should even attempt this!

The following week, we found ourselves at a show. It was so hectic! When Adam came out wearing his western clothes, even his older sister was impressed! His baggy jeans and oversized shirt were gone and he looked so tall and handsome!

Adam and Cheyenne were entered in two halter classes that weekend. As they entered the ring for the first time, his father, stepmother and a group of their family and friends approached it quietly. They had driven five hours to see the change in my child and to see his new companion (they had wanted to surprise Adam, as well). You could see Adam's nervousness, but Cheyenne acted as if she had done this all of her life. It's funny, the more names that get announced, the more you convince yourself you are there for the experience when you don't hear yours. After all, this was their first show and although you have hopes, you realize quickly that this takes experience. When they announced first place as Adam and Cheyenne, I broke out in tears. Adam gave Cheyenne a good rub and a hug, and collected his ribbon with a huge smile. His father and troop jumped up from their hiding spots and everyone cheered! They would move on to a Championship class of all winners in Cheyenne's age group.

As they came out of the ring, Adam realized how many of his friends and family were there. He was so happy to see them all supporting him! In the Championship class, there were six horses in the ring. When their second place win was announced, you couldn't hear anything over the roar of the crowd. Looking back, I realized how many people my (formerly distant and introverted) son had befriended that weekend. Even the people that were working the event knew who they were and were whistling and shouting. The first thing Adam did was turn to Cheyenne and love on her. His broad smile and look of accomplishment were unforgettable. They did equally as well in the Ranch Horse Conformation class.

Later that afternoon, Adam was called to the show office via loud speaker. I wasn't sure what to think. Had he gotten into trouble? Could habits from his past have come back? When he returned to the barn, there was cheering and clapping as he approached our end. There was my son, carrying a Reserve Champion Halter trophy! Everyone was slapping him on the back, shaking his hand, clapping and cheering. His smile again was such that my heart about burst for him (and you have no idea how guilty I felt for thinking my son had gotten into trouble). Boy, what a weekend we all had!

Summers don't last forever, and a few short weeks later it was time for Adam to go back to the city. He shed tears and whispered promises of frequent visits and future shows as he said goodbye to his new companion.

Over the months that followed, Adam's grades dramatically improved. He got out of the gang and helped the police turn evidence against them. He found new friends in a local saddle club. He found a wonderful friend in a retired woman from down the street. They help each other, one with wisdom, the other with odd jobs. They play games and tell stories.

What happened to Cheyenne, you ask? Adam got her for Christmas. Tears were shed when he opened a package containing her registration and transfer papers. She now stands like a queen as the Alpha mare in my pasture. Adam has trained her under saddle and they are still showing on that same circuit and doing well.

And Adam? He came to live with us at the end of the school year. He spent the summer interning with a farrier and a trainer. He attends high school and has a part time job. His short term goal is to earn enough money to get a truck and horse trailer so he can continue to show Cheyenne and take her on long trail rides. When he graduates, he wants to be a farrier and train green horses.

What no one else knows is that in the evening, I slip out to the pasture and it's my turn to whisper in Cheyenne's ear. I tell her how wonderful she is and thank her for saving my son.

(This story was previously published on the Horseheadquarters.com website)

Two horses and three cats get their daily meals from **Elizabeth Jones**. She also has an eighteen-year-old human who didn't inherit the horse-lover's gene but is a great daughter anyway. Elizabeth recently took on a new adventure when she accepted a position teaching high school English at a small K-12 school in central Missouri. During her lifetime, she has been a musician, a U.S. Marine, a college instructor, and a land surveying and mapping technician. She quips that she has lived the perfect life for a novelist, but is a poet at heart. She grew up in Missouri, but lived in Colorado, California, and Virginia before returning to her home state. She agrees the Show-Me State is a good place for a skeptic like herself. Elizabeth's mother placed her on a horse when she was six months old, and she has been hooked on equines since then. Most of the horses in her life have been easy-gaited horses, which Elizabeth appreciates both for the way they move and for their easy-going dispositions. She has also owned two Quarabs, the breed she says she would ride if there were no gaited horses.

My Miracle

By Elizabeth L. Jones

I didn't become aware of the degree of prejudice against mares until I considered selling my Walking Horse mare, and then I wondered what the fuss was about. Why would someone pass up a well trained mare just because of her gender? My mare is never difficult to handle when she is in season, although she can be more excitable and is particularly mean to my gelding at that time. But whenever I ride her, she is willing to go anywhere I ask her to go. I used to say that she would jump off a cliff if I wanted her to, but now I think she is smart enough to refuse that.

Ultimately, I did not sell my mare, and I think I would always have regretted it if I had. When I bought her, I intended to keep her for her entire life, and unless some financial disaster strikes, that is still my intention. It was only by chance that I found her in the first place, and I wasn't even looking for a horse. My mother went to a trail ride in Eminence, Missouri, and decided to buy a horse there. She lived in Colorado and already had a couple of horses but thought she would like to keep one in Missouri since I live there and she visited often.

On a Saturday drive from St. Louis to ride my mom's horse, Lady, I spotted a mouse-gray yearling with unusual white markings. The filly was too skittish for me to touch her since she had not been handled recently, so I admired her from a distance. I wanted to buy her almost immediately, but Lady was in foal, and my mother wanted me to help her raise and train the foal. Two months before the foaling date, we found a still-born foal in Lady's stall. A few weeks later I went back to Eminence to see if I could buy the filly.

I knew that her dam was my mom's mare, but I did not know that the filly earned her name by surviving near starvation during her first couple of weeks. Lady had herniated teats, which made it difficult for a newborn filly to suck. With some human help and her own persistence, Miracle survived to become the prettiest horse on the farm where she grew up, and the couple who bred her weren't certain they wanted to sell her yet.

She was small for a two-year-old, only 13.3 hands, and a little malnourished. Since I am only five feet tall, I expected her to be a good size for me, and the man who owned her agreed. Over the winter, she had turned black but kept her markings – four white legs to her hocks and knees, a wide blaze, a streak of white on her right cheek, and white on her belly. Her coat was flecked with white hairs, and I later learned that she was a black sabino instead of a black roan. A friend told me later that the white hairs in her coat, mane, and tail glistened like silver in the sunlight.

When I took Miracle home a few weeks later, she knew only three things: how to lead (sort of), how to stand tied (sort of), and how to pick up her feet. She had never had a bath nor ridden in a horse trailer. She had never worn a saddle, blanket, or bridle, and she had never seen asphalt. Although I had not owned a horse for years and had never started a horse completely from scratch, I took on Miracle's training with no misgivings. Fortunately, she was both easy to train and forgiving in nature.

To train her to take a bit, I just put a bridle on her. After ground driving her with a halter and then a bridle for a week or two, I climbed on her bareback and turned her both directions in a round pen. Over the next few weeks, she attempted some bucking and I fell off once, but I continued to ride her lightly a few times a week for the next year. She trusted me enough that within a couple of months, we rode out in nearby fields by ourselves, and she learned to walk back to the barn on a loose rein.

In the meantime, I fed her six pounds of grain a day and as much hay as she could eat. By the time she matured, she had grown five inches to reach 15 hands. She came to Colorado with me a couple of years later for a few months and then back to Missouri. We went to some horse shows in both states, but her heart has never been in arena riding. She is at her best on trails, willing to go anywhere I ask and tolerant of any vehicles, from motorcycles to tractor trailers.

One thing that I did not know about Walking Horses was that the running walk did not always come automatically. For months, I mistakenly schooled my filly in a stepping pace. Because I reinforced the incorrect gait, her gaits have never been perfect and I agonized over my attempts to correct my early mistake. I would not have minded the gait so much except that it has a slight jar that leaves my neck sore. But I had decided relatively early that she would be an "experimental" horse. I tried many different bits with her, finally settling on a French link snaffle. I bought an expensive saddle that I couldn't really afford and then had to resell it when it left a lump next to her backbone after a ride. I finally purchased a barely-used Wintec dressage saddle with a full set of adjustable gullets and have vowed to never ride a cutback saddle again. I would like to train her to drive, and maybe someday I will finally buy a cart and harness.

Now I just enjoy her as often as I can with my busy teaching schedule. I bought another Tennessee Walking Horse about three years ago, a gelding who is much better in an arena than on trails. Where Miracle picks her way around rocks and tree roots, the gelding doesn't pay much attention to his feet and trips over uneven ground. My gelding is frightened of anything unusual on trails, but my mare is alert, leaving little chance of man or beast sneaking up on us. In the winter, I trust her enough to ride bareback with just a rope halter, the best way to ride when there is snow on the ground and the temperature hovers around 20 degrees.

Best of all, after eight years with this mare, getting on her is like slipping on a well-fitted glove. Even though she is frisky in cool weather or when the air pressure is dropping, I know which way she is likely to leap and when she is about to drop her head to throw in a buck while we are cantering across a field. And when she is relaxed and moving out on a favorite trail, she hits that elusive running walk and my back loosens, my feet swing in time with her steps, and she is as smooth as silk.

Don't ask her to bow her head meekly
Or stand aside for a stallion –
With a burst of power
She rises on her back legs
Her white hooves flashing out.
Her long mane is a spray of black
Framing her head for a moment.
She spins around – another leap –
And then she returns to me:
My gentle and willing partner moving out
Boldly – to blaze a new trail.

Janet Hill was born in Detroit City and moved to Illinois when she was seven. She returned to Detroit City in 1948, followed by Carter Hill, the love of her life whom she married in 1952. Janet and Carter have two daughters and one son, four grandchildren, and six great grandchildren. She has taught three generations about the love of horsemanship. She and her husband moved back to the family farm in 1964, currently residing there with her two dogs, Romeo and Rufus ("the boys"), and four horses which continue to inspire her. Janet is 73 years young (in mind). She suffers from arthritis, has had two hip replacements, and has survived cancer. She often calls upon God and her passion for horses to continue to be an integral part of the horse world. Her riding buddy, when asked who she rides with, replies "an eight year old girl!" (Janet is guilty of loving to ride too long and too fast).

A Tribute to Lee Japhia

By Janet Hill

I first laid eyes on Lee Japhia in a snapshot, sent to me by a friend from whom I bought my first Arabian (a stallion, which my husband laid claim to before we got home). The picture was meant for someone looking for an Arabian filly; but as fate would have it, that person had already bought a filly. I looked at the picture lying on the kitchen table for a couple of weeks, thinking she was the prettiest horse I had ever seen. I was skeptical, however, because I knew her dam, and I did not care much for her looks.

I decided the only way to get this filly off my mind was to go and see her in person. I reasoned that after I actually saw for myself, I could forget her! I made the trip to my friend's house and told her my dilemma. I did not need another horse. I had seventeen head of horses and had spent my money on the aforementioned stallion. My friend brought Japhia out. Much to my dismay, she looked exactly like the picture — only more beautiful. Well, I knew I was hooked, which only further complicated my dilemma. As we walked back to the barn, we talked about other horses and alfalfa hay. She needed one thousand bales, and I needed Japhia. The wheels started turning, and we decided to agree on a barter system. I would supply her with one thousand bales of hay in return for Japhia. My friend delivered the mare to my house that weekend and picked up her one thousand bales of hay. I then embarked on my life with Japhia, or should I say on our life together because we became as one. Maybe because, as I often told her, only God, her mother, and I could love her, so she needed to do what I asked her to do. I assured her I would only ask it with tender loving care.

Japhia had an attitude and a personality to match her new-copper-penny color and flaxen mane and tail. She took very good care of herself so as not to get hurt, so that kept me safe as well. She was a one-person horse, to the point of resenting anyone else grooming her, saddling her, going into her stall, or even giving her a treat (which she would not take from a stranger). She had a heart as big as the sky, and she was tough as nails. There was no "quit" to her. She was always ready to go and I never had to ask her twice. It did not take long for her to let all seventeen horses know she was the alpha mare, and she held that position until she died of a heart attack the morning of December 25, 2000. I was not ready to let her go, but she did it her way and God's because I guess they knew I could not watch her fail slowly.

She was gone in less than ten minutes with no visible signs of suffering.

She was born May 17, 1975 and she was eighteen months old when I bought her. I worked with her and trained her myself, starting when she was almost three years old. By that time, we had a good understanding of each other consisting of respect, confidence, love, and trust. I told her she would have to grow up and be a horse by the time she was nine years old. I think she understood me, and I felt she had made it by the time she was seven. She surpassed my expectations and those of everyone else! I rode her on trails for two years, between the ages of three and five. Then we participated in organized trail rides in Missouri for 15 years between her ages of five and 17 years of age. I rode her in competitive and endurance distance riding for 10 years. Together, we completed over 3,000 miles in competition during her years of 7 to 17.

I always thought she had a few extra male hormones than normal mares, since her nicker was quite unique. People at trail rides and distance rides would ask who had the stallion at my trailer or stall. Her unique nicker could be heard all over camp when she heard my voice at another campsite. I believe she was calling me to come back and be with her, even if her companion was still there with her. I loved all the activities I did with her; the training, trail riding, conditioning, organized trail riding in Missouri, and competitive distance riding. During the training activities and competitions, I remained sensitive to her moods and feelings so that we could accomplish what I needed and asked her to do. I did this before I was aware or even knew about natural horsemanship by just following my gut feeling and my love of horses (mares especially). They really seem to be my passion and calling in life.

I have so many stories about each of these activities, but I will concentrate on my experiences getting her ready for the organized trail rides that occur at the Cross Country Trail Ride (CCTR) in Eminence, Missouri. I knew she must become acclimated to being tied on a picket line, so at home I would practice trail riding her 10 to 15 miles, come home, and tie her on a picket line I had put up in my front yard with her feed bucket and hay bag on it. That worked very well. There were some things I could not expose her to before she experienced the actual situation. Surprisingly enough, they turned out well too. My farrier, family, and friends told me I needed to sell her because she was going to kill me. They did not recognize the bond of understanding we developed so solidly during our first 5 years together. This bond never faltered during our time and miles together. Her intuition not to hurt herself translated into my safety as well. She always knew when things were not right or when something negative was going to happen before we got there. I gradually learned to listen to her, perhaps longer than it took for her to listen to me. We taught each other a lot. And we learned a lot from each other.

One time we were rounding a bend as we came into camp. In the middle of the road by the river, a horse and rider came galloping around the same bend, face to face with us. Not so awful one might think, except the horse had a big, blown-up inner tube around his neck, flopping with every hoof beat. Thank God and Japhia! She just "FROZE" as the horse and rider galloped on by!

Another time, while she was tied on the picket line in camp (this was after the encounter with the horse and inner tube), a group pulled into camp with a pickup truck full of swimmers and (of all things) inner tubes (used for floating down the river). Some of the people started throwing inner tubes out of the truck onto the ground. Much to my horror, one tube stayed upright and headed directly toward Japhia. I saw the fear in her eyes just before she flipped over. Fortunately, she made it back to her feet in a split second and just looked at the inner tube lying flat on the ground at her feet. It happened so fast none of the other six people saw her acrobatics on the picket line; it was another secret that Japhia and I shared (seeing that she was one of those crazy Arabian horses, you know!).

One hot August (a lot like the one we had in 2007) at CCTR, I was on the first all day fast ride with six more rides to come that week. As I have previously mentioned, Japhia was tough and had no quit. The all day fast rides were all about 20 to 25 miles long. Most of the horses were Tennessee Walkers, Standardbreds, or Fox Trotters. A person rode up beside me and asked what breed Japhia was. I replied that she was an Arabian; He had a Tennessee Walker. His remark to me was, "She will never make this ride and keep up; her legs are too short, and she is too fat!" I replied, "I think you are wrong, and I'm sure she will make the ride!" Well, Japhia and I finished the ride right behind the trail boss. The ironic element of this incident is that Japhia and I finished all seven all day fast rides together as one unit. The person who spoke his profound words about our ability rode three different Tennessee Walkers on the seven rides to be able to make all of them. A few of the other situations she had to get used to were crossing the Jacks Fork River belly deep, sometimes having to swim (I guess because of her short legs). She also dealt with canoes coming toward her, loud live band music, and fireworks. It was a wonderful journey. I enjoyed every minute of it.

She was to me a very special mare. I am sure a lot of horsewomen and horsemen have had a horse they feel the same way about. I think if you have one in your lifetime, you are wealthy. I remember a statement my one-room schoolhouse teacher always said, which is true of both people and horses: "If you can say you had one friend when you die you are a wealthy person. If you have more you are blessed."

Janet Hill is here pictured on that all day fast ride mentioned in the previous story. Janet was the first responder to an "invitation" for mare stories for this book, sending a beautiful letter about her experiences that just seemed so full of wisdom it had to be included in addition to her story about Lee Japhia. Here is most of that letter, containing Janet's wit and wisdom about mares.

I Love Mares!

By Janet Hill

When I think about my favorite mares, tips for working with temperamental mares, and helping mares get along with other horses, countless things come from my heart to my mind. My knowledge of horses is practically intuitive by now, from more than sixty years of experience. My family teases me, saying I live and breathe horses.

There is a term for my condition, although it does not comfort my family much. The term is hippophilia. Webster's definition of the term is "a horse lover." Currently, there is no known cure for it, and I hope there never will be.

There are a lot of good natural horsemen and women out there; a person just has to seek them out. In my younger years, I worked and trained horses from a gut feeling of love, kindness, and gentleness. I tried to understand them and interact with their body language, and I used my own intuitions and methods.

I was aware of the harsher ways of training, but I did not agree with them and I suffered a lot of ridicule for my beliefs. By following my instincts and believing in myself, I managed to forge enriching relationships with many horses and their people throughout the years. Finally, the instinctive method by which I have worked with my horses came to be known as natural horsemanship. I do not remember a time that I did not have this uncanny connection with the equine world. I live to look deep into their eyes, to observe the form of their majestic bodies, arched necks, honest faces, and proud displays of strength. There truly is a spiritual connection between horses and humans. I derive my own strength and courage from God and my love for horses.

The first horses I rode just happened to have been mares. I did not choose them; perhaps they chose me. My family acquired our horses when I was nine years old. I lived on a farm, and they were our workhorses. One was a four-year-old part Belgian, a one ton mare who was full of it; she liked to go! She was nervous and thought she was a thoroughbred. I remember riding her with a snaffle bit, work reins and bareback. I looked somewhat like a peanut astraddle her back. The other horse, an old grade mare complete with attitude, did not want to be ridden. I rode them both when they were not working in the field, essentially robbing them of their day off.

The first horse I considered my very own was also a four-year-old mare. She had belonged to a family with two children, twins, who were my age. They had other horses and did not like this mare because she was too hard to handle. When I went to visit, I had to ride her. My favorite aunt purchased her for me for $60, when I was eleven or twelve. I named her Flicka, and she soon became a central part of my life. I taught her tricks. I rode her to town to get groceries and tied them to the saddle horn in gunnysacks to carry them home. I had to walk her all the way home, much to my dismay. During wheat harvest, I carried crocks of water to the thrashers.

I remember the neighbor kids riding their horse to school, slapping it on the rump and sending it home. I thought that would be a great way to get to school, so I tried it too. There was only one problem. Flicka would not go home, so Miss Cress, the teacher of our one-room schoolhouse, would not allow me to bring her back to school.

Flicka was my faithful companion; I rode her incessantly. I had ridden her so much that at one point, I remember my father forbidding me to ride her for two whole weeks to allow her hooves to grow back out. That seemed like the longest two weeks of my life!

My next horse was a mare, too. She was a three-year-old who had been out in the pasture since she was a foal. She had never been handled and did not know anything. She didn't know what oats were or that she was supposed to eat them. I had the good fortune of starting from scratch with her. In those early days, I was actually learning along with my mounts, although I did not realize the experience I was gaining. I think that is the case with each and every horse that comes along our various paths.

Perhaps they are sent to teach us a particular lesson if we just take the time to learn what they have to teach us.

Moving on twenty years brings me to my next mare, Mariah, who was half Arab and half Quarter horse. My husband purchased her for me after we returned to Illinois following an extended absence. The mare cost us $200 and we had to send her to a trainer for sixty days. Upon picking her up from the trainer, he said he had done "all he could do." Her performance was inconsistent, and I worked her in an open field and finished her. I showed her in local shows and rode trails. My daughter showed her in English pleasure in 4-H shows, and I used her as a schooling horse for three students. I eventually sold her at the age of eighteen to a nine-year-old girl learning to ride. I took them on their first competitive trail ride and they placed second in the novice division.

I have owned and worked with approximately forty to fifty head of horses. Out of that number there were four geldings and two stallions and the rest were mares. I could write a story about every one, but the bottom line is: I love mares! Through the years, I have heard many people say they do not like mares, they hate to ride mares, and would not have a mare. People seem to lump mares into a group and say they are all a problem, and that I am crazy for liking and riding mares.

I get along quite well with mares. I thought perhaps I was just lucky and happened to have good mares. Then I read Linda Tellington-Jones' philosophy of dealing with problem horses. The horseman needs to reach out with love and respect because the horse doesn't have the problem – the person has a problem asking the horse what he wants the horse to do.

When I thought about why I like mares and why I get along with them, I came up with several thoughts, nothing scientific, just ideas that work for me. Mares have great personalities. They are always thinking, curious, loving and nurturing animals. However, when their hormones are raging, you have got to give them some room. Instead of asking for repetitious, boring and dull tasks, give them something to think about besides their hormones. Get them to use their left brain. Challenge their work and training with something different. Go with them; try to understand them, because they are not acting their "normal" selves.

As a stallion responds to his hormone level when he is near a mare in heat, likewise a mare responds to her estrus cycle. They are both responding to their natural, baser selves. We typically do not criticize the stallion for his hormonal reaction; we just say, "Oh that's natural for him to act that way." Why don't we offer the same amount of tolerance for a mare? When dealing with a mare in her estrus cycle, some people expect her to do what isn't normal or they will give her a drug. When a mare reacts to her body's hormone levels, you can administer drugs and possible confuse her – or you could work with her naturally. Which is the mark of a better horseman (or horsewoman)?

I suppose I would be considered a "natural horse-woman" because I would never give a mare drugs simply because she is going through her cycle. Drugs cause an alteration of the horse, thereby confusing it. People need to work with the mare or get a stallion or gelding, rather than alter the natural state of the mare. Using drugs could compromise the health of the horse. I am convinced that there is a direct correlation between the administration of these drugs and certain types of cancers in mares.

People want a calm, dependable horse that is easy to handle. You can have a well-behaved horse, but if you do not choose to deal appropriately with the hormone situation and appreciate it for what it is, then you geld a stallion, drug a mare, or use devices to control them, which can be cruel.

I have dealt with many mares that had more male than female tendencies. This can be caused by nature's hormonal mix or by tumors on the ovary. I did not see a need for drugs. I just kept the situation in mind and worked with the mare to help her through it. They were great mares. I did not consider them a problem, therefore, they weren't. The owner just has to understand mares. If you aren't willing to understand mares, then you shouldn't own them. You certainly should not criticize them for your lack of understanding and patience while working with them.

To summarize my advice, here are some tips.

- Use natural supplements to make the mare more comfortable, as opposed to drugs to make her conform or perform.
- Redirect her to think about other things; no dull or repetitious training sessions.
- Extra love, affection, attention and tolerance
- Stay a safe distance away from other horses; provide a "bubble" boundary
- Riding in a group with a stallion is like driving on ice. It pays to know your capabilities and stay within them. Allow yourself and your mare the space you need for a boundary of protection
- Use all natural grains for feed – corn, oats, bran, supplemented with pasture and alfalfa or grass hay

I have ridden mares in heat beside stallions with horse owners who are in control of their mounts with no problems. I have also ridden with those who are not in control. From my perspective over the years, it is not the horse with the problem; it is the human. I speak of these things from my heart and from my experience, but I also want to thank Linda Tellington-Jones and Pat and Linda Parelli for giving me more insight into all horses within the past fifteen years.

Lisa Waltrip has had horses since she was four years old growing up on the family farm in Jerseyville, Illinois. Currently, she has been raising and showing APHA and AQHA horses with her husband, Rich Metzger, on their seven acre place in Alton, Illinois. Lilly is Lisa's once-in-a-lifetime horse and she will own her forever. Lisa is an independent insurance representative with Secure Insurance & Financial Services, where she specializes in working with all the area seniors and also in Equine and Livestock Insurance. She may be contacted at 618-466-8800.

A Complete Miracle

By Lisa Waltrip

How could I have ever known that a trip to frozen Minnesota to look at a horse in December of 2001 would forever change my life? Not only did I find the horse that has been my soul-mate ever since, I also met one of my very best and dearest friends, Carmin Flowers.

I had been praying for a new show horse and when I received the video of Lilly, I immediately felt drawn to go see her even though she was 14 hours away in Minnesota and this was the dead of winter. Lilly was absolutely gorgeous on the video and she moved so soft and pretty she just floated across the ground. She had the perfect pleasure horse conformation, everything I would have looked for in a horse. A pretty head, big dark eyes, a long thin neck that tied in correctly to her chest and perfectly proportioned back and a big hip plus her hocks were strong and straight making her movement stellar. Her coat was a

291

shiny cherry sorrel and her mane a flashy flaxen mix. The details for the trip fell into place perfectly so I was hopeful that it was in Gods will. I was able to get a very reasonable flight and then an associate offered to pay for the airline tickets and the hotel bill for me. Soon, I was on my way to go see the horse that I felt God was leading me to.

I asked God to give me a sure sign if Lilly was the right horse for me when I got there. When Carmin took off Lilly's winter blanket, I immediately saw that she was even prettier than her video showed. Her soft brown eyes just melted my heart. She nuzzled me, introducing herself. I could tell right away she loved people and being ridden and wanted to be part of the family. When I rode her she walked, jogged and loped just the same for me as she did on the video. I just fell in love with her. I was so excited. It was a good thing that excitement masked the cold because it was only 24 degrees up there in the indoor arena in Minnesota when I was riding Lilly and normally I would have been freezing. Still, I needed a sign to be sure that this was the horse that God wanted me to have. When I went to lunch with Carmin to talk more about Lilly, I looked down in her truck's console and saw a tape of my favorite evangelist and it turned out it was Carmin's favorite too. In fact, she said she had been praying for the right person to buy Lilly because she wanted her to have a special home. That was my sign Lilly was the one for me.

I got Lilly home in January of 2002. During this same time I had been praying earnestly for God to give me the very best He had for my life. Little did I know how that was going to affect my life and Lilly's too.

I had great plans for our show career that year. Unfortunately, after only one horse show those plans were dashed when Lilly came up lame. Despite taking her to seven different vets, none were able to diagnose what was wrong with her. I was heartbroken. I just couldn't understand how God could give me such a wonderful show horse and now with her lameness she wasn't able to be shown. The more I prayed for God to fix Lilly the more it seemed she was never going to be sound again. Finally, God revealed to me that I had made Lilly an idol in my life and that He had to take her away from me if I truly wanted the best that He had for my life. I gave Lilly back to God and asked that His will for my life be done. I decided to take Lilly to one last vet to try to get her sound again. This vet was five hours away and it was a long shot, but I took Lilly there and miraculously he diagnosed her and recommended a treatment for her. I felt like God had given Lilly back to me. Again, little did I know what was in store next for my life and Lilly's too.

Lilly needed two joint injections 30 days apart to relieve the soreness in her fetlock joints. The first joint injection went off without a hitch and Lilly was again sound. I rejoiced. God had come through for Lilly and me. Then, for convenience sake, I tried a different vet to give Lilly's second injection and unfortunately, that was when disaster struck. Due to that vet's mistake, Lilly developed a joint infection in her left front fetlock. Since this condition is extremely serious, I took Lilly to a well respected equine hospital for treatment only to be told that they would do all they could to save Lilly but that she might die from the staph infection in the joint. At this point, I couldn't believe that I might lose my precious Lilly. That is when the first miracle happened. She spent 30 days being treated at the equine hospital and her fetlock looked like a big softball when she was finally released, but she was alive. The vet who treated her cautioned me that it was likely that Lilly would never be sound again as scar tissue would probably cause limited mobility in the joint. He recommended I breed Lilly because he felt she'd never return to the show pen again. I was absolutely crushed. I couldn't believe this cruel outcome. Still, I knew that God could heal Lilly and I began to pray earnestly for her. I promised God if He would restore Lilly that I would tell everyone about her miracle healing. In the meantime, I went ahead and bred Lilly just in case God's plan was not my plan.

That is when the second miracle happened. Five months after the joint infection, Lilly's fetlock joint looked absolutely normal. When I began to ride Lilly again she was sound. I actually cried tears of joy. I knew God had once again given Lilly back to me. My life would never be the same from what God taught me from this incredible trial. I knew whatever came my way that I could trust God and He would get me through it. I also knew that I could never let anything material come between my relationship with God or God could take it away from me.

That is when the third miracle happened. When I first purchased Lilly I had tried to no avail to get her registered paint horse papers even though she had a white stripe under her belly that should have qualified her. When Lilly was sound again, I decided to try one last time to try to get her papers. She was finally approved, but there was one hitch. Her quarter horse name was already taken in the paint horse breed, so I was told I needed to select a different name for Lilly. After careful consideration, I decided "Complete Miracle" was most fitting for Lilly's paint horse name because she is absolutely a complete miracle. Lilly has gone on to be a successful show horse in the paint horse breed and is due to have her third foal in January of 2008.

Through this incredible trial, I developed a strong friendship with Lilly's previous owner, Carmin, who kept Lilly in prayer the whole time. As promised, I have told Lilly's miracle story to everyone who would listen. When I was given the opportunity to write Lilly's story, I knew that God wanted to allow others to be blessed by it as much as I have been.

Denise Pederson lives on the family acreage in a small town in Central Alberta, Canada. She has been an avid horse lover since early in her childhood. In her youth, she was inseparable from her best friend, a little bay roan Appy gelding named Corkey. After being away from the acreage for several years, she is now able to enjoy the daily fun of Jaycee and Hayden. These times bring a sense of peace and joy to an all too busy work world, and you can't beat that blessing! Besides horses, Denise loves Southern Gospel music, Corvettes, and photography.

SW Seekers Gold Bar, aka "Jaycee"

By Denise Pederson

Jaycee and I met 5 years ago, in a moment of quick decision on my part. I had heard about her through a friend, and I said that I would keep an ear open for anyone looking for a horse, in no way thinking that it would be me! She had been shown and placed well, mostly ridden by a very capable 12 year old girl in the show arena. This was pretty well all I knew about her.

In a moment of frustration resulting from a Mexican stand off with my very sturdy, big foundation Quarter horse gelding, I left him tied to a tree out in my yard and walked into the house. I called the woman who owned this little show horse.

When I mentioned I was interested in her mare, she seemed a bit hesitant. She said she was not sure if she wanted to sell her, as her daughter's main show horse had been injured, and they had been using her.

Maybe I would be interested in one of her others that are for sale. I quickly told her no, I was only interested in that particular mare that I had been told about!

As we discussed the mare, it seemed obvious to both of us that she was sounding perfect for me! We made arrangements for me to go to her place, and she was still not 100% sure of selling her. My mom and I headed out to see this mare that same afternoon. I never would have dreamed that I would be considering buying a Sorrel Overo Paint (had to go look up what they looked like to be sure). One blue eye and one brown eye and a mare to boot!

So there I was. The lady hands me a halter, points to the horse and tells me she's the one. So out among the herd I go to halter this mare! I go up to this blue eyed, oh my goodness, rather skinny mare with a bad haircut, and I felt like I was having a moment in someone else's life! Yet, I had this feeling she would be coming home with me to live!

It took a week to make the deal, but home she came! The pastures were nil that year, and hay was scarce and very expensive. The deal factor narrowed down to the fact that I was an answer to this lady's prayer, as she was out of pasture and needed money for hay. We were both in awe of how God had worked out all the details of her prayer, just as she was believing for an answer!

The one thing that has totally amazed me about this mare, is that she has so much expression! She displays a "happy horse" look almost all the time, always looking forward to being with me. When my farrier came within a few days of getting her, her first impression was "that mare really likes you!" This same lady later said she couldn't believe how bonded we were, as she watched us at the fun horse shows that we participated in.

She is not a vocal mare at all, which may be why she seems to have so many expressions. She's a ham. She observes everything going on, no matter where she is. She actually watches the other horses doing the patterns in gymkhana events, all the way through right back to the gate. She loves little girls, and attention from people. She is a complete little flirt around geldings. She seems to sense if people are not partial to her and are pretending otherwise, as she is obviously standoffish toward that type of person! She is a Houdini, she is very smart and she does a perfect job in opening and even closing the gate in a trail class. As I would fumble with shutting the gate, she would take a deep breath, then push it with her nose, right on the mark! Even closing it too! She would always steal the show, but it was too funny to worry about the points we lost for her participation!

Jaycee has been nicknamed "The Princess." Is she pampered? You bet! She always has her ears forward as if to be saying, this is so nice and I feel so special! She is very protective of me. She does not tolerate other horses hanging around me and does not tolerate any horse getting in between the two of us, which gets a bit funny to watch, even if I am riding her! She is only top mare if there are no geldings or real bossy mares around.

I have seen Jaycee give her all and later discover she was actually hurting, plus I have watched her in situations that caused her to fight her way out. Instead of being scared silly after the mishap, she is calm and willing to go right back into the same area with no fear. I have had her gently refuse to load and be totally frustrated with her refusal, only again to realize she had a sore shoulder and back! I have watched her sigh in relief at the chiropractor and to stomp her foot after being adjusted for what she thinks has been too long!

Over the years, I have learned to respect that her actions have a reason, if she's not willing or has bucked. If I have not stayed in tune to her, if my pride or fear has overshadowed my awareness, she still has a very forgiving heart. She has also shown expressions of embarrassment and being sorry for overreacting, and I have had friends point this out to me, when my pride has affected my own observations.

Jaycee has a huge weakness for buns! Yes, the kind that we humans have our hamburgers in. She has to be kept under watchful eye when at a gathering with small children walking by with their hotdogs and burgers! Fortunately, there have been no casualties with the exception of my own bun being eaten up! She can smell a bun a mile away and can hear a rustling of a bread bag in my pocket, even if it is empty!

One day I mentioned to her, as I showed her a bun, that she would have to back up first before she could have the bun. She did this all on her own and I gave her half the bun. Before I could ask her to do it again, she backed up again and then waited for the rest of the bun! I swear she would sell the farm for a silly bread bun!

Jaycee is the first registered Paint mare I have ever had, and there is something very special about these Paints, as I am continually learning! The Paint seems to have a unique personality that is a true joy to be around. I would have never dreamed that in my heart there is a special love for a blue eyed sorrel overo Paint mare! And now we are anxiously awaiting the arrival of a bouncing baby foal in the spring of 2007!

UPDATE...

A bouncing baby colt named "Hayden" arrived safely on April 16, 2007 at 8:45 pm. My mom and I had the awesome experience to be present throughout this entire miracle of new life!

I must admit, I was very surprised on my first glance, to see minimal white on this little chestnut foal! Although the chance for a coat pattern like Jaycee's was 50/50, we all expected lots of color! His daddy is a beautiful chestnut/brownish AQHA stud named Betcha He's Smart. Hayden's registered name (APHA) is Betchahezablessing.

Hayden is able to enjoy all the attention he receives, because Jaycee is calm and relaxed around people. She has been like this right from the start, so that has been awesome! Sometimes she will intercept his attention, only because she would like some too!

Hayden has displayed a significant trait of his mom's, showing that he too is a "watcher." They don't just glance at something that is happening and go about their day. No, they watch the entire event from start to finish! For instance, my mom was painting at one end of the barn, and she felt she was being watched. Sure enough, there was Hayden peering through the fence! His total focus was on her every move and he stayed there for the duration of the job!

Jaycee has been known to do her share of this hilarious behavior too! Once at a local fun horse-show, I was sitting on her just behind the fence in the arena, planning to watch the event that was taking place. She looked over to her right to see a horse come into the arena through the gate. She then did a double take, as if to say "Oh he's CUTE!" The object of her new affection was a sporty looking Buckskin gelding named King. She would not take her eyes off of him even if that meant readjusting her view! She was very obvious in her "watching" which she continued until he exited the arena. Jaycee not only stole the show, she had us all in stitches laughing!

Oh, and by the way, Hayden has inherited another cute trait from Jaycee! Yes, of course, he LOVES bread buns!

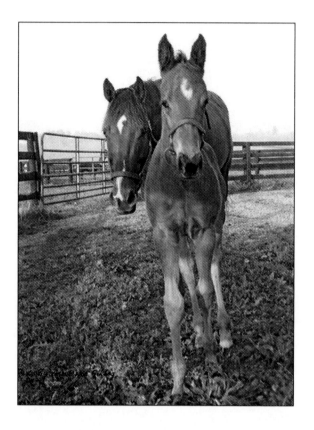

Joseph and Jackie King own and operate Indian Hills Thoroughbred Farm, Inc., a Thoroughbred breeding and foaling facility near Edwardsville, Illinois where three stallions stand and approximately 30 mares foal every year. Each mare and foal has their own story to tell; this is just one story of many.

First Born

By Jackie King

She's very quiet, subdued even. She's a Thoroughbred but looks like a small quarter horse. She is built tough, short, sweet and strong. She is smart; she understands your every move.

She has one flaw, a ripped nostril. Somehow, someway, it got there. It is obvious she experienced pain. Her flaw you never, ever see.

She raced and ended up with a new job, to become a broodmare. Only she knows the true experience of her first breeding. For certain she is poked, prodded and palpated. She is bred more than once, as it took her a few times to get pregnant. The humans involved treat her well and with respect. She in turn respects them.

She is finally pronounced in foal and returns home to her peaceful life of grazing on a field with friends. She has no idea what's growing inside.

Eleven months later and she gives only one sign, a big belly. No udder to speak of, so no waxing to warn birth is drawing near.

She is watched closely and medicated to increase milk production. She paws the ground and pushes against the wall. This goes on for a bit and then subsides for long periods of time. This is day one of the very early stages of her labor.

Day two brings on even more pawing and pushing. No sweating, no rolling—just the discomforts of labor. The problem for her — the labor never progresses.

A vet is called and she is grateful; her foal also grateful, anxious to get out of the womb. The water is broke and a colt is delivered. She never would have delivered on her own; this she knows is true.

She understands her job, and allows the colt to nurse. The night draws near and she is at peace with her new foal and, thankfully, comfortable. She appreciates the presence of humans and the ease they have provided.

She is a new mom; her name is Mamonia Gold.

Susan (Hadden) Pisarri owns Lionlamb Farm in Upstate New York with her husband David and two sons, Paul and Neil. She is a psychiatric nurse and a lifelong animal lover. Susan currently owns three Arabians. Draugas, a highly prized stallion, is a son of the legendary MS Santana. SB Elizabeth is pure Polish and presently in foal to Draugas. And last but never least, there is Susan's gelding and dear old friend, Derringer's Echo, otherwise known as Peanut. Susan and her husband are also active in the dog show community, showing and breeding Champion Rhodesian Ridgebacks, a breed originally created in Africa to hunt lions. Susan finds many parallels between Rhodesian Ridgebacks and Arabian horses. She says both breeds are independent, highly intelligent and sensitive, and that both Arabians and Ridgebacks have an exceptional amount of heart, and devotion to their people. Susan found that Ridgebacks possess the same combination of fearlessness of heart, and gentleness of spirit that drew her to Arabians – and that was the inspiration for LionLamb Ridgebacks. Visit her website: www.freewebs.com/lionlambfarm.

Promises Kept

By Susan Pisarri

Chell-Win Marana, better known as Marnie to all who knew her, was a hot blooded Arabian horse with a lot of issues. Only time and perseverance would reveal the incredible spirit that lay dormant in this once-in-a-lifetime mare. This story is dedicated to my beloved Marnie, my first horse, my friend, and my teacher of life's most valuable lessons.

I grew up in a single parent household; my parents divorced when my sister and I were very young, and my father passed away several years later. Money was tight, but I have learned that what is meant to be will always find a way. I was bitten by the horse bug at an early age, and I can remember going to sleep with my face buried in horse care encyclopedias and reading every book in The Black Stallion series. I can only guess my horse craziness was handed down from my mother, whose leased childhood pony Peaches brought her much joy for a fleeting couple of summers in her youth. Owning a horse at that time was unrealistic, but the dream was kept vividly alive by my active imagination. By day I daydreamed about cantering my black Arabian across the rolling fields behind the old Newbury Farm, where my grandmother lived and my mother was raised. By night, I fell asleep reading my horse books and quizzing myself about the uses of various grooming equipment listed in the horse care chapters. My favorite breeds were Arabians and Friesians, and that remains true today. I would fall asleep at night with the book against me opened to the Arabian page, as if the steed might jump out of the book and into my bedroom. Every ounce of me ached for a horse to call my own.

The years passed and I entered my adolescence, putting those equestrienne aspirations on hold for a time. I was 16 years old when I began struggling with depression and feeling discontented as though my life was without purpose. At 17, still feeling uninspired, the solution came to me all at once — I needed to find that part of myself I had left behind. The time had come to fulfill an old dream and find my first horse.

The question of "how" was not an easy one to answer. We were still living in a suburban apartment. My mom, a devoted single parent, did not have the means to purchase or care for a horse. Suddenly I knew what I needed to do. That day I marched into my guidance counselor's office with an unusual request. I wanted to graduate from high school early, effective immediately, and work full time to finance my horse habit while attending college part time. I was a good student with enough credits for a regents diploma already accounted for. After a bit more convincing, I was declared a graduate and secured a full time job.

A month later, the search for my first horse had begun. My mother and I went to look at a few prospects, but it wasn't until I responded to an ad for a 12-year-old Arabian mare that I was to find the horse destined to become my first.

I was too much a novice to notice that the mare was already caught and fully tacked when we arrived. I did not have much riding experience, and I dropped one of the reins the first time I rode her. She promptly trotted back to the barn and stood there. I figured if that's the worst she will do, I can handle this. There was no health exam, no follow up visit. We agreed to purchase her on the spot and a week later she was delivered to us. A kindly neighbor affectionately known as Uncle Bill allowed me to keep her at his 60 acre farm which was only half a mile away.

I still recall the excitement of purchasing my first halter, a bright red one with brass trim. How beautiful it would look against Marnie's dapple gray coat. The thrill of just grooming her, the smell of horse early on a chilly morning – I felt alive again! I had rediscovered the piece of me somehow left behind, and I was happy to have not only my first horse, but a beautiful Arabian mare to call my very own.

During the first week however, reality set in. I quickly learned about Marnie's many issues. She was impossible to catch, she reared, she could be very spooky, and when tied went into a blind panic. What was worse, she was so distraught from leaving her pretty yearling colt behind that she resented every moment of attention I thrust upon her. She didn't particularly like or trust people. I still adored her, but she was beginning to put fear in my heart, and what was worse, she knew it.

Uncle Bill could see that I was struggling in trying to handle this hot mare, and considering himself to be a lifelong horseman and owner of two horses himself, he offered to lend a hand. He caught her using grain and a bit of muscle, and tied her to a gate which she promptly broke rearing back in a panic. Twenty minutes later he handed me the lead rope, shook his head and mumbled that she ought to be shot. He said she was useless and would never be a good horse and walked away. I was devastated with few options left, and filled with self doubt. That night I called the sellers. They were willing to take the mare back, no refunds of course. I told them I'd let them know what I decided to do.

My mother found me at the barn the next morning, sitting on the ground crying, with an empty bag of carrots. We had a long talk about what to do with this impossible mare. Neither of us had the heart to return her. I managed to catch her that day, and I took her for a long walk. We walked together side by side while I told her about how long I had waited for her, how sorry I was that she had been taken away from her colt, and how sad I felt for her knowing that she had been bought and sold repeatedly throughout her 12 years of life without regard to the bonds or babies she had to leave behind. I still recall stopping that day at the top of a grassy knoll. I told her that perhaps she could be happy with me. I made a vow to her that day. I told her if only she could open her heart one last time, that I would never again allow it to be broken. I promised I would never sell her.

Those words must have traveled through the winds straight to God's ears and back down to settle deeply into the heart of that mare. I tell you, she came back home with me that day a different animal. She no longer viewed me as the enemy, and I no longer viewed her as a mistake. A friendship was born that day that would carry both of us through the next 18 years as true friends.

Marnie went on to become an extraordinary riding horse. In a year's time, I could ride her anywhere in just a halter. She had total faith in me and would willingly venture anywhere I pointed her. My confidence bloomed. She became a tremendous trail mount and even swam in deep water with me on her. In another year she became easy to catch, and would follow me without a lead anywhere. Years later, she taught my niece Jennifer to ride; and in her golden years, she even carried my five-year-old son Paul safely on the trails. What deep satisfaction it was to have the privilege of watching my small son beam with confidence atop my oldest and dearest friend. It is a memory I will cherish forever. I trusted her inexplicitly, and she never let me down.

When I bought her, the purchase separated her from her yearling son, and looking back I realize how devastated she was by this. I think a lot of her initial behavioral issues were due to her grieving the loss of that relationship. The former owners had told me she was such a loving mother that she would even steal foals from other mares and encourage them to nurse. A year later we ended up buying a yearling colt, a striking chestnut Arab like her son, and ironically sired by the same stallion. She immediately took to Peanut (Derringer's Echo) and mothered him; and being a very submissive boy, he adored her love and protection. They groomed each other daily and I literally never saw so much as a cross look between them during the 16 years that they loved one another. We had a third horse, Misty, a mare who was dominant over Peanut but beneath Marnie, and they had the typical horse pecking order interactions. But it was different for Peanut and Marnie. These two became lifelong companions, almost like mother and son.

Marnie was of good Crabbet breeding and stayed sound and active her entire life. We lost her at the age of 29 to her first and only colic. The night she passed is one that I will never forget.

When she was colicking, Peanut never left her side. All day and into the night while my husband and I walked Marnie, hoping the impaction might pass, he hung over the fence watching her. He didn't eat; he didn't drink. He was scared for her and knew she was in trouble. Her passing was very sudden, in the middle of the night. When she went down, he immediately started screaming and galloping wildly into the night air. A few minutes after we lost her we walked into the dark pasture to check on him, and he literally galloped across the field straight up to us. He stopped before me, then laid his head over my shoulder, resting the full weight of it on me like a hug. I threw my arms around him and bawled into his neck and I held him as we mourned together. He stayed in that position seeking consolation from me for several minutes before he finally lifted his head and walked to the gate bobbing his head, motioning to go to her. We opened the gate and let him go to her body, and after sniffing her for a few moments he raised his head to the midnight sky and started neighing loudly again. The emotion I saw in him that night touched me in a way that I can barely describe. His grief was so real; he was almost human that night.

I would love to be able to give a happy ending to Peanut's story. He went through a deep depression after Marnie died, brought out of it only by our love and attention. But he still longs for her. We have two other Arabians now and a miniature horse, but it's not the same relationship of love that he and Marnie shared.

There may be hope yet for that happy ending. Our Polish mare, SB Elizabeth, is now pregnant. She is bred to our stallion, Draugas, who was sired by the legendary National/Canadian Halter Champion MS Santana and possesses a unique blend of Polish and Crabbett blood. Draugas knows he is royalty, and he is the apple of my eye! He had a successful racing career in his youth but now enjoys an occasional trail ride.

The foal is ironically due on May 12, 2008, which would have been our beloved Marnie's 32nd birthday. Perhaps it is fate knocking; and just maybe, though this foal, Peanut may find that special love that he longs to experience once again.

The woman who bred Chell-Win Marana was Annette Winchell of Chell Win Farm in Western NY. Annette is not only a dear friend, but also an inspiration and I feel great fondness and respect for her. She has extensive knowledge of the bloodlines she sought to improve upon and truly understands form and function. She never compromises her principles and is the wisest person I have known. I am forever indebted to Annette for many years of guidance and support, and especially for having bred a mare such as Chell-Win Marana, who not only fulfilled a childhood dream, but who inspired a thousand dreams in the heart that loved her most.

Dawn Hadfield resides in her hometown of Collinsville, Illinois. She is actively involved in lay ministries and has followed many diverse interests during her lifetime, including horses, softball, playing Bluegrass music and ballroom, Latin & Country dancing. She speaks Spanish and French fluently, making her career in international business. Her house pets, Porky & Petunia (canine) and Samson & Delilah (feline) plus Emmy Lou (the equine member of the family), are amongst her closest companions. Her personal relationship with Jesus Christ is integral to all else in her life.

"Emmy Lou"

By Dawn Hadfield

All my life I've dreamed of owning a big ol' hefty 16-hand Paint gelding. Who knows why? We horse lovers are attracted to different color schemes, sizes and breeds for varying reasons. I tend to like splashy colors. Give me a tall, stocky horse that requires a step ladder for mounting! Give me a Paint, Appy, Gray or Palomino any day of the week. While I think a rich, deep Sorrel is very pretty, it has simply never been my *"mane"* attraction (if you'll pardon the pun). The sorrel is simply not what I, personally, would look for when in the horse market.

"Don't buy a mare," many people told me. *"Whatever you do, don't buy a mare." "They're too moody." "They have attitudes – even worse if you get an Alpha." "Wait 'til you have to deal with one being in heat."*

After being some 27 years removed from the world of horse ownership — surprise, surprise! I am now the proud owner of a 17-year-old 15.1 hand Sorrel Quarter Horse Mare named Smooth Intimidator, or "Emmy Lou," as I like to call her. Who would ever have guessed? I ended up with precisely what I was not looking for in horse flesh, and I could not be more pleased. We seem to get along like two peas in a pod. I love to see her pretty red coat glisten in the sun like a bright copper penny. This mare has some of the best ground manners of any horse I've ever known. She is relaxed and compliant. I question if this is due to her trainer's good efforts or just her natural-born disposition or some combination thereof. Needless to say, Emmy Lou has changed my mind about mares.

There seems to be a "moody mare" stereotype that dogs these four-legged beasts. Perhaps it takes a moody mare to know a moody mare. We females have a way about us, you know (big grin). Perhaps Emmy Lou doesn't always care for *my* moody mare attitude. Some times my day doesn't go quite as planned. Some times I just don't feel 100% well. Some days I am sluggish, unenergetic, unenthused or irritable and just need a little space. I have learned to respect Emmy with that same type of space. I get the impression that she is more content to be left alone to enjoy her chow rather than for me to stay in the stall fussing over her. There is no reason for me to not give her this space. She is entitled, as am I when my female *druthers* come into play. We females have a lot in common!

For some years of my youth, I was blessed to have a best buddy, Becky, whose dad owned land to harbor her horse and pony, along with some cattle.

During that time, I owned three geldings that bunked at Becky's. Those days were among my best childhood memories. It seemed that most horse people I knew back then owned a gelding. And still today mares do not seem to be the gender of equine preference. My, but I have learned how important is the relationship between horse and owner rather than to focus on our list of criteria, of what we think we want in a horse.

When you're born with the passion for horses you never lose it (Am I singing your song?). For a time I looked to buy some land, but could not find what would accommodate both my needs <u>and</u> my pocket book. Since I believe strongly in taking everything to the Lord in prayer, I began praying about what possibilities there may be for me to make a re-entrance into the wonderful world of horses. God led me to Arlington Stables, in Granite City, Illinois, where I now have lots of new horse-loving friends some of whom (stable owners included) are steadfast believers in Jesus Christ, as I am. During my second visit to Arlington, I met Emmy. Her big brown eyes and long lashes flashed at me from behind the bars of her stall. While she was not what I had in mind, I remember thinking what a pretty little gal she was. As I looked at her more, I even thought to myself, *"Hmm, I wouldn't mind owning you some day."* As it turned out, her owner was in poor health and in need of some horse caretaking. I spent the next 15 months helping to care for Emmy a few days a week. Needless to say we knew each other quite well by the time her owner was willing to sell and I was in a position to buy her. Not everyone who is in the market for a horse will have that kind of opportunity. But I did learn from that experience, that it is very wise for horse and prospective new owner to spend as much time as possible together prior to making the purchase. For me, there were no surprises. I knew all of this mare's good traits right along with her few hitches and glitches. Emmy and I plan to stay together until either she goes to that great pasture in the sky or I go to my "Heavenly Home" on the range.

There are some things that Emmy doesn't like, such as getting into a trailer, having her head tied too tight and another horse's nose landing on her rump. *"Well Emmy, perhaps you should know there are some things your owner doesn't like either, such as scary movies, flying, the whir of a chain saw and driving across bridges, especially those bridges over water."* Could it be we have more in common with our horses than we realize? Oh I get on airplanes – but I never like them. By the same token, my Emmy Lou does get into and out of trailers, but a small amount of balking and fussing lets you know she is never too crazy about it. Considering she was in a trailer accident when she was very young, I can't blame her. Some times I have to hear chain saws or drive across bridges. But I never like being exposed to either. Occasionally, when flipping channels I see scary movie previews – so I close my eyes and cover my ears, while singing real loud (Quite the visual isn't it?). By the same token, Emmy probably won't ever like her head being tied too tight or having another horse's nose on her rump. But she is learning to tolerate both much better all the time.

A children's song says, *"He's still workin' on me, to make me what I ought to be . . ."* So while God keeps workin' on me, I guess I'll keep working on Emmy Lou. Besides, Emmy's worst problems are possibly nothing more than her owner's ignorance in how to deal with them. Don't sell your mare (or any other horse) short. Help is available. There are knowledgeable, experienced horse people everywhere and most are glad to help!

At age 17 (about 53 in human years), Emmy is still learning to deal with her fears and anxieties and at age 47 I am still learning to deal with mine. God's Word (I Peter 5:7) says to *"cast all your anxiety on Him because He cares for you."* In some similar fashion, perhaps we horse owners ask our four-legged beasts to cast their anxieties (those things that cause them grief or fear) on us, as their owners, because we will lead them safely through the peril and will not, intentionally, expose them to harm. With some patience and instruction from a few well-seasoned horse handlers, we are working to conquer my mare's age-old fears.

Whether I'll ever own the 16-hand paint gelding of my dreams remains to be seen. Maybe now I will want a 16-hand paint *"mare"* instead! For now, though, I only have eyes for Emmy.

Cynthia M. Medina has been a professional in the horse business for over 25 years, and a B graduate of Brush Run Pony Club, where her love of horses started. She is now actively involved with Silver Springs Pony Club. She became a certified riding instructor in the early 80's, teaching and training off and on throughout the years even during her jockey career. Yes, Cynthia was a professional jockey for 18 years and one of 20 female jockeys to ever win over 1,000 races! While her horsemanship skills and love of horses developed during her Pony Club years, her race track experiences allowed her to nurture, refine, and hone those skills. And she thoroughly enjoys passing along this knowledge to others. Since retiring from racing in September, 2004, Cynthia still works in the horse industry — teaching, training, writing about and painting these magnificent creatures that touch her soul. She says she can't picture her life without horses. Visit her website at www.cmmbarnbrats.com.

And Down the Stretch They Come!

By Cynthia M. Medina

Do I have an interesting mare story? Hmmm. Where do I start? Being on the race track for twenty years, eighteen of them as a jockey, I met and fell in love with many wonderful mares. Most of the mares I rode seemed to try just a little bit harder, as if they too had something to prove. This of course was something I could relate with. Win the heart of a mare, and you have really done something!

In loving memory of her late owner and trainer and my dear friend Ann Hobbs, I will tell you about Secret Doctor. Ann passed away from cancer, but while she was on this Earth, she was a great horse-woman — someone I looked up to and learned a lot from. She too had developed a wonderful bond with Secret Doctor from the moment she laid eyes on her. She saw something very special in this mare. She saw "heart." Having heart isn't something you can train into a horse; it comes from some place deep within.

Ann acquired Secret Doctor, or "Doc" as she was known around the barn, back in August of 1990 from owner/trainer Ray Leaf. Doc stood about 15.3 and was a lovely dark bay, the color of rich chocolate, with a white star. She had the kindest eyes and a sweet disposition. There was something very soulful about those eyes, as though she was older and wiser than her years.

Here's a little fun-fact: Doc started her racing career (at the age of three) at Fairmount Park in Collinsville, Illinois, and finished her racing career at Mountaineer Park. I started my racing career at Mountaineer Park and finished mine at Fairmount Park. Doc raced 120 times and won 19 races and was on the board a total of 60 times. That's 50% in the money, as we say on the track. Which is a pretty good record. Like I said, the mare had heart.

One thing that Ann believed (and I agree), is that after a horse raced they should go home to the farm for a few days to a week for some much needed "Rest and Relaxation!" She once told me, "the horse will tell you when it's ready to start back into training." And Doc was no exception.

Doc had one phobia or quirk, and that was traile-ring. She hated to get on the trailer. It didn't matter what kind of trailer it was or if you were hauling her from home to the track or from the track back home, she hated to get on the trailer. Some mares will kick out or rear up when they feel threatened by the confinement of a trailer, but not Doc. She just refused to take one step into that dark abyss on wheels!

I've never seen a mare so agile and light on her feet. She could wiggle her body in every way possible just to avoid getting on the trailer. But with enough people around to keep her straight, she would eventually walk calmly in. One thing about Doc and her sweet disposition, you never had to worry about being kicked by her, which was a good thing especially if you were the person standing behind her.

One person would lead her in and two would stand behind her off to each side, keeping their hands firmly on her butt so she couldn't wiggle away. With that arrangement, she would walk calmly in and take her spot. But sometimes there just aren't enough people around when you need them.

It was during one of Doc's layups (I believe it was her second lay up since Ann had owned her) that we (Ann and I) noticed that Doc kept herself pretty busy. A lay up is when you give a horse some time off to just rest his body and mind, either due to an injury or just because he has raced a long time and needs a break. Most horses literally do lounge around for the most part when they go to the farm for some R & R. They might have two or three days in the beginning where they get full of themselves and run and play. Then they settle in, enjoy the green grass, bask in the sunshine and on a hot day splash around in the pool. But not Doc. She kept herself fit, even during a lay up.

Our farm routine was pretty much the standard. After feeding the horses in the morning, they would get turned out in the pastures and their stalls would be cleaned. On cold rainy days, when we couldn't turn the horses out in the pasture, we would turn them out two at a time in the shed row. The shed row ran the full length of the barn, about 120 feet, and was about 20 feet wide. Two horses would have plenty of room to stretch their legs, play a bit and roll in the fluffy shavings that lined the floor.

When I would take Doc to the pasture, she would walk calmly at my side, never acting fussy or antsy. Unlike some of the other horses who would get excited and giggy heading out to pasture. Walking with Doc was like walking with a friend. She seemed to understand my every mood and feeling.

When I was in a happy mood, she seemed truly happy too, giving me a brisk walk to the pasture gate, with lots of positive energy in her step but no pulling. If I wasn't feeling good, or if I was sad or blue, she walked a bit slower, staying just a little bit closer almost as if offering me her shoulder for support or to cry on.

When I unhooked her lead rope, she would turn quietly and trot away. She would then begin her daily fitness routine of trotting around the perimeter of the pasture fence line. She was never in a super excited state, but she just seemed to know what to do to keep herself fit. Doc seemed to do it with the mental intensity of a person who trains for marathons. She would get in the zone and just do her morning jog, for about ten or fifteen minutes every day.

Sometimes the other horses would join her for a lap, but then they quickly settled in to their favorite past time, munching grass. Doc would settle into munching grass after her work out. Then she became just another horse in the pasture, eating grass and basking in the sunshine or splashing in the mud (or better yet rolling in it!).

When it was time for Doc to get back into racing shape, it really didn't take long to get her ready – she had already been keeping herself fit. I really became attached to Doc during her R & R and before taking her to the track to gallop, I would often take her out on the trails to hack out a bit. Doc seemed to thoroughly enjoy our hacks through the woods, up and down hills. I could tell she was having fun.

Then came the day she had to ship into the track to continue her race training, and we had a terrible time getting her on the trailer. Doc in her usual quiet protest was saying, "Why can't I just stay here and train?" I kept getting that vibe from her, like a voice in my head. But I wasn't her jockey at this time. I was just exercising her at the farm. Her jockey was a friend of mine and he felt she needed to get to the track to really get race fit. He couldn't imagine her being fit enough to race from working out at the farm.

I convinced Ann that Doc was pretty fit and she wouldn't need to be at the track too long before she raced, as she hated it there. So three weeks before her first race back, Doc went to the track. She needed a published work out or two before she raced. My friend the jockey who was gong to ride Doc, was very impressed at how fit she was from her farm workouts. And in Doc's first two races back, she finished two very strong thirds.

I remember Doc's fourth race back – it was pouring rain and the track was sloppy. My friend was riding her and I was riding another mare in the same race. The mare I rode didn't really care for an "off" track, and I was doing my best to get us around that sloppy track without incident as she struggled with the footing.

Being in this race with Doc but not riding her really gave me more insight into Doc's personality and I watched her for most of the race. She and my jockey friend seemed to be out of sync. He was trying to send her to the lead out of the gate, and she hated being rushed. Around the turn, he began to fight her, trying to hold her down on the rail, which only made her drift out more. Down the stretch, he got a bit too aggressive with the whip. I could see Doc getting more upset and frustrated. But I couldn't say anything – they were about five lengths in front of me. I wanted to scream, "Leave her alone, and let her do it her way!" He wouldn't have heard me, and more than likely he wouldn't have listened anyway.

After crossing the finish line, we pulled up and headed back to the paddock. My mare wasn't handling the footing, so I opted to trot home at a pace she was comfortable with. Doc was about ten lengths in front of me and cantering rhythmically home. That's when she decided to get even with her jockey. As I mentioned, the track was sloppy and it was pouring down rain. The overhead lights were gleaming off the water on the track, and that was all the excuse Doc needed. At the 7/8 pole she ducked out a bit and off toppled her jockey, landing with a splat in the gushy mud. He was unhurt – well, with the exception of his pride!

I couldn't help but tell him he deserved what he got, for trying to make Doc do more than she could do. I told him this mare will give you her heart and soul if you "ask" her instead of trying to manhandle or force her to do it. He of course blamed it on the reflection of the light on the water that spooked her. But I knew different. Doc had planned his dismount with the strategic timing of a general in battle.

The next time Doc was to race, I teased my friend, "Hey, don't get too aggressive with Doc or you'll end up on the ground again!" I was joking, of course – or was I? But Doc wasn't joking. He tried to ride her the same way he had done in the previous race, and again while galloping out after the race, she ducked out at the same spot and left him sitting in the sand. I swear I could hear her laughing as she did it! I couldn't resist. I just had to give him the old "I told you so!" as he came back into the jocks' room.

Two other male jockeys rode Doc for her next four races. If they were too pushy, she would do her ducking thing with them after the race. One of the jockeys actually came off, and he said he'd never ride her again. And he didn't. Which was good, because Doc didn't like him at all. He was much too aggressive with her, and she hated it.

My jockey friend who had previously ridden Doc had a double call and couldn't ride her, so he suggested that Ann should let me ride her – as I seemed to know the mare better than anyone. Personally, I think he did it just to see if she would do her ducking thing with me. She didn't, not ever, in 34 races to be exact, in which I rode her. But then again, I did know this mare like the back of my hand, and we worked great together.

It was when I started riding Doc that I mentioned to Ann (her trainer) that I thought Doc would prefer to run from the farm. She liked being at the farm, she kept herself fit and she liked the pace at the farm, and she was happiest there. Ann agreed. She too had noticed that Doc lost weight and seemed unhappy while at the track.

So over the next four years that I rode Doc, that is what we did. Doc was trained at home, and I could tell she was thankful to me for listening to her and being her voice. Doc's workout regimen consisted of swimming when the weather allowed it, hacking out trotting through woods and up and down hills, and cantering and slow gallops along the edges of the big farm fields. But she also did her own thing to keep fit, whether it was trotting along the pasture fence line, trotting back and forth in the shed row or swimming herself in the pond.

I noticed that when we started training her at the farm and she only had to ship in to the track to race, she began loading in the trailer with ease. If there was a long gap between races, we would ship her to the track for a published work and then take her back home until race day. Knowing she would come back home after a race or a published workout seemed to make the difference for her.

I rode Doc off and on for four years, for a total of 34 of her starts, and I hit the board nineteen times. 10 wins, 6 seconds, and 3 thirds, which is a pretty good record. Whenever my agent had previously booked me for a different mount and I couldn't ride Doc, I made sure to tell whatever jockey rode her, about her quirks. I also tried to get a female jockey on her as much as possible, as they would listen to me. The guys had their own agenda, and when they got physical, she did her ducking thing. Sometimes they would come off and sometimes not. But you couldn't blame the mare for trying to stand up for herself.

Doc was like any other race horse, in having her own quirks or way of doing things. Like most mares, if you "ask" for what you want, not "tell" her what to do, she would give you 110% every time she stepped a hoof on the track.

Doc would occasionally drift around the top turn just past the 3/8 pole. Instead of trying to crank her head around and try to hold her in, I found if I just dropped my weight into my inside stirrup and pressed my whip (down and uncocked) into her shoulder, she would stay in. But if you tried to crank her in, it just made it worse and by the time you turned for home you would be out in the middle of the track wasting a ton of ground.

Doc also knew the pace that was comfortable for her, and was appreciative of a jockey that would let her run her own race. She didn't like to be hustled out of the gate or hit a lot with the whip. I learned a lot about Doc and about mares in general from Doc, and

I used what I learned from her on other mares I rode during my 18 year career as a jockey.

I learned that mares may be more sensitive than colts and geldings, but once you have won the heart of a mare, you have a soul mate. The only way to win the heart of a mare is through respect. Doc is definitely one of the top ten best mares I ever rode, and every time I talk about some of the best horses I ever rode, she always comes to mind.

Ann retired Doc in January of 1996 after running only two races that year. She decided to breed Doc, hoping she would pass along that wonderful winning spirit and heart to her offspring. I moved away in June of 1996 and started racing at Fairmount Park in Illinois, where Doc had come from. I heard that Doc did indeed have one foal, a colt they named Mr. Doctor, who raced twelve times and won only one race. I hope that wherever Doc is today she is happy, as she deserves it.

Ann passed away after a long battle with cancer shortly after I left Mountaineer Park to head here to the Midwest. I hope she is smiling down on me as I write this story about one of the greatest little mares to ever race. She may not have been anything more than a "cheap claimer" – and I say that with true affection – but she had heart. Many blessings to you Doc wherever you may be.

Betsy Kelleher once owned this mare for only two months, but it was a memorable experience! This photo of Mandy was taken at a horse show with Mandy's new owner in the saddle. Mandy was one of those stories that "could have been," but story endings aren't always what we originally have in mind.

Mandy Was Mine Once...

By Betsy Kelleher

Sometimes a horse comes along that you just *know* could be something really special...but for some reason you don't or can't make it happen. I saw Mandy the day after I lost old Samson. I did not feel drawn to her at first; her ears were back and she seemed irritated at the flies. Mandy was a large flea-bitten gray Arab, almost 16 hands and quite round. My husband liked her, however, and bought her for me, thinking she was a bargain. I was told she had been abused and rescued and they didn't even know how old she was.

I owned Mandy only a few months, but I will never forget her. In that short time, she captured my heart. I admired her smooth, beautiful movement and I saw tremendous potential in her style and personality. She had a slow Western Pleasure jog and she also had a magnificent extended trot. She had power and ability and she was beautiful. She had a willing disposition in spite of her fears. I knew Mandy could have done dressage, jumping, anything I ever wanted to do with a horse, but I knew it would take a long time and a lot of patience and hard work. Mandy needed to learn to trust the humans around her. Aside from being an Arab mare, her biggest problem seemed to be a super sensitive body combined with a fear of being hurt. She would move sideways while I tried to put a saddle on her, and when the saddle fell, she freaked out. In time, she calmed down but not while I owned her.

One special memory bound me to Mandy. Two weeks after I got her, I was in her stall just petting her and being with her, and we had a supernatural bonding moment. As I stood with my left hand on her neck and my right hand on her face, looking at her scars and thinking about what might have been done to her...something strange happened. Perhaps Mandy was allowing me a glimpse of her past abuse. Perhaps a heavenly Spirit was in her stall with us. I suddenly felt as though Mandy and I were surrounded by a powerful Presence that enveloped us both like a warm, thick cloud. I felt that we were standing on "holy ground." She stood very still, and I remember feeling afraid to move, and then I began to cry, feeling an unexpectedly strong emotion of empathy for her past suffering. I told her again and again how very sorry I was. It was a remarkable gift of understanding and I believed at that moment that Mandy and I would be able to fix her problem and she would be whole again. But it didn't work out that way.

Her fearful, nervous nature and her size had me really scared and my fears only made hers worse. After a few frightening incidents while fastening the saddle, I gave up riding and concentrated on "desensitizing" touch therapy. I knew what to do, and ground work didn't scare me. But I wanted a horse I could ride!

She had broken the crossties once when I was putting the saddle on her. The mere tightening of the girth set her off. Another time I took her to a park to ride, and tied her to the trailer. I tried to be very careful while putting the saddle on her back and slowly bringing the girth up to fasten it. She suddenly freaked out, and for a moment I thought sure she was going to break loose. I loaded her back up in the trailer and came back to the barn, where I saddled her in the stall and rode around the nearby fields. Once I was in the saddle, she didn't give me any problem being ridden. Fastening the saddle brought out her biggest problem.

For one whole week, I worked with her in the indoor arena every day with only a saddle pad. I would lay it on her back and move it around, letting it slide just a little, gradually letting it fall to the ground beside her. The first time it fell off her back, she jumped a good 15 feet. By the end of the week, when it fell beside her, she was moving only two or three feet. I felt we were making progress.

I asked a young friend to ride her in the indoor arena while I watched. She seemed very sensitive to leg pressure, yet I was told she was trained from leg more than rein. But when you asked for a canter, she would put her ears back and would stop or give a little buck. She had a sensitive mouth and sensitive sides and she demanded a light touch!

People around me were starting to express concern. I tried to see the situation from the eyes of family and friends who were thinking of my emotional state and my safety. I had let this mare become a consuming frustration. I was nervous and I cried easily. I wasn't sleeping well and I was exhausted. I wanted desperately to "cure" Mandy of her dangerous and fearful reactions so I could enjoy riding…but I wasn't ready to deal with putting the saddle on her!

I wanted with all my heart to see Mandy become the horse I envisioned her to be. Was I selfish…or was it pride? I believed that Mandy was the chance of a lifetime. But I felt that my time for such an experience was past. I'd had that kind of relationship with a difficult mare once before. I knew what it would take. And for what? Would I ever do all the things with Mandy that she could accomplish with the right training? She needed a younger rider, perhaps a trainer, a more courageous rider with higher goals.

The day I traded Mandy for Traveller was one of the most difficult in my life, although I have never for one moment regretted having Traveller, the most reliable trail horse I've ever ridden. I traded her off to a trainer who worked with her for almost three years before finding a new owner.

A true partnership should allow both partners to grow, fulfilling the potential within and finding joy in becoming the most one can be. Fear prevents both joy and growth. My fears couldn't help Mandy;

she had enough of her own. Perhaps I tried too hard to "fix" her. But how do you know what it might become...if you don't keep trying? A true partnership takes time...but it develops because something inside you says to keep going after it. It comes from struggle and patience...from finding the right touch and the right response.

I visited Mandy one time in the trainers pasture after trading her off. I walked to the fence and called her, and she came eagerly toward me. She reached out and put her nose on me, then sniffed at me, all over me wherever she could reach. I had just been with Traveller and his smell was certainly still on me. Mandy looked me right in the eye and gave a disgusted shove with her head then turned and walked away. I called to her again, but she would not come. She knew.

Mandy was a challenge because she had a mind of her own. When she put her ears back because she didn't like the leg pressure, it scared me to death! But her next owner laughed at her spunk and said that Mandy was a tremendous amount of fun. Mandy became a different horse than she was when I owned her. Someone else had helped Mandy find trust in humans. But even three years later, her new owner told me, "She's real tense. And so sensitive! She doesn't spook that badly, but she gets excited around other horses and she seems scared of people." That's the Mandy I remember. I've heard that still another woman later bought Mandy, and I've lost contact with her.

Sometimes I wish I'd kept Mandy. But only because I think she might have been the dressage horse I've never had. I watched her in a show once, as she jumped two-footers with ease and grace. I felt a bit of envy, but I didn't miss all the years of hard work it would have taken me to get her to that point. I keep telling myself, we can't have everything we want...if we aren't willing to work for it.

Cherie Duggan lives with her husband, Jay, and children, Jonathan and Hannah, in northern Michigan. She works as a grant writer for a hospital foundation and enjoys reading, travel, helping out with church activities and spending time with her family. In the spring of 2008, the Duggan family will be growing to include two children from Ethiopia. Cherie became a first-time horse owner three years ago and enjoys her novice status, since it means she will never run out of things to learn and experience with her equine friends.

Sadie's Journey

By Cherie Duggan

Her head was lowered, ears flat back, lips snarling as she came at me. My breath jerked in jagged bursts. I had seen documentaries on wild horses. I knew exactly the dominance game she was playing with me, and I began to run! The barn was only seventy-five feet away, and I would be safe inside. I could hear her hooves in the dirt behind me, but like a child hiding from danger under the bed, I was too afraid to look. I reached the barn, my hands trembling so violently that I couldn't unlatch the door. My heart jolted adrenaline to every extremity. The chain finally loosened, and I scraped through the emerging opening. Stumbling onto the hay-covered floor, I slid the door shut.

My knees turned to water, and in relief, I sobbed—great heaving sobs of fear and despair. I knew nothing about horses, not a single thing, except that they consumed my dreams every day and every night as a child. Back then, my family didn't have the resources to own one. Now that I was an adult and my daughter loved horses too, my husband agreed to a tiny barn—barely more than a lean-to shelter—and fenced in a small pasture. Hannah and I were in business!

Sadie was given to us for free. We were told she was so gentle, so willing, so compliant that she had been sold as a child's lesson horse to a riding stable. As the new owners were closing the trailer door, she exploded out of the trailer in fear, falling backwards onto her left hip. Barely able to walk, hobbling for months, the vet gave her a 50-50 percent chance of recovery. Full of naivety and with a new shelter ready for my first horse, I said we would give her a loving home on the chance that she may recover.

Now, here I was doubled over my knocking knees, trembling and sobbing, while a so-gentle-a-baby-can-ride mare paced outside ready to attack. I could hear her snorting and pawing, and I prayed scattered thoughts. "God, I'm scared to death. Okay, You can see that! I really can't get rid of this horse yet, not after all my husband has done. He'd be so mad at me! But I cannot keep her! I can't even open the door! This is really bad. She can smell my fear from out there." I remember the sense of amazement that knees actually do "knock together" in intense fear!

I considered for awhile that as a responsible adult, I did have to feed Sadie. Somehow. I peeked out between the door and the wall. Sadie was looking the other way distracted by a passing biker. Soundlessly,

I gathered a flake of hay and slid the door open. With a giant heave, I pitched the hay in one direction and blindly ran the opposite.

Without eye contact with anyone as I entered the house, I dialed the number for our dog's vet. How irritated would she be with my weekend emergency question: "What do I do if I'm too scared to go into my new horse's pasture?" She must have heard my quaking voice and in mercy offered a trainer's number.

The trainer arrived that afternoon and guardedly approached my violent mare. After a few minutes, she strode to where I stood, safely on the outside of the fence. She was smiling: "This is a lovely mare. She just needs you to tell her that you are her leader." She showed me how to walk confidently, lead her, move her and swing a rope to back Sadie off. I watched in sheer awe as she confined my mare to an open stall with the point of her index finger.

Three years later and two horses into this, I am pleased to say that Sadie IS a very lovely mare. I will be forever grateful that I did not give up on my passion when I was tempted so many times to do so. Absolute thoughts used to pour through me: I was not raised around horses and cannot overcome this handicap; I am not a tough girl—in fact, rather wimpy; I am not cut out for this; I'm not strong enough; I can't overcome this fear because Sadie can smell it.

Many things have helped me, but most of all understanding, knowledge and accepting incremental progress. Understanding is important for both Sadie and me. First, I needed to understand her.

She is a timid horse that over-reacts to her fear. If another horse comes up too quickly from behind, she will swing her hind quarters around, ready to defend herself — to kick before being kicked. For the first several months I owned her, I could not pick out her hoofs. If I leaned on her hard enough to lift her leg, she would slam it down quickly. Her previous owner told me to smack her when she did that. Unfortunately, hitting her only increased her anxiety to the point that Sadie would not even stand still. The right answer was to retreat and spend time massaging her legs until Sadie learned to understand me—that I meant her no harm. Today, with a gentle squeeze of her chestnut, she will dangle her hoof for me to grasp.

Knowledge has come through education—veraciously reading, watching my daughter take a few riding lessons and attending a Parelli event. I went with a skeptical attitude but was hooked within the opening sequence. Two gorgeous horses erupted from the arena entrance, galloping and exuberantly bucking, whirling, seemingly playing to the music. After several minutes, from the center of the huge arena, the Parellis silently invited their horses to them with a beckoning index finger. The magnificent animals immediately circled and gently trotted to them.

I was hooked! Yep, I bought the DVD series and it has been worth every dollar and a whole lot more. The program breaks learning into incremental steps. Filled with insight and humor, I hear the instruction and then watch other new learners working with their horses. After working on each goal with Sadie, we mark our progress off on a chart. When a new task is introduced, my first thought is often, "I'm not sure if we will ever be able to do that!" But then I look back at the things Sadie and I have checked off and remember that I felt that way then as well. Confidence is growing! If something isn't working, instead of thinking things like, "I should give up— I'm not tough enough to handle this," I sit down and figure out where the breakdown in communication or understanding might be.

The answer for me is not to ignore my fear or "push through it," but instead, to back up to a point where I feel no fear. If I feel fear when riding, I get off, even if it means I am teased by fellow riders when walking my horse along a road because I am not confident near the traffic. A loud truck passed and Sadie was fine. Next time I probably will not get off. I believe that trusting myself to not put myself in danger eases the need for anxiety.

While Sadie and I have miles and miles of learning yet to travel, we enjoy the journey. Small successes bring enormous joy when we have come so far. Just yesterday, I was able to reintroduce the trailer to her after a three year hiatus. She most certainly remembered her prior experience, but with gentle requests on my part and patience, she quietly stepped in and stood for fifteen minutes!

A few weeks back, I accidentally left the barn door open and was riding my other mare, Savanna, in the lower pasture. Sadie was taking full advantage of the situation. Foraging for hay, her front half had disappeared into the barn.

"Hey Sadie," I called to get her attention. She craned her neck to see me, and I gave her "The Look."

"Uh-uh, girl. Back," I said and shook my index finger at her as I had been taught by Parelli. Without stopping to think about whether I could really enforce that request from so far away, she backed herself out of the barn, pouting at me.

An enormous sense of accomplishment washed over me! Strange as it may seem over such a small task, the major obstacles of misunderstanding, miscommunication and fear that both Sadie and I have overcome make each success very meaningful. I raced around the lower pasture on Savanna, grinning to myself at the thought that I just directed my horse from 100 feet away with my index finger!

This was my Suzie

This photo is of the very same Savanna mentioned in the previous story, with Cherie Duggan, her owner and the author of both stories. This photo was taken one week before Savanna died from colic. Cherie owned her only eight weeks.

For Savanna

By Cherie Duggan

*For Savanna...The delight of my day, the
sunshine of my mind, the dream of a little
girl who loved you long before she knew
you.*

You consumed my dreams every afternoon as a
child. A golden palomino, you and I galloped
bareback over grassy hills. Never stopping to rest,
we flew. A gentle spirit who would only be guided by
our friendship, you would come running from open
fields at my smile. I heard your hooves pounding in
the night and it set my heart free. Breathing in your
mane, we would fly away.

When I was young, my second grade parent-
teacher conference was dominated by the teacher's
plea on my behalf to find me a horse—she had
never known a little girl so consumed. Our family's resources could never include a horse, and I

knew better than to ask. Mom enrolled me in 4-H's "Horseless Horse Club" where we made posters about horse breeds, hungrily listened to horse owners tell us every detail about their horses, and generally rubbed salt into open wounds twice a month. For my birthdays, with a twist of guilt over the expense, I would invite a friend to Springbrook Riding Stable. We would carefully select our mounts from a paddock of twenty beauties and ride through the woods following the owner, Cindy, or her daughter, Dove (who was younger than me and probably had no idea what a charmed life she led). I knew I wasn't really riding—that my horse was just tromping after her leader—but it had to suffice.

What happens to a child's dream snuffed out by reality, forgotten by necessity? It smolders, growing in intensity for thirty years until quietly, unexpectedly a piece of kindling softly lands. The embers ignite into open flame. Savanna, I prayed for you and longed for you again. My precious husband wanted to fulfill my dream, and after two years of searching, we found you! You were golden and lightly dappled with a thick white mane covering your neck and flowing even below, a white blaze, soft black muzzle and kind eyes.

Savanna, your heart was so big. You trusted implicitly. You would never buck, rear, bolt, bite, pin your ears, wring your tail, stamp your foot, or refuse. Could another horse exist so kind? We built a friendship and rode over the grassy hills. You were so willing, but if you saw something suspicious, you would freeze at high alert. Trembling, you would slowly look back at me. I would rub your neck and say, "You're alright, Savanna," and you would believe me. If I asked you to walk, we would walk together. If I asked you to trot, we would trot together. When I asked you to run, breathing in your mane, we would fly away.

We flew through the deep woods, up a sandy two-track, enveloped by autumn colors and the smell of dry leaves. I leaned my face back in the sun, closed my eyes and like a child, whooped in glee! We rustled through the leaves while the sun warmed our skin and splashed up the river. I have never felt so free, and I knew—after all these years— it was you!

Seven days ago, it never entered my mind that I would lose you within the week. For three nights and three days, three vets, my friends, my family and I worked to help you through colic. The vet said when the pain became too intense you would give in and writhe, but you never did, Savanna. You just gently accepted the pain, bravely, stoically.

And now you are gone. I didn't believe there were any tears left in me until we buried you today. My heart is broken and my dreams are shattered. We had such a short time together, but I knew you and loved you my whole life. The night you died, the sky was clear black and the stars bright. Alone in the silent pasture at 3 A.M., you told me you couldn't keep fighting any longer. You rested your warm face against me, and we sobbed. I saw deep into the heavens, and I knew that God could see straight down to where we were, and we cried, "Why?" Truly, there is no answer.

But this much I do know: that You, God, are good. You love me and gave me the gift of Savanna. You feel grief as I suffer, and I feel You reaching down to comfort me in the embraces and kindness of family and friends. Through my friend, Dove—the same Dove who led me on trail rides at Springbrook Stables—who spent the night with Savanna when I couldn't. Through my husband, who simply does not cry, but has cried with me every day. Through the words of sorrow and prayer and the tears of family and friends. Even through a childhood friend who buried Savanna and refused payment—You, my Father, tenderly reach down to say that You hurt when I hurt and that You love me.

This I also know: Savanna, the delight of my day, the sunshine of my mind, the dream of a little girl who loved you long before she knew you, God has promised that someday, all will be well.

Cathy Robinson is 47 and she works for the State of South Carolina in the Bureau of Water. She started riding a few years ago, and Mattie, an ex-race horse, is the first horse she has owned. Cathy and Mattie are learning about riding and jumping from Cathy's instructor, Dawn Cooper, at Country Springs Equestrian Center, Pelion, SC. When Cathy's granddaughters visit, they like to ride Mattie bareback while Cathy leads. They all consider Mattie to be their family horse. Mattie's photo is also on the stable's website at www.countryspringsequestrian-center.com.

Mattie's Journal

By Cathy Robinson

This is actually my own journal, as much as Mattie's. Before I got Mattie, I would watch movies about horses and cry because I wanted my own horse! I rode as a child, but that was just trail riding. Now I have my very own horse. It is not as easy as people think it is. This is my record of our first eight months together.

FEBRUARY, 2007 - The day I first saw Mattie, she looked at me with those sweet eyes and face and I was in love. Mattie is chestnut with a white blaze and one white sock. She is a seven-year-old off track thoroughbred (OTTB). She was not fast enough for racing, so her owners made her a brood mare and bred her too young. She had trouble and the foal died. She can no longer have a baby, so the owner did not want her and sold her to a couple who split up and didn't feed her. The next owner's health got bad, and she sold Mattie to a girl who planned to resell her. I had called that girl about a horse that had already sold and she told me about Mattie. She was asking more than I had, but she agreed to accept what I had as the price. I wanted a horse that could jump and a horse I could put my two granddaughters on to just walk around. When I went to try Mattie, I didn't know anything about OTTBs and I had only been riding for a year and a half. I trotted her, but was too scared to ask for a canter (which I love to do)! Not knowing about race horses, I pulled back to stop and it only made her go faster. I was near panic when the girl told me to pull only one rein. Mattie stopped and I got off. I looked at other horses the next day, but I knew that Mattie was the one for me, even though I was scared of her. I had been riding a 14 hand horse and she is a little over 16 hands! Big difference! But I knew she had very kind eyes and was really sweet.

MARCH - Mattie is boarded at a 100 acre stable, with a nice new stall, 11 other horses, trails, two arenas and three different pastures. I travel 40 minutes to visit her and I see her almost every day. I had first taken her to my brother's place in the country, but then I moved her to the stable owned by my riding instructor. Dawn went to college for four years to learn about horses. Mattie is sweet with me, but I have seen her misbehave with Dawn a few times, mostly when being shod. And this tells me she is a mare: she will kick the stall when the white horse she doesn't like is next door. I don't think Mattie is an alpha mare but she's not at the bottom, either.

When I put her out to pasture, I love seeing her take off to get to the other horses. Her back legs go

under and she hunches down low and takes off fast!
I don't see how she was not fast enough for the race
track!

MAY - On Mother's Day, Mattie somehow got
hurt and had sixteen stitches in her nose under the
eyes. We don't know how it happened — her stall is
brand new and very nicely made. We looked carefully and couldn't find anything that may have hurt
her. A storm the night before may have spooked her.
I love her so much that if I could never ride her again,
I would still keep her.

JUNE - Mattie is still green but very smart and
willing to please as long as she knows what I want.
She learns fast. We are learning together! She is so
kind and loving toward me. The other day she propped
her head on top of my head. That would have made a
great picture! And I love it when she shakes her head
yes at me. She does spook easily, but doesn't take off
and run. She just jumps then calms down when I talk
to her. I am not a strong or experienced rider, but I
am learning! I know they say horses don't love but
they do! She has not done anything to try to hurt me
or get me off. I believe she loves me to ride her.

Mattie is a little stubborn when she is in season.
She makes me work hard to get what I want and to
make her listen.

The photo of Mattie and me was taken after we
went for a walk together. I don't want her to think I
only come to ride her, so I often just give her a bath,
go on walks with her or run together with her on the
ground. She loves that!

I really love Mattie! We all love her. She is part of our family and I think she knows it. She really seems to love her new life. I wonder if she has ever been truly loved in her seven years. Maybe she knows she has a real family now and that I will never get rid of her. I want to sell my house someday and get one with land so I can bring her home! I also want to get another horse to go with her. I read that OTTB's are the most loving horses once they bond with you. I believe it, having one myself. But then again, I have not owned anything else so how would I know?

When my granddaughters first came with me, Mattie would turn her back on them and stand in a corner. One day she smelled them, and from then on, she has been different. She seems to look forward to their visits. I saw one weekend how she greeted my youngest as if she was saying "Hello, I know you!" And of course my granddaughter loved it! She rides bareback while I hold the lead rope.

One Saturday, we had a mock horse show and Mattie and I came in fourth every time with five in the class. Mattie needs to slow down. I have gotten used to fast, so "slow" doesn't feel right anymore. During lessons, Mattie and I are working on slow. Mattie often wants to canter but Dawn said to keep at a walk and trot at first. I can't stand it and neither can Mattie, but we try to listen. I want to canter so badly, but I'm scared. I know one day I will be able to feel Mattie's speed and feel safe.

I almost fell off during a lesson when Mattie broke into a canter when I asked for a trot. It caught be off guard, but I stayed on. I will be more careful from now on (it did scare me a little).

Mattie likes to jump! I put up a cross rail one day while my husband watched me ride — we have done those before. Then I put up a vertical for the first time. She did just fine, but we both need practice.

During one of my lessons, we got to canter with the rest of the class! I was really happy and so was Mattie. Just when I was having fun, a storm brought the lesson to an end. I think Mattie and I do better when we are in the ring alone, but it is good for us to be in a group.

JULY - Mattie jumped two and a half feet over a vertical and had a shoeing the next day. Then she was lame, so I took her out of her stall to let her graze and just spend time with her. Sometimes after I gave her a bath she rubs my back with her head.

She loves her snacks and knows that she is getting something when she sees me. One day I left them in the stall while getting something from the tack room. When I came back she had knocked the jug over and was eating a pile on the floor! I won't do that again.

I like working in the arena. I've been watching some dressage and I think it is really neat how they dance together! So if jumping is too much for Mattie, we will do dressage instead! She is still fast when starting the canter but she will slow down. One day, when I got off her, she nudged me back to the saddle with her head. That was so cool!

We are learning together and I really like that. I feel we are growing closer each month, and I know we are trusting each other more. I see it in our riding.

I never thought I would get as far with Mattie as I have in this short period of time. I could have gotten a horse that was better trained, but I am retraining her a lot on my own, and I am really enjoying it!

With four people now in our group, we trotted over poles, four in a row, with a cross rail after that and another cross rail on the other side. I can see Mattie getting better and braver! She is coming along very well with the other horses in the arena with us. At first she was fast and paid more attention to the other horses than to me, but now it is easier. I would rather canter in the small arena. I am scared the big arena looks too much like a race track.

When Mattie refused the first cross rail, Dawn made us step over it. She went over after that but I had to use more leg. One night Mattie did not want to jump and kept running out on me. I called Dawn to help me and it took less than five minutes to fix it so we could end on a good note. She had not done that before. I worked on the canter for a few laps and she started to get fast, so I brought her back down to a trot. I made her go over the jump four times each way. I guess we'll have good days and bad!

SEPTEMBER — Things happen! Mattie and another horse (a new boarder) started kicking each other and she had to get 20 stitches in her leg between her butt and the upper back leg. She has to stay in her stall until the stitches come out, so riding is out for a few weeks. Now I will ride other horses and Dawn says it will help my confidence with the canter.

When I rode another horse, I went to the stable an hour early so I could spend time with Mattie first. I cut grass and fed her and spent time with her. Then I rode a paint for my lesson and I did a lot of cantering! I could hear Mattie calling while we were riding. I went back to her stall later to talk to her and give her treats. One day I spent about three hours with Mattie so she would know she is loved, just grooming and talking. I told her we would ride again soon.

After riding another horse, I could feel my legs because he took a lot more leg than I was used to using. Mattie responds good to my leg yields — I guess that is what riding one horse will do for you. Riding another horse showed me that. I had a good time but I really wished I was riding Mattie.

I took Mattie out for an hour and grazed her on grass and groomed her, then watched her roll in the dirt! I took her back in her stall and cleaned her wound. Then she rubbed her back end on her stall and tore out some stitches! There is a hole that will probably leave a scar.

While Mattie was healing, I rode a 16-hand paint horse at Hitchcock Woods one Saturday. That place has about 2000 acres! It was my first outing. We walked, trotted, cantered and jumped. I have not cantered like that in a long time and I really enjoyed it. I can't wait until Mattie is ready for that and I can ride her with the confidence I had on that ride.

OCTOBER - A friend is going to work with us to get my canter seat better. I am going to ride my girl as much as possible before it gets too cold. I am taking Mattie to a show the end of the month, just so she can see what goes on. I have not been to a show before. Riding lessons are going better, with more cantering. When Mattie gets a little fast, I slow her with half halts and she responds. I am always a little scared before asking, but I want to canter so badly that I usually find my courage. If it doesn't feel right, I won't ask.

Dawn asked if I would rather go over a cross rail and come out at a canter, which I like better. So we did that and Mattie was nice and slow. We did about four laps around the arena and I was not scared. Mattie and I are both still green, but not as green as we were! She loves to canter. After I ask the first time she is ready to go and usually does not want to stop. During one lesson, she did stop whenever I asked, and she wanted to go back into the canter, but didn't until I asked! That is better than before, when it sometimes took three laps to get her to stop.

My granddaughters now ride in the saddle and hold the reins. I walk ahead and Mattie follows me wherever I go.

We have spent several months getting Mattie to slow down. We have come a long way. Dawn said we scared her in the beginning, but now she says Mattie poses no danger to me. She was fast and green and I was unstable on her. It took work to get where we are now, but it was well worth it. Sometimes I get asked if I love my husband as much as I love Mattie, and I say it's a different kind of love. When Dawn tells me how far we have come, I know we will go a lot further — I just feel it! I will have many more entries in Mattie's journal but all of them will end the same. I love Mattie, and I never knew how much I would love riding!

Doreen Davis is a "50 year young" horsewoman who has been involved with Arabians for over 30 years. She enjoys trail riding, and is working towards competing in competitive trail and endurance with her Arabian mare, Brandy, pictured here with her. Brandy is the mare Doreen acquired after the unexpected death of her mare, Breezy, the focal point of her story. Outside of her horse interests, Doreen also enjoys gardening, reading, fitness, and spending time with her family which consists of her husband, Bob, and her son, Logan. She also shares her home with three cats, a dog, and numerous fish.

She Wasn't Very Fancy

By Doreen Davis

There we stood. It was a single track trail, down a short but very steep embankment to a creek. We had been riding for hours without any opportunity to offer the horses water, and there the creek lay, just a short distance from us. Down this short, steep, muddy embankment. My mare dropped her head and looked at the trail. It didn't look too bad to me.

I was riding Breezy, a small and quiet cherry red Arabian mare. She wasn't very fancy. She wasn't very demonstrative. But she was very loyal, and she was very steady. I had purchased Breezy as a yearling, years ago. Something about her just grabbed me the first time I met her. Something about that huge blaze, those two tall stockings, that quiet personality. I named her Breezy in my mind before I got home, and purchased her via the telephone the next day.

Breezy refused the trail, whirling on her hindquarters and stepping away. The trail still did not

369

look that bad to me, and I pointed my mare towards it once more. I kept my legs firm on her sides and told her to move forward. I could tell that Breezy still did not care for this approach, but I had told her to go. She began down the track, head down, ears up. After taking several muddy steps down the embankment, we began to sink, Breezy's front feet becoming entrenched in the mud. We were facing downhill on the steep slope. Breezy froze but her feet continued to sink. The saddle began to slip forward, slowly creeping up Breezy's neck.

When I introduced the new filly into the herd at home, the only gelding in the small group of horses was mine. His name was Kenai, a grey Arabian who was almost completely blind in one eye. He hated her, charging her and refusing to allow her anywhere near him. Over time, as often occurs, the herd dynamics changed and Kenai accepted Breezy. You rarely saw him chase her anymore as she would graze quietly near him, slowly and steadily inching closer. Some changes in my personal life forced changes in my horse's lives as well. Kenai and Breezy moved to a new home where they grazed side by side, alone but content, the bond between them slowly deepening. Even as the bond between Kenai and Breezy grew stronger, Kenai remained always the leader. He decided where to graze, when to drink, when to go to the barn. Breezy in her quiet manner always followed where he led. One morning, when I arrived at the barn, I noticed things were very different. Breezy was leading. Kenai was following. I watched the two horses moving along one of the pasture trails. Breezy was quietly moving along, but Kenai, Kenai was moving differently, with his head at her hip. I continued to watch and I realized, no, not AT her hip, ON her hip; touching her hip, his cheek resting completely and trustingly, on her hip. When I approached my horses, I realized what had happened. Kenai had injured his good eye, which caused it to swell completely shut. He was essentially blind. Breezy had understood Kenai's need, and offered her hip and her eyes to him. She maintained physical contact with him, lending him support and guidance until he could see again.

As the saddle continued to slip forward, I realized I was in a bad situation. I was very close to going over Breezy's head, and Breezy's position was compromised, with a real possibility of my weight toppling her onto me as I fell. Bracing my hands against her neck and leaning back as much as I could, I found myself lost, with no idea what to do. Breezy understood from my body position and the loose reins, that I had no direction to offer, and acted quickly and with assurance. She lifted and pivoted her front end onto solid ground, standing perpendicular to the muddy trail. She steadied herself then chose her path, plunging through the brush to return us to the trail at the top of the embankment.

Understanding what she had done for Kenai, I stood there and rubbed her face and neck and said, "Oh, Breezy! What a good girl!"

Understanding what she had done for me, dismounting, I stood there; rubbing her face and her neck, and said, "Oh Breezy! What a good girl!"

Breezy wasn't a perfect horse. She wasn't very fancy. She wasn't very demonstrative. But Breezy was very loyal, and Breezy was very steady.

Oh, Breezy! What a good girl you were.

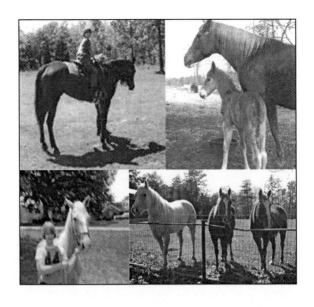

Top left going clockwise: Annie; Twist and baby; Windi, Dell and Twist; and Sheba. **For Lynette Partridge-Schneider**, animals have been more than just a lifetime adventure; her love of animals is a passion. Since her first horse, Lynette has remained involved in the equine industry. She has gained her judging certification through Purdue Multi-state Judging Clinic certified for 4-H and open all-breed horses shows, Illinois Judging clinic certified for 4-H and open all-breed horse shows, North Carolina certified for 4-H and open all-breed horses shows. After being in the human medical field for 20 years, Lynette decided to turn her full attention to animals, although having been involved with animals, especially horses and dogs, for over 30 years. She became certified as an equine/livestock appraiser, equine sport massage therapist (graduate of Equissage), equine and canine body worker plus numerous modalities including but not limited to Reiki, acupressure, trigger point and behavior problems. It is to be stressed that alternative methods are not necessarily intended to take the place of standard veterinarian medicine, but are intended to compliment standard methods. Her website is www.quailridgeequine.com.

Mares: From My First Horse to Present

by: H. Lynette Partridge-Schneider

When you are told that one of your first spoken words was "Hooree" (Horse), you are probably hooked for life. I know I have been. When your first horse is a mare, then not only are you on a big adventure; it is one you want again and again.

My first horse/mare came in to my life when I was 10 years old. Sheba was a 10 year old palomino appendix quarter horse. When I first found Sheba in the paper, she was owned by someone in the military. I went to see her and there was this special something between us. The owner saw it and even cut her price so that I could buy her and a saddle. The adventure of many years began. At the time, I had long blonde hair, my grand-daddy teased me when riding across the pasture that all you could see was blonde mane – Sheba's and mine.

Sheba was my best friend, partner in adventure and the best of teachers. She taught me about herds and how human, especially women and horses join together to form a herd. In a herd environment, the lead horses are the caretakers. These horses are the ones willing to put the safety and concerns of the group ahead of their own. As a result, the leadership is established as the herd recognizes the ones that care for them. It is also noted that attention is paid to the things important for the herd as a whole – not just themselves.

Sheba taught me the leadership role is earned. There is a quiet respect that builds between humans and horses; especially between women and horses. My first mare, Sheba, taught me respect for others, boundaries and taking care of living, breathing creature is an honor, not a chore. To go out in extreme weather to check on my horse and be rewarded with nickers of "I am glad you are here" was always worth it.

Sheba surprised me a few months after I got her with her saddle not fitting and she was becoming cinchy. The veterinarian was called and to everyone's surprise, Sheba was in foal. When she might be due was a guess at this stage of gestation. The veterinarian had said within a month or two. The previous owner had no idea she had been exposed to a stallion.

Talking about a learning experience, Sheba gave birth on Valentine's Day to a buckskin colt. An unusual snow for Georgia had hit putting 12+ inches of snow on the ground to walk through to get to the barn where I discovered the new addition.

Talking about new experiences and learning about horses, this new foal added to my education. I learned so much watching Sheba and this foal. As an eleven year old, I learned more about protectiveness, care giving as well as boundaries during the growing foal's first months. Sheba showed me patience and small lessons on training a youngster. How everyone makes mistakes, can be forgiven and given another chance.

Sheba was tolerant of my learning curves in owning horses. From the time Sheba entered my life until she went to a new girl to teach her when I went off to college, I had many lessons and adventures while growing up to an adult.

After college and starting my career, I was able to get back into horses. I had never lost that love and need of the connection between women and horses. Although, my first horse was to be a stallion, eventually I did get another mare.

Twist is an interesting mare. She had been in a pasture and had nothing done to her for a long time. I was told she was not a friendly horse. I found just the opposite. After riding her and being told they had never seen her move or act that way, I knew she and I were destined for an adventure that is continuing to this day.

Twist, like so many women, wanted to be understood and loved. Twist has the gentlest, biggest brown eyes that ached to be bright again. She seemed to looking for someone to give her a big hug.

Owning Twist taught me different lessons than Sheba. Twist taught me about gaining trust after hurt and rejection. For a mare that was described as unfriendly, would not nicker and doesn't take treats, I discovered a mare yearning for love and partnership. Twist was a mare that just wanted attention and has thrived on it. As with women that have been hurt and lost trust in others, mares are cautious of letting the guard down, again. Twist was no different. As Sheba has taught me lessons of patience and being a caretaker, Twist was in need of a leader that put her needs first.

Twist and I continued to grow into a partnership. Grooming, riding sessions, and daily chore routines brought Twist out of her shell. Twist showed she was really a chatty Cathy, nickering and wanting attention and letting you know she was ready for her treats. Working with Twist, being the leader she needed and caretaker, gaining her trust that she readily gave back.

When I bred Twist to my stallion, she proved how much she trusted me by allowing me to help when she foaled. She was and still is with her babies a proud mama. Twist likes to show off her babies and will push them toward me to show me how good she has done. Although, protective and hating weaning time, she trusts me to take care of her and her babies.

My lessons I had learned from other mares were profound, but nothing prepared me for the lessons and experiences I learned from Annie. Annie was an older mare when I got her, but full of spunk and vinegar. She was this mahogany bay colored that shined gold in the sunlight. When I got her she was a great addition to my broodmare band that I was putting together for my stallion. Annie, became so much more than just another horse, she was a teacher and friend.

With Annie, I really got into the study of alternative healing methods. Annie had bad knees from running barrels in her younger days; I learned from a fellow therapist how cold laser treatments can make a difference. This encouraged me to keep reading and studying holistic and alternative healing, which now has become a lifelong passion; all due to my horses. Annie blossomed with alternative healing, her movement improved with the cold laser as did her arthritis.

That was not her biggest lesson to teach me. Annie was like this grand lady. She was patient with babies, young riders and other horses, especially rescues. She was the caretaker of the herd and took the role of lead mare. Her methods were quiet leadership and guidance, especially with the young horses and rescues that I took in.

Annie was patient and gracious to the end. As she grew older, especially over 25 years old, she had issues with going from grass pasture to hay and would get gas colic episodes. She and I shared a special bond, so much so, that she would allow me to massage her stomach in between her legs while waiting for the veterinarian to arrive. In many cases, the episode would end before the veterinarian would get there from massaging her stomach and back. I would be right there in the middle of her legs and she would relax. She looked to me as her lead mare as the herd looked to her.

Annie's last winter was hard on her, but she taught me the greatest lesson, dying with dignity. Annie was a tough mare and enjoyed her special treatments and care as she aged. She chose her time to leave this earth. I was grateful for her doing so as I had told her I couldn't make that choice. She died taking a nap in her favorite spot. She is buried on the hill near the barn that over-looks the pasture she ruled. Annie was dignity and graciousness in the form of a horse. I miss her still and have shed tears remembering her in this story.

The year Annie passed away, I also lost my stallion. In the same year, Twist had given birth to a palomino filly; I named Windi after her grand-dam. Windi was a wonderful combination of her sire and grand-dam; just everything I had hoped to produce from my stallion. Annie had been Windi's nanny and buddy before she passed.

Windi was everything I had hoped for as a breeder of quarter horses. She had conformation, type and a brain. Boy, does she have a brain. Windi as a youngster and to date is too smart for her own good.

Windi has a personality all her own. She is a follower that would like to be a leader; she is a clown but can be serious. She makes me laugh at her antics. I can't stay mad at her even when I want to due to her playfulness and zeal for life.

Windi for all her playfulness, she is a quick learner and you have to work hard to keep her attention. She gets the lesson and wants to move ahead even before you think she is ready. Windi gave me back the excitement of the partnership women and horses have, especially women and mares have. Her sire and Annie had passed on, but Windi's demand for attention kept me going.

When Twist gave birth to Dell, Windi showed me what she had inherited from her dam – patience and a deep maternal instinct. Windi was a great nanny and buddy for Dell, taking over Annie's role. Although, she has not had a foal, I suspect Windi will be a good mother like Twist has always been.

Windi, as all the mares before her and those to come after have shared their personalities, quirks, trust and themselves with me. I feel lucky to have had these wonderful mares as teachers. From Sheba who was my childhood to Twist, Annie and Windi that were and are part of my adulthood experiences, each have taught a different lesson.

Mares have a personality and essence all their own. Each has to be handled differently, if you don't believe it – just ask one. One method of training won't work. You have to work with the individual mare and her ability to learn. Other mares have entered my life than just the ones mentioned. Most recently, the mares have been thoroughbreds instead of quarter horses. Thoroughbreds have a different energy than quarter horses, as well as completely different type personality. I am looking forward to learning new lessons with these mares. As with the mares of my past, I am certain there are more lessons in my future.

Leo Buscaglia in his book, *Living, Loving, and Learning,* describes best how the power of giving to another creature, even a horse, especially a mare can change one's life. *"Too often we underestimate the power of a touch, a smile, a kind word, a listening ear, an honest compliment, or the smallest act of caring, all of which have the potential to turn a life around."*

Marita Wassman is a founding officer, Program Director and serves as vice president for the Ride On St. Louis, Inc., Board of Directors. Marita is a certified therapeutic instructor since 1998, with the North American Riding for the Handicapped. Marita has over 30 years experience with a variety of equestrian enterprises and has trained at Rolling Acres Stable under Liz Young Millard, a member of the 1968 U.S. Equestrian Team. Marita professionally worked with Otis Brown Stables of St. Louis and LePere Thoroughbred Training Center in Illinois. Marita was the head instructor at Pecan Tree Farm in Houston, Texas. During her tenure as instructor, the number of riding students increased rapidly while she also volunteered with a special needs riding stable. Marita gained broad knowledge and experience with the equine assisted therapy stable and continues to devote herself to the industry. (Photo of Lucy by Mary Hammel)

I Love Lucy

By Marita Wassman

Ride On St. Louis (ROSL), an equine assisted therapy center, was only in its third year, so getting a phone call in regards to a possible free horse for the organization was still very new and exciting. We needed another horse for the therapy team. Main points that I remember of the conversation were, "We have an Appie mare, about 14 years old, that we must find a home for, since we are moving. She's been a good family horse for the past four years." Although the caller wished to share many details about the horse and her current life situation, she was hurried and had an urgent tone. "It's understandable having limited time when moving," I thought. We chatted about scheduling an evaluation for the horse. Surprisingly to me, she agreed to Saturday, even though she would not be home to meet me.

The morning was bright, crisp and sunny, and made for a pleasant drive to evaluate the mare. Mary, our center's barn manager (Barn Goddess a more exact title), was reading the directions to me in the car. I could see the house ahead, level with the street and a pale green valley dropping behind, sprinkled with all sizes of cedar trees. There was about an acre pond settled directly behind the house in the center of the property, and gold flashes of the sun reflected in our eyes. The whole scene made a beautiful view as we approached. We could see a small metal shed down the sloping back yard and the entire picture seemed a family horse haven, except, now coming into view — barbed wire.

It was rusty, old, crooked, and often changed from two to three strands or one and intertwined with the cedars. We scanned the new surroundings as we searched for a place to park, trying to get a glimpse of the possible new team member. The only distinctions from the gravel road and parking area to the newly constructed two-story house were some sparse blades of grass and weeds. Not wasting any time, Mary and I grabbed the tack, lunge line, and whip, along with a beach ball, and headed down the hill to the back lot. We found what would be called a gate, and after trying to figure out the wire hook, had to end up crawling between a strategic point of wire to slide over to the other side.

Across the pond, we could see two horses, darkened by the contrasting brightness, start to make their way to greet us. They were not in any hurry while they plodded each step around the pond with their heads low to the ground. My first thought was, "They must be very laid back horses." As they approached on the brown rocky path and came into better view, we could see the lead horse was the Appaloosa, Lucy, which we were to evaluate. She lacked any tone along her top line, had a dull, thick winter coat, and was in poor condition. She was about 15.2 hands and first impressions were good confirmation with thick bones. The only noticeable spark about her was a small gleam of interest in her eye for the unexpected company. Following nose to tail behind Lucy was a small Tennessee Walking Horse, bay gelding. We gasped as he came into sight. This little guy was absolutely a picture for the Humane Society ads. You could count every bone in his body. Mary and I were horrified and amazed he could still stand. Almost in panic mode, we thought, "He needs to eat." Searching quickly around the shed we found a round brown stemmy blob held together with twine. The single round bale of hay packed tight with mold, did not have any parts suitable for consumption. As we investigated more of the surroundings, a young man started his way down the hill from the house.

"Mom told me you wanted to look at Lucy."

"Yes," I confirmed as I also made introductions. I immediately questioned the feed times for the horses and found out they were fed grain a couple times a week. They had no other hay on the premises. I sensed my deluge of questions started to create some defensiveness. The care, or lack of, for the horses was appalling; but guided by my Christian upbringing, I knew I must be sensitive to the plain ignorance of the owners.

The little shed built on a gravel floor had two stalls with Dutch doors to the outside wall of the building. The teenager said they dumped a scoop of grain in each of the stalls and the horses are free to walk in or out of the stalls. No schedule, no effort to make certain of the amount each horse had. Lucy must gulp her serving down and head over to finish the other portion, too. "Could we give them some feed now?" I requested. With that, we directed each horse to enter into a stall. I shut the half doors and proceeded to meet Lucy after she had finished her little amount of grain.

She truly seemed interested in meeting me and exploring something new. I had set the boy on a mission to find any grooming supplies they owned while I patted Lucy from head to hoof. He finally came up with a brush. Sending him again, he also found a hoof pick. Lucy watched everything I did. Since she behaved with the best manners, I decided to toss the ball around to see her response (We use many toys in our therapy program and I like to check out the horse's reactions to something they may never have seen before). Lucy only moved toward the ball to investigate it better and was wholly pleased to let the ball roll over her back and hit the chat floor. This was a wonderful reaction we love to see; no fear or hesitation, only interest.

Meeting no resistance with tacking up, we were set to move on to the next phase. I usually plan to lunge the horse first. This helps to evaluate what training the horse may have had, reveals more of its personality, and gives me a good view of its gait and movement before I hop on. Finding a small level area next to the shed, I led Lucy out. Giving her some lead on the lunge, I had her walk some circles. I don't think she had ever been asked this before, but was quick to understand and did not seem to mind. "Ok, let's see what kind of trot you have." Giving two clicks and a flick of the whip, I received no reaction. Repeating again, she still offered no trot or even quickened pace. "Well," Thinking to my self, "I guess I need to be clearer with my request since she hasn't got a clue." Now moving into driving body language and getting close enough to tap the whip, I could tell Lucy understood what I wanted. She did not try to spin out, flee, stop or what I hoped for, break into a trot. Puzzled with this "nothing" reaction, I tried to read her face and movement. She did not appear lazy; she did not even get defensive. She had the same tempo walk as earlier that morning from the path around the pond and to the food waiting in her stall. As I assessed their working conditions – it must be the footing! Although it appeared to have some grassy/weedy growth, the horses were standing on rocks with only enough powdery dirt to camouflage the hard lumps. This mare knew that when she trotted, it hurt; and no matter what I wanted, it was not worth her feet hurting.

Again, I started with questions. The boy said they mainly rode the horses on the road. "I have to really make her run, and she'll only do it for a little bit." He implied to tarnish Lucy's character. "Do you have any place that is flat *without* rocks?" I hoped there was a secret spot behind some cedar. "The top of the hill on the side of the house has some dirt," He offered. We headed up the other side of the lot. As we led Lucy, she confirmed our suspicion as we watched her strategically place each hoof step. She had learned exactly how to protect her feet to walk on the rocky ground. The top of the hill only offered a straight dirt stretch along the barbed wired to trot her out in hand. I did not get much of an evaluation in, but loved Lucy's attitude and really just wanted to save her. And what about her pasture mate?

You can imagine the non-stop chatter on the car ride home. We wanted to report this situation to the Humane Society immediately, but would the family be offended and cancel the possible donation? They were moving out of state anyway. Mary and I decided the sooner we could get the horse donated, the better she would be. We also thought that if necessary, we would offer to take the TW gelding just to rescue him, too.

Lucy has more confidence than any horse I have ever met. This quality benefits Ride On St. Louis in many ways. Being the Alpha mare, she keeps watch over the other seven horses in our herd and keeps the peace. Although five of the horses are easy going, independent, and can be led away from the herd without excitement, they all still depend on Lucy. When she is in the pasture, there is an increased calmness. When anything new comes along, she is the leader who checks it out for the herd. She chases away stray dogs and greets trucks or equipment with eagerness.

During one session at our program, all the staff and volunteers laughed because they could not believe that Lucy wanted to challenge a rhino. Ok, it was an enlarged, laminated photo of a rhino tacked up on the fence. Our riders were playing a matching game with animal cards. Lucy stood with her neck arched and snorted at the lifelike picture. "This can't be happening with a photo," I thought, but she had no reaction with the zebra, giraffe or hippo! We even moved the picture to our indoor arena for the next day's classes, and she had the same reaction! I also witnessed her standing in cross ties while a stall door literally fell off its hinges. She and I noticed the slow, slight tipping of the huge door at the same moment. With uncanny accuracy, she stepped her body a few inches to the side as the door came crashing to the floor missing her belly by mere inches. Her head stayed centered in the ties. That was it, nothing else, merely a step over to be out of the way. I was more surprised than she.

We have many different riders who benefit from riding Lucy. Some clients who are in wheel chairs gain trunk strength from her steady and smooth gait. Because she has a large girth and round back, her broad body offers the most secure base for these children with poor balance. She is very trustworthy for our independent sport riders who lack leg strength. They need a dependable mount that will not spook or make abrupt moves that could topple their seat. Lucy is terrific!

Oh, I mentioned we have eight horses — six and Lucy are very calm. However, the last horse is my thoroughbred mare. She is another story in herself, a huge scaredy–cat that is afraid of her shadow. She also was in need of rescuing about 17 years ago, so how fortunate it is to have Lucy to balance it all out!

When we hauled Lucy home seven years ago, the vet was concerned with her respiratory rate. She probably had not done anything to work her lungs or heart in the four years of living on rock. We started long reining, riding, and conditioning her with good food and vitamins. She is beautiful now, and for your peace of mind, the TW gelding went to a new home shortly after we adopted Lucy!

Lucy is now 22 and I am seeing some signs of aging. I hate to think what will happen when she is no longer our fearless leader. I know that somehow, God will keep ROSL's herd happy when the time comes that Lucy is no longer around. For now – I Love Lucy!

About Ride On St. Louis...

ROSL began in 1998 as a small backyard operation on two acres in the director's backyard in Oakville, Missouri. In 2001, ROSL relocated the program to the Estate of the late Fred and Mabel-Ruth Anheuser, heirs of the family that founded the Anheuser-Busch Company. The use of this facility is through courtesy of the Anheuser Permanent Fund. In addition, the Anheuser Permanent Fund donated the construction of The Buttercup indoor riding arena, named in honor of the Anheuser's World Champion Saddlebred. ROSL will always hold deep appreciation and admiration to Ms. Dorothy Hatfield, the niece of Mr. & Mrs. Anheuser, who was instrumental in granting this tremendous gift to ROSL and the surrounding community.

The program mission is to use hippotherapy (therapy with the aid of a horse) and/or therapeutic horsemanship to achieve emotional, mental and physical benefits for the developmentally and physically disabled, as well as the disadvantaged youth of the community. Ride On St. Louis was founded to serve all for the greater glory, honor, and love of God. We value the use of prayer and recognize our dependence on God. The center promotes volunteerism, the willing spirit of service, the offering of good works, and the duty of caring and the giving of love with an openness of heart to receive and know God's Peace and Joy in return. www.rideonstl.org

Sylvia Roper and her husband Joel (married 39 years) are members of Equestrian Ministries International, South Carolina chapter (www.scequestrianministries.com) and Sylvia is a past secretary/treasurer. They also are members of Grace Equestrian Ministries, one of seven fellowships under the SCEM umbrella. They were instrumental in starting the local Happy Trails Cowboy Church (www.htcowboychurch.com). They have four Tennessee Walking Horses on their Dry Ridge Farm, plus a gelding currently out on loan, and they belong to Piedmont Saddle Club. Their daughter Joy and her husband Gary have two children, Kevan (age five) and Mikalah (age nine). Sylvia's other interests include writing, both fiction and non-fiction, and she belongs to The Christian Writers Den, a local club. Sylvia's current equine riding partner is Shadows Night Watcher (Shadow), a 15.3 hand, twelve-year-old gelding and former show horse. She also rides Ericka's Precious Moment (Precious), a 14.3 hand seven-year-old mare that her granddaughter Mikalah now claims as her own. Sylvia works part time as an Administrative Assistant. She teaches 4th grade Sunday school at Standing Springs Baptist Church, Simpsonville, SC. Sylvia and her husband have ridden in South and North Carolina, Georgia, Kentucky, Virginia, and Florida.

On the Winds of Heaven With Abbey

By Sylvia Roper

"Delight yourself also in the Lord, and he will give you the desires and secret petitions of your heart." [1]

B old, black and beautiful. The words formed in my mind as my husband and I watched her go by, neck arched, large head nodding, tail fanning out behind her. The cold, wet mist of that Saturday afternoon didn't deflate my husband's enthusiasm one iota as he watched her with two giggling girls upon her back. She glided by in the damp vapor like a magical horse found only in dreams.

She's gone now and this narrative is a tribute to her. We called her Abbey, and this is her story.

In the summer of 1994, my husband's handsome gelding, Blaze, developed ringbone arthritis, and was no longer serviceable as a trail riding companion.

We had three horses at the time: Blaze, Shadow and Lady. Blaze and Shadow were twelve years old. Lady was around twenty and retired. All were Tennessee Walking Horses. An avid rider, Joel needed another horse, and quickly. So we began asking the Father to lead us to a new horse.

I think my husband prayed more than I did. I really didn't want to bother our Heavenly Father with such an insignificant, pitiful request, when so much hurt and pain goes on in the world. I mean, He's a really busy God, right? His time is hectic with healing folks' bodies and spirits, anointing pastors, saving souls — would He really be interested in our selfish request for a horse?

My husband's faith, however, was stronger than mine, so he did his own private praying, asking God to lead him to the right horse, the horse He'd chosen.

On a cold, wet Saturday afternoon in January 1995, we drove to an auction in Oconee County, just to look around. We didn't even take a trailer with us. As we walked through all the holding stalls and looked at each horse, we weren't drawn to any particular one. There were black ones, spotted ones, bays and grays . . . geldings, stallions, mares and yearlings; quarter horses, grade horses, mules, ponies and donkeys.

What my husband wanted, however, was a black Tennessee Walking Horse, preferably a mare. The horses being offered for sale that damp afternoon didn't meet his standards, so I thought that God wasn't going to answer our prayers – at least not that day.

I was wrong, as I would discover later.

Our search took us outside into the open lot, where we watched different horses being paraded around, their owners hoping to catch the eye of a potential buyer. Two teenage girls were astride her, guiding her with only a rope hooked to her halter. We watched as she sashayed by. Awestruck, my husband and I watched as they rode her back and forth several times in the misty rain. She moved with the style of a show horse beneath her amateur riders.

"I believe that's a Walking Horse," my husband said, as he watched her. I agreed. She moved with exquisite, fluid grace, her head nodding in unison with her four-beat gait. Convinced he'd found a jewel among stones, Joel walked away to find the person who'd brought the horse to the auction.

Long moments later, he returned, all excited. She was indeed a Tennessee Walking Horse and the owner had decided to sell her for an odd reason. Telling me about it, my husband was a bit incredulous, "They said they didn't want her because she won't trot! Can you believe that?" He turned to stare as the teenagers rode by again . . . on the elegant black mare who refused to do a gait that was unnatural for her.

Tennessee Walking Horses are not supposed to trot. They are capable of several gaits – the canter, the rack, the gallop, to name a few. However, what they are famous for is the four-beat gait called a flat-foot walk, or, in higher gear, a running walk. It's a very a smooth ride that does not bounce the rider up and down as the trot does.

There was one drawback: she was within a few months of being fifteen years old. My previously excited husband became somewhat discouraged. He'd wanted a horse no older than ten. Still, he liked what he saw — an intelligent, good-looking mare, exhibiting a willingness to go, with the smooth, gliding gait he desired.

It was time for the auction to begin and the pretty black mare that had captured my husband's heart was led away. We went inside the dusty barn and took our seats on the stadium benches with the other bidders. Many horses were shown that afternoon, but we eagerly waited for the spirited mare with the white sock on her right hind foot. It was the only white spot on her otherwise jet black coat.

Then she was ridden in, and we watched, holding our breaths, listening to the auctioneer, sure that we'd hear "Sold!" at any moment. Her price was in the $800 range, not a bad price, but she was a no-sell. We thought perhaps it was her age – or her breed. The quarter horse is the most popular breed in this state, not the TWH. Looking back later, I understood the reason she didn't sell; God had intervened. She was there for my husband and no one else.

Joel did not bid on her. I looked at him, an unasked question forming in my mind. As though he heard me, he said "I'm not going bid on her. She's too old." He wanted her but he was letting her age cloud his judgment.

We watched as she was led away, rejected, unappreciated – back to the dimly lit stalls. My husband may have been uncertain, as well as I, but our Heavenly Father's decision was unquestionable. Of course, neither of us knew this, because we weren't viewing the situation through spiritual eyes.

He had led us to His choice, but we couldn't see past the number 15. She was middle-aged, over-the-hill, no longer youthful. My husband wanted a young horse, full of stamina and fire. Sometimes we can't see what is right in front of us because we're looking through a smoky glass – one clouded with doubt and hesitation.

There were no other horses that captured our interest, so we left the auction, disappointed that God hadn't answered our prayer, or so we thought. On the way home, we stopped at a restaurant about thirty minutes from the auction barn. During the drive to the restaurant, in the restaurant and during our meal, my husband kept talking about the horse we'd watched and admired and left behind. He bemoaned the fact that he hadn't bid on her.

"I should have bought that horse," he said, over and over. He was 99% sure that she was God's answer to his prayer. She was black, his favorite color for a horse. She was a mare, which he preferred. She had exhibited the ability to do the flat foot and running walk, even under the hands of two inexperienced teenagers. She was a Tennessee Walker, the only breed he would consider purchasing. However, there was the age factor. Still, he felt deep inside that she belonged with him. He was at war with himself.

Finally, I said, "Well, if you feel that strongly, let's go back when we finish here. If she's still there, we'll take that as a sign from God that she belongs with us." My one concern was that she'd be gone – that we'd missed our chance. But I kept that thought to myself.

To our relief, she was still standing in a stall, as though patiently waiting for our return. We petted her, stroking her head and neck. My husband spoke softly to her, asking her if she would like to come home with us. Her large, soft, brown eyes seemed to telepathically send a confirming message to my husband, as though she was saying, "I've been waiting for you. What took you so long?"

We quickly found the owner and told him that we were interested in the "black walking horse." He was busy talking with others and didn't respond right away. Again, I worried that the horse had already been sold. We waited an agonizing two minutes before he turned his full attention on us. "I'll come down fifty dollars and no more," he said rather brusquely.

We were expecting to pay the full price. Not one to argue, Joel whipped out his checkbook and quickly wrote the check, becoming the proud new owner of a fifteen year old mare with a thick black coat, big, trusting eyes and one white sock. Then it hit us . . . we hadn't brought a trailer! We talked incessantly about our "new horse" all the way home and back, finally convinced that God had sent us to Oconee County on that particular afternoon just so we would discover the beautiful Tennessee Walking Horse who wouldn't *trot* for its owners.

We led her to our trailer and someone offered to help load her, as she was looking just a tad anxious. "All she needs is a good shot of penicillin," the stranger said as she stepped into the trailer.

Red flags went up. Doubt showed its ugly face. I thought, did God really lead us to this horse, or were we just too eager to take one back home with us? True, she was pretty, talented, and she was a TWH; but if she was sick . . . just what had we bought? Why would she need penicillin? I pushed the disturbing thoughts aside and joined my excited husband in the truck.

"Do you think she's sick?" I asked him, quoting the stranger's remark. "Naw," he replied. "She's just tired and hungry. She'll be fine." Okay, I thought – if he's not concerned, I won't be either. I dropped the subject.

As we drove home, we contemplated various pet names for our newest addition. Her registered name, according to her papers, was Stocks Ebony Lady. Stocks didn't seem appropriate, we already had a horse named Lady, and Ebony just didn't have the right ring. We took turns suggesting different names, and nothing sounded quite right. After a while, I suggested 'Ebbie', a play on her middle name. Over the roar of the diesel engine, my husband thought I said 'Abbey' and the name clicked. It seemed to suit her; there was no further discussion.

After we'd gotten home and put Abbey in a dry stall, with grain, hay, and water, we went into the house, still feeling the excitement of having a 'new' horse. We'd even decided that 15 years wasn't all that old, anyway. My husband sat in his recliner to study her registration papers. Within moments, he was exclaiming in an excited voice, "Do you know her father, Super Stock, was the TWHBEA[2] World's Grand Champion in 1977?" Abbey had excellent blood lines. God had supplied a horse with just the right qualities, and added a bonus – a horse with a stunning pedigree. Joel was in seventh heaven.

As time progressed, I became convinced, as did my husband, that God brought us and Abbey together on that cold, rainy afternoon for several reasons, the main one being to teach us to trust Him. God gave my husband the kind of horse he'd wished for . . . gentle, intelligent, willing, a horse who enjoyed being ridden. God also knew that I would someday need a trusty, patient horse to help me overcome my inherent fear of riding. He could see down the road and know that we'd have a grandchild who would be a horse lover like us and that Abbey would be her teacher. Lastly, I believe God led us to Abbey so that her life would be saved. Had Abbey not come home with us that cold, wet rainy night, I am firmly convinced she would not have lived to fulfill God's plans for her.

My husband began riding her around our home, which at that time, was surrounded by a forest, with a creek running through the property. He was testing her, to see just what her abilities were, and to check out her gaits. As he began down the hill toward the creek, Abbey balked. Up she went, high into the air on her back legs. Down she came, and again my husband asked her to cross the creek. Abbey again resisted. She looked so powerful, so determined to have her way, but in the end she obeyed my husband's command and crossed the creek. Under her new master's experienced hands, she began her training.

Weekly, sometimes daily, Joel rode her on a track he'd built on our land. Around and around they went, until she was doing the slow walk and the running walk perfectly. As he worked with her, he discovered that she was exactly what he'd prayed for. He'd found his next trail horse.

Soon we were trail riding again, me on my gelding, Shadow, and Joel astride Abbey. She exhibited great stamina and a willingness to go. She loved long dirt roads, where she would go into her running walk, with her head nodding and tail flying out. I would watch as my husband rode ahead of me, his body never moving as he sat tall in the saddle.

After a few trail rides, we noticed that Abbey breathed heavily, and would cough a few times at the very beginning, but as she 'got her wind' the coughing ceased. During late spring, we took Abbey and Shadow on a trail ride in the mountainous terrain of Oconee County, to an area locals refer to as Rocky Gap. To my delight, my husband let me, the novice, ride his new horse. While climbing a hill, Abbey began coughing violently – heaving, as some would call it. It really worried me. What is wrong with her, I wondered. Did we buy a sick and dying horse?

"Are you trying to kill my horse," my husband asked quietly as we came to a plateau and stopped. I could hear the concern in his voice. Abbey was breathing hard, but we had just finished some strenuous riding. After a fifteen minute rest, she seemed to be okay. However, we both agreed that a visit to the vet was in order.

The vet's diagnosis was disturbing. Abbey was indeed sick. I had never heard of COPD, chronic obstructive pulmonary disease. I listened to the diagnosis with a breaking heart, and watched as Abbey coughed up a green, vile-looking discharge after being given a shot. The vet said that Abbey had been left untreated after becoming ill with a respiratory illness, resulting in the disease and irreversible lung damage. I felt terrible. We had been riding a sick horse. She'd had an infection and we had not known it. However, Abbey was a fighter. After the shot, she began to get better.

We removed her from the barn, with its dusty environment, and left her outdoors. She fared better in open air. And with medication, proper nutrition and lots of TLC, Abbey proved that she was God-sent. Although the coughing never went away entirely, the infection did, and she coughed less and not as violently. She became my husband's all-time favorite horse, taking him on many trail rides all over South Carolina, North Carolina, Georgia, Kentucky, Tennessee, and Virginia.

In the fall of 1996, our daughter joined us on a camping trip/trail ride adventure at Manchester State Forest in the lower part of the state. We took Abbey, Shadow and a racking mare I had purchased the summer of 1996 and was afraid to ride. Our daughter, who had inherited her father's riding skills, rode Beauty with aplomb.

On our second day there, my husband let me ride his beloved Abbey. Joel rode Shadow, as our daughter followed on Beauty. As we sped down one of the red clay roads that Manchester State Forest is famous for, I had no idea that we were going at breakneck speed. All I knew was that I was sitting astride the smoothest, fastest horse I'd ever ridden, without a care in the world.

After a few moments I heard my daughter yell out, "Mother, slow down. We can't keep up!" She sounded far away.

I didn't want to stop. Abbey was so easy to ride. All I had to do was sit there as she flew down the road. I was still a novice rider, but that didn't concern Abbey. She knew what to do and she did it very well. My husband told me later that my hair flew straight back. He told me that I had no idea how fast Abbey and I were going.

I had only one word for the experience: exhilarating. We dubbed her as our "road horse" because she excelled when ridden on an open, flat road of packed soil. She did equally well on the grassy surfaces, or sandy trails.

At age 18, Abbey produced a look-a-like filly, Stocks Midnight Glory, or Dixie as we call her. During Dixie's nursing stage, Joel rode Beauty. I still was not fully confident with her. At my husband's coaxing, however, I did finally learn to trust Beauty, and we eventually became good friends and trail partners. But that's another story.

A few years later, after Beauty's untimely death due to colic, I once again looked to Abbey. She had become our granddaughter's teacher, but I was without a horse. At age twenty-one, Abbey willingly became my new full-time riding partner.

When Abbey was twenty-two years old, I rode her at Mount Rogers, VA, known for its, rocky mountainous terrain. At that time, Dixie was four years old. Sure-footed Abbey, with her damaged lungs, and advanced years, fared much better than her offspring, who stumbled and fell among the rocky trails. Dixie was also afraid of cows, which we encountered along some of the trails at Mount Rogers. Nothing bothered Abbey. She just looked straight ahead, intent on her way, never flinching, never hesitating, always eager to go forward.

I began to bond with Abbey. For two years, she was my trail horse. Under her tutorage, I gained confidence in my riding skills. She made me feel secure and safe in a group of riders. Her smooth gait made it easy to stay seated and balanced in the saddle. I began to love horseback riding more and more. When we went with groups, it was Abbey who set the pace, leading the pack.

As I think of her I am reminded that God answers prayers in ways and for reasons that we do not at first discern. Abbey needed a good family to take care of her for her remaining years on earth. My husband needed a good natured, intelligent, willing horse. God also knew that I would need a good horse at some point in my life – one that I could trust and depend on.

Our granddaughter, Mikalah, was born in 1998. We discovered, early on, that she'd been born with a deep love for horses. When Mikalah was five and Abbey was twenty-three, they became a team. Phase three of God's plan had come to fruition.

At age twenty-five, Abbey was still working. She had been trained several years earlier, quite easily, to pull a wagon. Over the years, we took her to parades, where she patiently pulled the wagon down streets lined with adults and children, their faces aglow with the spirit of Christmas.

She also pulled the wagon at church festivals where she stood still afterwards, enjoying the praise and hugs of delighted senior citizens and children. She was steady as a rock at an outdoor Christmas pageant, pretending to be the Roman steed to a Roman Soldier (my husband). The camel was of no concern to her. With arched neck and flared nostrils, she played the part to perfection.

In 2006, we decided to retire her. She was 26 years old. Her labored breathing had become a major concern. The medication was doing little to help ease the struggle to inhale and exhale. Her stomach muscles worked overtime to expel the air from in her lungs. Still, some days she appeared to be fine and would run across the pasture, right behind her daughter Dixie, and Precious, a mare I had purchased in 2002.

We had hoped that she would live long enough to teach our grandson, Kevan, not to fear horses, but to love and respect them. He did not inherit his sister's affection for horses. If Abbey's lungs hold out, I told myself, she'll teach Kevan to get over his fear and he too, will learn the joys associated with caring for and partnering with one God's greatest creatures . . . and perhaps His favorite. But Abbey's time on earth was coming to an end.

The heat wave of August 2007 took its toll. It was 102 degrees the day Abbey became ill. Her old, damaged lungs gave out, and the struggle to breath led to colic. I prayed for God to heal her. After all, she wasn't arthritic, she wasn't thin as some older horses become, plus she was so loved and so needed. We weren't ready to let her go.

The morning before her last day, I watched her run in from the pasture, to be fed with Dixie and Precious. She seemed fine. Look at old Abbey go, I thought.

The next morning, she was too sick to stand for very long. Every breath was a struggle and she was in great pain with colic. Although weak and tired, she obediently loaded onto the trailer, standing strong during the forty-five minute trip to the vet clinic. We hoped and prayed for the best. We weren't ready to give her up. God had given her to us for twelve years – couldn't he let her stay a few more? This thought kept running through my mind. She was old, but the thought of losing her hurt too much.

Two vets were waiting for us at the clinic, and immediately gave Abby their full attention. Aware of her COPD, one of them administered a steroid shot to ease her labored breathing. An IV was started and we were told to go home and wait. The love and tender care they were showing for our beloved friend gave me hope.

Well aware of her long struggle with COPD, one of them commented about her will to survive. "She's a fighter," he said. We said our goodbyes to our friend and left. We were optimistic as we returned home. The vet had promised to call with news – good or bad. We prayed for a miracle.

"She's too far gone." Those were the words my husband heard at 2:00 PM, on August 7, 2007. Heartbreaking words that could lead to only one decision: euthanasia. Unwilling to make a decision without my presence, he told the vet he'd call back, and waited for me to get home from work.

At 2:15 PM, I entered our home and immediately asked about our beloved mare. "It's not good," he said quietly. "She's not going to make it."

I made the fateful call. "How is she?" I asked, already knowing the answer. "Not good," the vet said. "She took a turn for the worse. She's in a great deal of pain."

With tears streaming down my face, I gave them permission to administer the shot that would ease her pain and take her life. My husband and I could not bring ourselves to return to the clinic. Seeing her loaded onto the "death trailer" and being put down wasn't something we wanted to experience. We'd done that with Beauty, and the memory wasn't pleasant. We'd said our last goodbye that morning. Neither of us wanted to see her as a sick, old horse, unable to get her breath, groaning in agony with the pains of colic. We preferred to remember Abbey as she'd once been. It made the pain of loss easier to endure.

At 5:00 PM that evening, we fed our remaining horses. Even though there was one less horse to feed, the task seemed more difficult. A beloved member of our horse family was gone. Her feed bucket hung on the fence – empty. Our other horses seemed unusually quiet, as though mourning the loss of their equine friend, the grandmother of the herd.

A few days after she was put down, my husband told me one morning that he'd dreamed of riding Abbey and that she'd been young and healthy. My heart broke for him. She had been, after all, his horse. He had simply loaned her to me and our granddaughter.

Abbey had fulfilled her purpose. She had done what God had intended. She brought love, happiness and fun into our lives; and memories that will be cherished for a very long time. She brought my husband many pleasurable hours of riding. She gave us a beautiful filly, as black and beautiful as her mother, to love and enjoy. She helped this greenhorn rider to overcome an innate fear of horses. My granddaughter learned her basic skills upon Abbey's strong back. Our daughter, Joy, even had her time with Abbey. She was the horse we would choose when friends and family brought their children for an afternoon ride in the yard.

Some mornings, during these chilly fall days, before the cool mist disappears, I see the ghost of Abbey running across the pasture, her head high, her tail fanning out behind her, whinnying into morning light, welcoming the dawn of day. Stocks Ebony Lady, affectionately called Abbey, is gone. The date and time of her death is forever burned into our memories. She will not be forgotten.

I don't know if my husband will precede me on our journey to the mansions God is preparing for his children, but I do believe Abbey will be waiting there, with healthy lungs and a spirit of fire to welcome the first arrival. I believe my mare Beauty will be there too, and Blaze, and all our other horses we've lost, and that my husband and I will someday take turns riding them, and together we will go for unforgettable rides in pristine forests and down long roads that seem to go on forever.

While you're waiting Abbey, run through the green grass and down those long, straight roads. Throw your tail high, raise your head and whinny at your equine buddies. Flare your nostrils and breathe deeply, filling your healed lungs with Heavenly air. Someday, I'll climb upon your strong back again... and we'll ride on the winds of Heaven.

[1] The Amplified Bible. Psalm 37:4
[2] Tennessee Walking Horse Breeders and Exhibitors Association

Ginger's story is another by Betsy Kelleher. Ginger is a special old mare that belongs to her husband, Russell, shown here in the saddle. Ginger is a newer addition to the Kelleher's horse family, but she has proven to be just what Russ wanted in a kind, safe trail horse.

Ginger's a Keeper

By Betsy Kelleher

Our first sight of the mare we were wanting to buy for my husband wasn't the best. Tied to a tree, her ears were back at a nearby horse, and she looked nothing like the photos we'd seen. Those photos, taken the previous summer, showed a lovely chestnut or bay glow. Now, the first day of April, she still had a shaggy coat, rough and dry, almost sorrel. And she definitely looked all of her almost 20 years.

My husband wanted to drive on by and forget the deal. I felt we needed to give the mare a chance. I had driven almost three hours against the wind (later learned we had gusts up to 50 mph), pulling a two horse trailer with my gelding in there alone to meet these people at a park where we could try out this mare. I wasn't ready to turn around and go back without being sure we didn't want her.

It would be my husband's first mare, sort of. He had bought another mare three years earlier because he fell in love with her at first sight, but then she turned out to have a headstrong alpha nature that he didn't like! I ended up riding her and falling in love with her myself. Then he bought a young gelding, that had recently bucked him off, and now I was also riding that horse.

After purposely not looking for a mare for a long time, I had finally decided that maybe that was exactly what my husband needed. His back problems from handling bales of hay had prompted his doctor to advise him to stop riding. But we didn't want to give it up, so I was looking for a safe, reliable mount with an easy gait, and he wanted a horse he could have a good relationship with. I had talked to the owners of this mare a few times, and liked all the answers except one. I had asked if she had an affectionate nature, and I was told, she doesn't come to you when called, but she won't run away from you. And I told myself, maybe you can't have everything. Safety first this time. She was a registered Missouri Fox Trotter, about 15 hands, and had a nice smooth gait. She had been ridden by their young son for 4 years and was no longer able to keep up with his desire to go fast for several hours of family trail riding.

My husband rode Ginger that day, and I rode my Rocky. It was cool and windy, but we had a nice ride for almost an hour. Heading back to our parking area, we were riding on the road when I saw two motor-cycles coming toward us. If I'd been riding my mare, I might have had a heart attack on the spot! I wasn't sure what Rocky would do, and I was very happy to see his reaction. Ears forward and alert, Rocky watched the two motorcycles pass without moving. Ginger also stood quietly, seemingly oblivious of the noisy things. We went back to our trailer and loaded her up.

Ginger has since shed her winter coat and "Boss Man's Beauty" has emerged. For six months, we have watched her attitude become more friendly, more accepting, and more alert. Her eyes show increased interest and energy. I tried several different supplements for her arthritis, and the current combination of Missing Link Plus and MSM has made a noticeable difference. Missing Link is a vitamin for older horses and the Plus is glucosamine. I also give her a supplement for hooves.

Her hooves were good and strong, though dry, but her frogs were in very bad condition and the summer heat and dryness of 2007 almost destroyed her heels. Fighting thrush and cracked heels at the same time was a challenge, but I finally saw improvement, and I will monitor her feet more closely from now on. I've always believed in keeping a salt block in the stall, but taking out two full muck buckets of wet sawdust every morning had its toll on my husband's back. We removed the salt block, and I started adding minerals in her feed. The drier stall helped with her thrush problems and my husband's attitude!

Another reason the thrush got bad was because I couldn't pick up her back feet for more than two seconds, especially the left rear! I discovered I could pick up that foot and bring it forward with less trouble, yet she would stomp it down quickly when

I brought it back. The vet said this might indicate arthritis in the hock.

One day, the crossties weren't available and I had to work in a different area, so I asked Russ to hold her. He was stroking her face and she loved it. I did the front two feet and went back for the right hind. I noticed she was standing with that foot resting on the toe, instead of standing flat footed as usual. I knelt down and picked out the foot with my hoof pick, and she left it still while I worked. I applied the thrush medicine and she stood quietly. Then I went to the left hind, the foot I had trouble with. I told Ginger, if she would tip up that toe like she did the other one, I wouldn't have to pick it up. I knelt down beside that foot, and pushed on the heel. She promptly tipped up the foot, resting it on the toe, just as I wanted. I was amazed, but very happy that this had worked out so well. I cleaned out the frog and she stood there quietly, still enjoying my husband's stroking and petting. I was finally able to apply the thrush medicine adequately to the right place!

I couldn't wait to see if Ginger would do it again, to tip up that foot for me, resting on the toe, so I could work on it. Previously, I had struggled to pick up the foot while she edged away from me. Even when I picked it up, she stomped the foot down before I could do anything with it! I wasn't sure if she was being protective, or if it was a physical problem with her hip or leg. But now I had a way of doing what needed to be done! And yes, she did cooperate better after that, sometimes needing patient encouragement, but letting me work on the foot as she tipped it on edge. And when the farrier does her feet, he puts that foot up on his stand, with the canvas sling to hold it, and she accepts that.

It didn't hurt that my husband was rubbing and stroking her head. It seemed to distract and calm her immeasurably, almost putting her to sleep! I've always believed that when a horse and owner work through problems together, they bond from it. When a horse has a problem and the owner is able to fix it, I believe the horse knows she is loved and cared for.

A vet recommended giving Bute for a week, then adding MSM to her feed, to see how it might affect her ability to pick up the hind feet. I soon discovered that I could pick up both back feet and she could hold them up for me while I worked on them.

The next time my husband and I rode together, he had a different Ginger. As we rode, she kept up with my gelding instead of lagging behind. As I rode a bit faster up a little incline in the trail, Russ was surprised when Ginger cantered up without being asked. After the ride, I was able to clean out all four hooves and Ginger actually held up that left hind while I rubbed in a conditioner and she did not put it down until I was finished! I knew something was working. Picking up her feet before a ride isn't as easy as picking up her feet after the ride. So gradually, we are figuring out what the problems and solutions are.

This old mare is the perfect trail horse for my husband! She is as bombproof as they come, and doesn't mind when I take off in a faster gait and leave her behind. She also has a nice smooth gait when asked. Russ can relax and enjoy our rides now, and he says he loves her more with every ride. I am overjoyed to see the bond my husband has developed with this mare. I was also able to put a young inexperienced granddaughter on her in the outdoor arena one day, and I trusted Ginger to take care of her as she rode all by herself.

Ginger is turned out with my two geldings and gets along fine with them. At first, she squealed quite a bit now and then, even when they weren't anywhere near her! The "Moody Mare" supplement from Silver Lining Herbs seems to have ended that. I hardly ever hear her squeal anymore. My old gelding is especially fond of her, and they usually stand together at one end of the paddock, while Rocky goes his separate way.

One day we rode past a pile of junk which included a bed mattress wrapped in plastic that was torn and waving in the wind. My gelding stopped suddenly upon seeing it, maybe 50 feet ahead, and clearly was saying he did not want to go further. But Ginger walked on by us, past the pile of junk, just looking at it and walking on without missing a step. Rocky walked on beside her, staying close. Next time we passed that pile of junk with the mattress, Rocky hardly noticed. Guess he figured if Ginger didn't see anything scary about it, he wouldn't either. She was a quieting influence when Rocky needed it.

I have traced Ginger's bloodlines on the internet, including Zane Gray and Zane's Boss Man, and also Banner's Shepherd and Banner's Jubilee. I have tried to contact former owners, with questions regarding a couple things that concern me. I would like to know how many babies she has had, and if she has ever been used under harness. There are some hard lumpy pads, maybe calcium deposits, near her tail and on her side.

She was cinchy, the former owner had told us, but not too bad. At first, she would swing her head around each time we fastened the girth, even though we were careful to take it slow. Then I worked to figure out whether this was a painful thing or just a past memory. I pushed on every bump and spot on her back, with no reactions. And she has several bumps. At first, I thought they might be uncomfortable under the saddle. Next, I put a surcingle on her, tightening it very gradually, noting that it did not go over any of the bumps. Not much problem there, either. I told my husband to just put the saddle on her back and wait a few minutes before tightening it up. That worked wonders, which proved to me that we were simply dealing with a memory of past pain. The cinchiness is practically gone now.

A mare like Ginger is a special creature. She is a sweet old gal, even if she does assert herself at times with a lifted foot. She has never connected, but she is simply able to say "get away" when she needs to. She seems to be happy in her current situation, and I tell her almost every day that I am glad she is ours. When she came, she would only accept the grain-based horse treats. Now, she loves carrots, apples, and mints as well. I was told she was out on pasture with other horses, without grain or supplements. She now has grain and grass hay, with several different supplements, is gaining weight which she needed, and her summer hair coat is shiny like the photos we had seen.

The way she rides with my husband is worth everything we can do to keep her comfortable and safe for as long as possible.

AnnMarie Cross is cofounder and president of Crosswinds Equine Rescue, Inc., a 501c3 nonprofit horse rescue in Illinois. AnnMarie holds a BS from Cornell University in Animal Science, and has been riding, showing, and training horses on and off for 20 years. Whenever possible, CWER focuses their efforts on rehabilitating and retraining "dangerous" and "unfix-able" horses to become productive members of the equine community. Like most small nonprofits, CWER survives on donations from a small number of dedicated supporters, and every dollar makes a difference. Unlike most nonprofits, CWER pays no salaries and has no mortgage. The Cross family owns the property personally, so that every dollar goes toward helping the horses. CWER proudly boasts of placing more than 35 horses in its first three years into "normal" lives — as lesson horses, show mounts, trail riders, and a few retired companions. Visit www.cwer.org for more information.

Adapting an Alpha Authority
(Taming the Terrible Tess)
By AnnMarie Cross

A dominant mare can be an intimidating creature. Millions of years of evolution have told
her it is her job to lead her herd, to prod the timid,
to control the aggressive, to protect the foals. Her
dam, her dam's dam, and every other dam she's ever
met has told her that her genetics have given her this
place of power and responsibility. Then, in walks
some foolish human who thinks that simply because
he or she provides a tub of grain now and then to
this mare who perhaps decides to be so kind as to
allow them to touch her glorious coat or sit upon her
majestic back, that suddenly the human is in charge
of the herd and she is to step down.

Just as instinct teaches a human parent to grasp
for a child's arm in a moment of danger, every
instinct in our alpha mare's body tells her to put such
a foolish beast in its place and advise it to get out of

her way so that she can go back to her job. It is her duty to manage her herd and protect the future of her little band. We can't expect the filly of an alpha mare raised in a normal herd to step away and give up her authority without training and cooperation, any more than we can expect any horse to understand to yield to pressure on a lead, to step onto a horse trailer, or any other skill that requires them to allow trained behaviors to override instinct.

What humans so often forget, is that with horses — as with nearly every companion animal — instead of fighting to 'break bad habits', we can work with our partners, and find ways to use their instinctive behaviors to help us, and to help the other animals in our care. Just as the hunting instinct of a well bred dog can be used to our benefit, so are the massive muscles of a well bred draft, and the natural cunning and skill of a bred cutting horse. So, too, can the inherent traits in an alpha mare lead to an amazing partnership between human and horse.

Alpha mares exist for a reason. In the wild, her job was to oversee the herd. It was her job to keep a bunch of attention-span-challenged, selfish animals working together to protect one another. It was up to her to ensure watch was kept, foals were protected, aggressive outsiders weren't allowed to steal crucial resources or injuring or running off the ill or young, leaving them exposed to predators. And, yes, it was her job to ensure that the stallion kept his harem, and that he created the ideal filly — HER filly — to take her place, and ensure the herd would continue on to the next generation.

Now, put her in OUR world. Ask her to live in a pasture — likely a relatively small space — likely with a smaller herd. Likely with multiple males who don't really understand that they are no longer stallions, but who also have never lived in a harem scenario and don't really understand what their genetic instincts tell them should be the norm — a single stallion free to breed a private harem of mares. Ask her to deal with ever-changing groups of horses in her block. Expect her to be willing to allow less dominant animals to enter and exit the pasture without her leading — keeping them safe as her genetics tells her she must. Insist she allow others equal time at the hay stacks, even though her survival-of-the-fittest instincts say that the weakest, the least valuable, may be left to starve so that the strong survive. And, ask her to submit not to a single alpha human — which, for her would be like submitting to a more dominant alpha mare or tolerating an overly dominant stallion — but to submit to the whims of EVERY human who walks into her world, despite so many clearly showing submission in some scenarios, aggression in others, and overall having a horrible lack of manners and lack of understanding of how to communicate in her millions-year-old language.

And you say we encounter problems with alpha mares?

Instead, imagine for a moment making a partnership with an alpha mare comparable to that of a wild herd's stallion and his alpha mare. She has jobs which are hers, and the stallion leaves her free to do those — maintaining the pecking order, protecting the smallest/weakest/oldest, mothering foals and weanlings, patrolling the pastures. You, her 'stallion' partner, instead, ask her permission to enter her pasture. You ask for her partnership in your efforts to work with HER herd, when adding or removing a new member, or taking a horse out for other reasons such as riding a different mount. While your first round pen and other training sessions MUST begin with an alpha/submission discussion—one which you must continue until you win — to have a PARTNERSHIP with your alpha mare, you've GOT to make her your partner. Just as with a spouse, you ASK for her cooperation, you request her support, and you give her love and affection and meet her needs in return. The end result? There's NO equine partner in this world like the partnership between a respectful "whisperer" horse owner and his or her truly alpha mare. Your alpha mare will carry you with pride and respect through situations where a lesser mare or, heaven forbid, the average gelding would turn and run. More than that, as her partner, it is her genetic duty to protect YOU, to stand by you in battle, and to ensure your future to ensure HER genetics future. As such, she will protect you against an aggressive horse — or any animal for that matter — that she feels is threatening her partner. She will fulfill requests that an average mare would turn her nose to — so long as the positive reinforcement is there which indicates you ARE her partner, and you appreciate all she is doing at your request.

Let's talk about a truly Alpha mare, and the possibilities that partnership can bring. Meet Tess.

Tess arrived at our rescue a coming 3 year old registered Clydesdale alpha mare who had been allowed
to dominate and abuse humans since a very young
age. She had also been penned in a small space 'to
control her' with 2 other horses...so small, she had
never learned to canter. The result? She was VERY
angry with humanity, and took it out on every human
every chance she got. The first day I handled this
mare, I was turning her out in a paddock twice the
size where she'd grown. I walked her through the
gate, turned her toward me, and took my eyes off her
for a second to latch the gate. She reared and swung
both hooves inches from my face, then pivoted and
fired both hind hooves at my head. Minutes later, she
and I had our first round pen discussion in which Tess
came to understand that I was an alpha mare, higher
ranking than her, and with the ability to make her
run until she truly submitted. We earned each other's
respect that day.

Tess was to be Michael's horse, however, not
mine. That would be a good decision in the long run
— she would always resent my refusing to allow her
absolute dominance over the females on my farm.
Mike, on the other hand, while he HAD to begin with a
lesson in submission, he quickly worked with Tess to
form a partnership. He showed her respect and refused
to allow disobedience or aggression, but primarily
focused upon being equals, and upon showing her
how to earn praise and love instead of being aggressive and getting punished. Tess had arrived in late
November. In March, Mike and Tess began riding.
In May, Tess was providing lead line pony rides at

public events, with literally hundreds of children feeding her treats, being led on her back. When Mike and Tess ride, Tess is capable of performing intro level dressage work, basic jumping, and hours-long trail rides with power and grace. When another rider is on her back without her partner by her side, Tess is opinionated and challenging — even to me, despite our truce and mutual respect on the ground. Mike steps into her vision, and nothing matters but Mike. She will halt on his voice command from hundreds of yards away, despite any rider behavior. She will come to him at a moment's notice, and she will walk as if carrying a child made of glass despite a rider pounding her sides with their heels, if he only asks.

Recently, we had a very aggressive dominant yearling mare in for training. She was not responding as we would have liked to her round pen training. She would work with us, but there was always aggression underneath, and no trust was forming. Mike chose to turn her out in a small paddock next to our pasture for the afternoon with a pony, in hopes that horsey companionship might help get her on track. Tess and her herd were in the 30 acre pasture adjacent to the paddock. Mike turned the mare out and walked into Tess's pasture to visit with his big mare and to tell her not to bother the filly across the fence. As he entered the big pasture, he realized the filly intended to jump the pasture fence to get in with the big herd. He started running toward the filly, hollering at her to not jump the fence. The filly cleared the fence and, apparently, it appeared to Tess that the filly was charging at Mike. Tess flew past Mike and cornered the filly instantly, pinning her in a corner and showing absolute alpha dominance over the filly. The filly showed complete submission to the now 5-year old, 2000 lb Tess and, once Mike convinced Tess that he would be fine, she stepped back to allow him to walk the filly out of the big pasture and return her to the training round pen.

Make no mistake. The filly understood immediately that Tess was alpha on this entire farm, but also that Tess had bowed to Mike's leadership. Instantly, the filly was cooperative and responsive, respectful and manageable. Her training progressed beautifully from there forward. (She was not allowed to go into any adjacent pastures again, to ensure that Tess didn't threaten her any further.)

There isn't a gelding in the world who would've attempted to protect Mike in such a manner. There isn't a gelding in the world who would've dominated an aggressive mare, then handed her to his human handler for reprimand.

In general, geldings are quiet, laid back, social creatures who seek male horses for companionship and make for easy going, dependable riding horses. But their genetics lend them to protecting themselves and being aloof and distant animals. An average ranked mare is used to following, not leading, not creating a partnership that consumes her world. An alpha mare, however, can be as engrossed in her relationship with a human partner as she would've been with her wild herd.

AnnMarie Cross has written a second story, about another horse rescued by Crosswinds Equine Rescue, Inc., now in a new facility at Sidell, Illinois. This mare named Factor has touched a special place in AnnMarie's heart. AnnMarie holds a B.S. from Cornell University in Animal Science, and has been riding, showing and training horses on and off for 20 years.

Chiropractic Saves a Life (Factor's Story)

By AnnMarie Cross

One strange fall evening, we got a call. A woman knew of a thoroughbred brood mare who was going to be sold to slaughter. She knew nothing about her except that the mare was to be sold for meat, and that she saw life in the mare — a spark in her eye, a spirit in her soul, or whatever you may believe in. She saw passion still in this horse who hadn't managed to carry the coveted twins full term. We didn't have space or time for another horse. We couldn't take her in, but we would try to help her find the mare a place. We tried everything we could to find Factor a home directly, but the mare's day had come, and no one could take her. So we went to bring her home. We managed to make room for just one more.

The timid mare looked at me with those soft, liquid eyes. Of course, she couldn't know what we had saved her from, that her life was very likely over without us. She was frightened, but yet she reached, just ever so slightly, to me. And, when it came time to load on the trailer, she followed me up and stood quietly beside me like a pro, like we'd been partners for years.

That very day, this darling mare began to have the strangest of effects on me. She stretched my trust and confidence like no horse had ever done. Her quiet, easy demeanor and soft eye convinced me to unload her alone when my husband hadn't yet made it back to the truck from a phone call. She convinced me to sit, quietly, on a bucket in the corner of her stall, reading a book...just to be near her, and to give her a chance to be near me.

Some weeks later, we started playing in the round pen together, just exploring one another. I was working to gain her trust, she to regain her muscle and composure, her strength and her personality. In a matter of minutes, she was standing beside me, handing me her trust like a delicate flower. She was showing me the fire in her eyes, nuzzling me cautiously, begging me to prove that I truly was who I seemed.

Soon, we were riding together. This petite fine boned broodmare, it turns out, had first been an unsuccessful racehorse. We hadn't been concerned with her pedigree before bringing her home, but we knew now that she was French-born, with incredible bloodlines including Native Dancer. At 17, she had 7 foals we knew of, and likely others that were unregistered. She had lost one set of twins, and may well have given birth to others.

With every step, with every day, she reached to me, and insisted I reach into myself. She pulled confidence from me, sometimes kicking and screaming. Years ago I had broken my back falling into a show jump, and I swore I would never jump again. Yet, with her beneath me, I found myself taking jumping lessons at a local stable, and flying over simple fences. Soon after, I found myself back in the show ring. Amazingly, I would "wake up" after a ride to find that she and I had been soaring over natural obstacles on a local trail ride despite never having been comfortable over rigid jumps even in my best days.

Her delicate features were overshadowed by her incredibly exceptional conformation. Most guessed her age at less than 10; many marveled when her teeth proved she truly was more than 16 years of age.

I've had a lifelong interest in dressage, but no access and undoubtedly no natural talent. With Factor guiding me, I marveled to find myself talking to a lady at a local park, who turned out to be a former Rolex rider who lived just miles from me, and started working with us when she could. Then, with the mare and my husband both nudging me, I found myself going to the east coast for a week long "dressage camp" where I learned enough basics to continue to explore and enjoy the little mare even more and ever more. After careful planning and yet another few "lucky stars" that 'the princess' seemed to drop into my life, Factor and I together got to spend a week out east learning more about what came so naturally to her and what I worked so eagerly to try to match myself.

One day, I planned to ride my beloved mare, the gentle magnificent beauty who has given me so much, taught me so much, helped me give myself so much. To my horror, she collapsed at my feet almost immediately after bridling her. I swore, right there, she was going to die in my arms. As I removed her bridle, she came to her feet again and stood beside me, not quaking with fear, but trusting me to ensure whatever had been wrong would not happen again. When I rebridled her (not believing the equipment we've used for years together could possibly have caused her to fall), she again pulled back, knees collapsed, and fell beside me.

Our equine chiropractor assured me that this wasn't a permanent issue, that the odds were very good that he could help her. It turned out that a misalignment at her poll was causing pressure on the blood flow to her brain if she pulled back while bridled. Once he adjusted it, she was able to be herself again. After several scary evenings of testing and testing again, we were confirmed she WAS fine, and ready to ride again. Now, Factor is back to riding, and loving the work she does.

At first, I truly wasn't sure I could bring myself to ever bridle her again. I was prepared to just ask her to live the rest of her life at my side as my friend, as my companion. She has given me so much. And, once again, she has amazed me and given me something so much more. When I thought she was leaving me, she reached to me, came back to me, stood beside me once more. I wasn't sure I could ask her to ever do more than that again. She had already, always, done so much for me. But she so loves her work and seems so pleased to be doing it. On my worst of days, I can look at my photos on my desk of her playing in our pasture, or of us in the show ring, and remember all we've shared, and smile. To think, this mare was "unwanted" and would've been someone's dinner. Instead, she's my partner and my dearest equine friend.

Helen Farley was born and raised in St. Louis, Missouri. She is a registered nurse employed as a legal nurse consultant. She currently resides in St. Peters, Missouri, with her husband and their five children. Her extended family includes two dogs and two horses – a gelding named Chief, and Abby, her wonderful mare.

Kindred Females

By Helen Farley

I have always considered myself a horse person. I was bitten by the bug early in my youth and spent many years riding, caring for and just loving horses. Two in particular stand out in my childhood to this day, and both were mares.

When I was 42 I stepped back and looked at my life. I was fulfilled and complete with one exception. And so I made the decision to revisit my first love. I wanted to combine my passion for horses with my family. With my husband's blessing I scoured the internet for the perfect horse for our lives. One of the criteria that weighed heavily was that it be a mare. Mares had always represented to me a combination of feminine beauty, strength and power, gentle love and fierce will. Their personalities ran deep. I didn't **rule out** a gelding, but I really was drawn to buying a mare.

The first time I saw Abby, I fell in love with her. There really isn't another way to describe it. She came strolling up from the pasture among the others in her herd with an easy pace and gentle eyes. She radiated femininity and power at the same time in a glorious sense to me. Once I saw her, it was as if the other horses evaporated from view and she walked alone. She was not a strikingly beautiful horse in a flashy sense; in fact she was quite small with a compact, muscular build and a simple bay color among large palominos and paints. But I knew instantly: She was *it.*

There is talk of alpha mares, but Abby was *not* one of those. In fact, we were warned that she'd been at the bottom of the pecking order and really had a hard time of it. Still she had an undeniable combination of feminine depth and complexity (wisdom?) that I very much appreciated. And so on a blustery October evening we made our purchase and brought our new horse "home" to a boarding stable. My husband had ridden at this place as a youth and knew the owners well. We were very comfortable taking her there.

I remember getting on Abby for the first time and feeling completely incompetent. Had I really *done* this before? I didn't know what to do with my upper torso, let alone my arms. When I reminded myself that it had been nearly a quarter of a century since I'd last ridden a horse, I allowed it to become a learning – or re-learning experience. And what a powerful journey I was about to engage in.

Our family and Abby spent the winter months getting to know each other, or at least trying to. She rode fair in the arena, although she was new to any ring; she had only seen trails and fields her entire life up to this point. She wasn't **happy** to be there, going along in monotonous circles for no apparent reason. My husband and I took turns riding her at walks and trots around the rings. We led the children around on her. It seemed to be going well enough, though it was as close to the blind leading the blind as one can imagine. We brushed her, saddled her, gave her treats and were genuinely fearful when the unexpected came up – a spook here, a pulling back there. She remained patient with us all.

Abby initially struggled in the small group of mares she was turned out with. After several months of nasty bite and kick marks and various signs of torment cautiously monitored by the barn manager, she finally found her way and even bonded with the others. I was amazed and grateful that while she was not the alpha mare, she held her own and demanded respect.

Spring came, and as winter melted away, we were able to ride Abby more frequently. And that is when the behavior problems began in full force: A buck here and there when changing gaits, increasingly frequent exaggerated spooking, even the occasional bolt. It was all extremely unpredictable. Abby became anxious around us, nervous. I was the only one with enough determination to override my fear of her. When I'd bring out the saddle she would flinch and prance to the side. When I tried to get on her, she would actually jump away. If I was lucky enough to get seated, she seemed overcome with panic, frozen until springing forward. She didn't turn, she *spun* and *darted*. She didn't walk, she *leapt*. Sudden movement in the saddle invited a bolt. She would go along on a trail and suddenly become completely unnerved. My husband had two nasty falls from her.

Something obviously wasn't right. Abby was annoyed, hurting, irritated or a combination of all of those. My husband came from the school of firm correction. If a horse spooks, you naturally take it back to what scared it. If a horse bucks, you must show it that it is wrong to do so. I did not agree that Abby needed something along the lines of stricter discipline. To me, her behavior warranted further investigation from the angle that something was hurting or scaring her. My husband did not agree, pointing out how her living situation hadn't changed, her feed hadn't changed, her handling hadn't changed. Surely this was behavior related. And so, the lines were drawn. My husband expressed concern for my safety and went on to purchase his own lovely paint gelding, shaking his head and genuinely worrying about my safety.

Through these changes with Abby, I refused to lose faith in her. I felt a connection continue to form, even though we had lost the typical horse/rider relationship. Although I often feared what she would do and what would set her off, I was determined to continue loving and caring for her. I remember many times when I'd take her saddle off, she would turn to look at me, sigh, and then step closer to me. It was heartbreaking.

I was at a loss, and so naturally I reached out to others. I asked experienced people for advice and help. I asked the barn manager, the owner of the stable, other boarders, the trainer. I posted questions online. What could be wrong? What did this sound like? And *every* person answered in resounding, unanimous agreement, one by one: "You have a mare."

This response floored me. How could knowledgeable people with such vast experience and obvious intelligence tell me that? How could they actually *believe* it? Was it just an excuse because they really didn't know what was going wrong? I began to realize over time that it was truly a firm, solid belief held by many, if not most, horse people. I began to hear it over and over again: *Mares are no good.* "Look at our line of trail horses," a stable owner told me one day, nearly laughing at my lack of knowledge and/or common sense about this issue. "We don't have *one mare*." She went on to explain that they are simply crazy, unpredictable in general, and basically mean – *because they are mares*. "The only thing mares are good for" she added, "is to make baby geldings." I remember literally stepping back a bit. Somehow I found this disturbing to hear, especially from another woman. It was unsettling to me that a female would sell out on the issue of a horse being – well, female! There was something that I had never put into words, or even fully thought through, that I felt with Abby – a feminine kinship perhaps? Yet I never offered a defense against something that was apparently so universally accepted.

A barn manager described to me his view on mares: "It's like they have one of those kids' games in their heads – you know, that has a board with holes and the marbles that roll around? Some days the marbles roll right into the holes and fit perfectly and you have a darn good day. But others – well those marbles just roll and roll."

The other boarders meant well. They were all wonderful, kind people. But their disdain of mares was absolutely firm. "When are you going to sell that mare and get a nice, calm gelding?" one asked every time she'd see me leading Abby. At one point I half-heartedly challenged her and said, "While she's having problems, I can't exactly try to sell her." To which the boarder responded as if I were a naïve child, "THAT'S when you take her to the auction and get yourself a GOOD horse. Get yourself a *gelding*." Another boarder watched me ride Abby and after much thought said, "I wouldn't get on that mare. I wouldn't get on that *thing*. I'd be scared to death of what she'd do." I did a double take, and she added, "Sell her to some teenager – they love crazy stuff like her…I mean, who wouldn't want her if they just LOOKED at her?" That made me feel a little better, but it still hurt. In other words, she was pretty enough, but *hopelessly* insane – because she was a…SHE.

Something about this talk of mares made me even more defensive of Abby. Being female was *part* of her, who she was…being strong enough to give life and feminine enough to nurture it. All things aside, wasn't that in itself powerful enough to admire?

Though I vowed to stand by her, difficulty with Abby grew until I was genuinely concerned for my safety. I just didn't know how far she'd go. I remember concluding that I had to do something and deal with this problem directly. I realized that I had to admit and accept that possibly I was not advanced enough to work properly with Abby. That perhaps she was "too much" horse? The progression of poor behavior baffled me. She was settled into her home, appeared happy and healthy. She was sound. Finally, on the darkest of days I blamed myself for somehow "ruining" her. I could not forgive myself for that – what if another owner could bring her back and erase any damage I'd done? I didn't want to lose her, but wasn't selfish enough to not let her go if that was really best for her.

And so, I reached out the only other way I knew – on the internet. I read much on mares, riding, and the development of bad habits. I was overwhelmed. Where to start? What if she *was* misbehaving because she was female? I remember shaking my head in disgust at myself. How could *I* fall into that overly simplistic trap?

During the next several weeks I broke down and forced myself to face the fact that letting Abby go might be in her best interest. Clearly *we* weren't progressing but her unruly behaviors *were*. She was to the point that when her saddle was brought from the tack room she would almost flip over sideways.

If it was in her best interest, I would not *sell* Abby; I would find a good home to give her to, as long as I was allowed to visit. I panicked when I thought of what could happen to her, especially with her behavior. In one last attempt to find help, I looked on the internet for a horse rescue that might offer some advice. I emailed several, pleading for suggestions or answers. I received a response from one and arrangements were made for a visit within the week. I am grateful to AnnMarie Cross and her husband Mike, of Crosswinds Equine Rescue, for coming to rescue Abby and me! They were like angels in my time of need, swooping in to shed a positive light on everything. When they came, they identified the problem immediately: Abby was hurting. The used saddle that was sold to me as a perfect fit for her had been causing terrible pain. As I was shown, it was worn in places that needed padding, bent where it should've been straight and straight where it should've been bent. Everything made sense – the bolting, the fear that seemingly came out of nowhere, the bucking. I felt foolish but elated at the same time: Abby's behavior was from a physical problem, and had absolutely nothing to do with the fact that she'd been born female! I could deal with this!

And so we started over. Abby rested for a full month – with absolutely no riding. During this rest, she and I *really* got to know each other. We spent numerous hours together on ground work and building trust. She learned to lunge beautifully. We took walks. She was groomed like she'd never been groomed before. We *enjoyed* each others' company.

She nickered at the sight of me. Something clicked, and we have never looked back. With new well-fitting tack and a gentler hand, life with her became a bonding experience and a true delight. We took small steps to complete trust in each other.

Abby and I have built an amazing relationship and I will always consider it one of the great achievements of my life. She looks to me for reassurance and when she does she *is* reassured. And through it all she has truly been as watchful of me and my safety as I am of hers.

My husband and I were invited on a trail ride to a state park not quite one year after we bought Abby. It was the ultimate test for us. I don't think anyone who went *wasn't* concerned about how we would do. Abby, after all, had a reputation. I had to smile to myself when I realized that she was the only mare in the group.

It was a glorious day. From loading her into the trailer to the trail ride filled with bicycles, yelling children, barking dogs and deep water, we completely enjoyed ourselves and each other. Abby passed with flying colors. She was my trusted, steady mount. She came through for me and I have never been so proud of her. We were pros, and in fact, handled every obstacle as well or better than anyone else there. She put plenty of geldings to shame that day.

My children adore Abby, but they have a healthy respect for who she is, and that is not necessarily a horse for them to ride. She has helped them understand that each horse, just as each person, is an individual. They are enjoying learning to *care* for both

Abby and our docile gelding, Chief. They are learning to *ride* Chief. They appreciate that he is calmer and generally more predictable. It is interesting, however, to see my only daughter inexplicably drawn to Abby. I don't think I imagine it that Abby is also drawn to her.

I will grow old with Abby. I will care for her until the end of her days. Sharing the seasons, sensing our trust and enjoying life from the back of a horse once called hopeless because of her gender, has been nothing short of a spiritual experience for me.

Abby is a mare, and that is such a *small* part of all of who she is, and yet such a *huge* part at the same time. It makes her heart bigger, her loyalty stronger and her tenacity clearer. It gives her personality such vivid dimensions. I know how far to push her and what is too much to ask, and she in turn knows the same of me. There is a respect between us that isn't describable in words, but stems from the bond we share – a bond between horse and human, true companions and most of all, two kindred females.

To order additional copies of

MARES!
(Ya Gotta LOVE 'em)

Fifty Stories to Aid and Inspire Mare Owners
Compiled by Betsy Kelleher

Visit Website: Goduseshorses.com

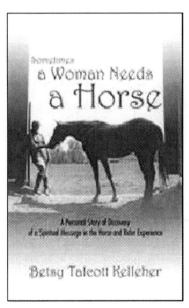

**If you enjoyed these stories about mares,
Here is another story
by the author who compiled this book!**

Sometimes a Woman Needs a Horse!
A Personal Story of Discovery of a Spiritual
Message in the Horse and Rider Experience

Copyright 2004 by
Betsy Talcott
Kelleher
Packaged by Pleasant
Word
ISBN 1-4141-0261-5

To order by phone
with credit card,
call 1-877-421-7323
Retail price: $17.99

Or visit author's
website
www.goduseshorses.
com

Betsy Kelleher has written a story about the training of her first mare, Fanny, which goes beyond the "how-to" of developing partnership with a horse. Betsy shares the excitement of competitive trail riding and the amazing influence of Sally Swift's basic Centered Riding principles. While training Fanny, working to instill trust and obedience, Betsy realizes that God is working with her in much the same way. Through the details, principles and experiences of her horse and rider relationship, Betsy shares her discovery of a spiritual parallel between horse training and Christian discipleship.

Printed in the United States
201124BV00001B/67-273/A

9 781604 775471